0.07

MERRYN SOMERSET WEBB is editor of the respected weekly financial magazine *MoneyWeek*. She has regular columns in the *Sunday Times*, the *Spectator* and *Saga Magazine* and has written for a variety of other publications including *Harpers* and *The Week*. Merryn is also a frequent radio and television commentator on financial matters. She lives in London with her husband and young daughter.

Love Is Not Enough

The Smart Woman's Guide to Making (and Keeping) Money

HarperPress

An Imprint of HarperCollinsPublishers

UNIVERSITY OF CHICHESTER

Harper Press
An Imprint of HarperCollins*Publishers*
77–85 Fulham Palace Road
Hammersmith, London W6 8JB

www.harpercollins.co.uk
Visit our authors' blog: www.fifthestate.co.uk

Published by Harper Press 2007

A catalogue record for this book is available from the British Library

ISBN-13: 978-0-00-723518-6
ISBN-10: 0-00-723518-6

Set in Fairfield

Illustrations of characters and hand lettering © www.joygosney.co.uk
Illustrations except 65, 71, 72, 194 © Sarah Hayes 2007

Printed and bound in Great Britain by Clays Ltd, St Ives plc

Contents

Love Is Not Enough is in large part the result of hundreds of conversations with women about their finances. My thanks to all those women for their openess. In particular I'd like to thank my sisters, mother and grandmother all of whom spent a great deal more time than I know they would have liked talking to me about their money and their happiness. Other vital contributions came from Gillian Tett, Riko Sakurai, James Ferguson, Tim Somerset Webb, Ashe Peacock, Caroline Bennett, Katy Light, Gabrielle Jourdan, Caroline Law, Heather McGregor, Naomi Caine, Suzette Field, Pheobe Crawsahw, Charlotte de Panafieu, Verity Williams and most often of all from my husband Sandy Cross. I'd also like to thank Nick Reid, Euan Stuart and Craig Davidson for checking for mistakes (although any that remain are of course still my responsibility).

Introduction

For most of my twenties, when I thought about my future, I imagined all sorts of delightful things. Country houses and sunshine, long weekends by the Italian lakes, Christmas in the Caribbean, happy children riding brand-new bicycles, lazy mornings drinking coffee in cafés and sparkling-glassed conservatories, a wardrobe full of high-heeled shoes and cashmere jerseys, sports cars and speedboats. But the one thing I never thought about was the path from my current life to this new one.

How was this splendid future lifestyle to be financed? Would I inherit a few million from a distant relative? Win the lottery? Suddenly see my good career change to a great one as I started and quickly sold a fabulous small business or was promoted so far so fast that my salary and million-pound bonuses would take care of it? Or was I perhaps hoping for another kind of facilitator of the future? I think that a part of me – despite a strongly feminist upbringing – couldn't help but assume that my fantasies would be paid for by someone else. By my very own Prince Charming. My truth is that deep down, despite love of my own career and pride in my financial independence, I long thought of the day when I would meet the man I intended to stay with for ever, the one who would be the father of my children, as the day most of my problems would end. Not only would my emotional burdens be shared but I would no longer have to worry about pensions, the housing ladder, savings, the stock market, bills and the like. I'd keep working and earning of course, but my Prince Charming would take all those boring things off my plate and chuck in a shopping allowance as a bonus. Yes, as far as I was concerned money was a man thing.

So I didn't really worry about it that much. I made good money and did the bare minimum to look after it – I tried to keep out of debt, made sure I saved a little money and got the cheapest mortgage I could find when I bought my flat – but long-term planning? None. In my twenties I earned a generous salary at an investment bank. But when I resigned at 29 I had almost nothing to show for it (except for many, many pairs of shoes, long-term sleep deprivation and a heroic tolerance for alcohol). While I was working I wasn't leveraging my earnings into long-term financial independence. I was effectively starting my financial life from scratch each month. Sound familiar?

Prince Charming isn't coming

I'm not alone in having spent much of my adult life hoping for, worse, planning for, a let-out clause. A survey of all my (many) sisters and my friends, independent career women every one, shows that almost all of them, loath as they are to admit it, feel the same. They all know how they're paying for their next holiday but very few of them have any idea how their retirement might be financed. Why? Because they assume that they won't be financing it themselves. Someone else will. A recent survey by National Savings and Investments showed that 45% of women say that a healthy bank balance is their top priority when looking for a partner. Only 22% of men said the same. The women also said that a man didn't become desirable until he was earning £50,000; they expected men to have hefty stashes of cash for them to spend – they assumed that potential partners would have an average of £24,000 in savings. The men surveyed expected partners to have only around £15,000 saved up.

There is nothing wrong with hoping for a financial let-out clause, be it a lottery win or a rich husband (neither are intrinsically bad things, in fact they are both rather good things). The problem comes when we put too much faith – consciously or subconsciously – in the idea that our financial futures will be sorted out by this kind of external force. Because the odds are they won't be.

Let's look at the lottery. Imagine a huge room filled to the top with 10,000 books. In one book, on one page, inside one O in the middle of a sentence somewhere, is a tiny dot. You have a pin. You must choose a random book. Then you must close your eyes, open the book and stick the pin in it. It is about as likely that you will hit the dot as it is that you will win the lottery in any one week. Indeed the odds of you winning the lottery are so low that they are pretty much the same whether you buy a ticket or not. That's not really something to depend on.

And nor for that matter is Prince Charming. He may well turn up – many, maybe most, of us find real love in our lives in the end – but when he does he probably won't be quite what you had in mind. Your PC could be poor himself. He could be a high earner who is useless with money. He could be only a short-term PC – you could leave him or he could leave you. Let's not forget that nearly 50% of UK marriages end in divorce. Either way, you can't rely on either his arrival or his long-term support. Love is a wonderful thing but rare is the woman who finds that it comes with a full cheque book.

Even if it does, you do need to ask yourself if you really want to leave yourself dependent on a man for money for ever. I used to think that it would be just fine, but I don't any more. I've been working and taking care of myself for over a decade and I don't think I could be happy constantly having to ask someone else for money. When I was on honeymoon my debit card suddenly stopped working for no apparent reason, leaving me totally without cash and dependent on my husband for the two weeks we were away. The honeymoon was a gift from him to me so being cashless presented no major problems. It did, however, give me a hint of what it might be like to be dependent in less romantic conditions. When you've only been married a few weeks it isn't hard to ask your husband to give you money to buy some postcards but would you really want still to be doing it after ten years of marriage? I get the feeling that once you've earned your own money you'll find that for the rest of your life you'd prefer to make it than to take it. That means that even after you have married you still have to have an eye to your independence: you need your own savings and your own source of income to fall back on.

Face it: you aren't going to win the lottery and the lottery of love is never going to pay out to your full satisfaction. You've got to look after yourself.

Times are tough

Unfortunately for women, the time when we have no choice but to confront our own finances and plan for our own futures has coincided with a period when things are pretty tough. All the things our parents seemed to take for granted – being able to buy a house, support as many children as they got around to having and then retire in reasonable comfort – seem far out of reach today. I met a man a few weeks ago who had joined the BBC as a graduate trainee 50 years ago on a starting salary of £500 a year.

It wasn't much, he said, but he and his wife still managed to buy a flat in London's South Kensington in which to start their lives together. 'South Kensington,' I said, 'how much was that?' 'Five hundred pounds,' he said. Now South Kensington wasn't as smart 50 years ago as it is now, but just imagine being able to buy a flat in central London for the same as a graduate trainee's salary (around £20,000) today. How much easier would that make life?

The same man has – like most of his generation – a final salary pension scheme. He has never really had to worry much about his retirement, his company did that for him and now they pay him a nice pension every year. That won't happen to our generation: current state pensions are tiny and by the time we retire they are going to be even tinier – if they exist at all. These days if you want to survive in any style in your old age you are going to have to come up with the cash for it yourself. You are going to have to work harder than your parents and probably retire later. At the same time, taxes have recently risen enormously – you pay tax on almost everything. On your clothes, your food, your shoes, your alcohol, your petrol, your car, your aeroplane flights, your insurance and on all your investments. Overall, 40% of the nation's wealth disappears into the deep pockets of the state. Nobody really knows where it goes after that but one thing is certain: it won't be around to bail you out when you can't pay your bills in your seventies.

Oh, and don't expect to inherit enough money to make it all OK either. Not only is the government intent on making sure that inheritance tax eventually hits everyone with two pennies to rub together but your parents are now likely to be living well into their eighties. That cash you had your eye on? The odds are they'll still be spending it when you're in your sixties. The fact is that young people today are at a serious disadvantage financially compared to previous generations. We are, says think tank Reform, the IPOD generation – insecure, pressured, overtaxed and debt-ridden.

But just as the serious demands on your money – housing, pensions, tax and so on – have become more intense so has the pressure to consume non-essentials. As most of us have everything we need the only way for companies to grow their profits is to sell us stuff we don't need. And that's exactly what they do – with enormous skill. So successful has the advertising and marketing industry been that half of us appear genuinely to think that we need £20 scrubbing lotions to get clean and £500 handbags to look acceptable when we go out for dinner. We've got too many obligations – or we think we have too many obligations – and not enough cash. How, we think, can we possibly live a reasonable lifestyle and still save enough so that we aren't living off dog food in our old age?

The answer is that we can do so if we take control of our money rather than letting it control us. That means understanding it, talking about it and making it work for us. It also means being comfortable with it – knowing that using money well is neither embarrassing nor intimidating. Too many women still think money is a dirty word, still think that being rubbish with money is somehow feminine and still refuse to have proper conversations about it. In the last 100 years we have made huge leaps both in the workplace (I don't think there are many who would still claim that men are necessarily better lawyers, managers or doctors than women) and outside the workplace (men still don't do as much housework or childcare as we do but the fact that they should is pretty firmly established), but there is one more step to take before we can say we have tried properly to create real equality with men – we have to start sorting out our own finances.

Back in the 1970s feminists got very worked up about the ongoing passivity among women when it came to money. We could cope with going out into the workplace and making the money, but investing it? Buying houses with it? Arranging pensions with it? In the 1970s we thought that all those things should be dealt with by men. But the really absurd thing is that 30-odd years on nothing has changed: many of us – in our heart of hearts – still do. We see a brown envelope in the post and we either ignore it or hand it on to someone else.

When was the last time you had a conversation about money with a girlfriend? For many of us the answer is never. Men talk about money, they exchange stock and fund tips, they compare mortgage deals and the cost of new cars and boast to each other about their financial successes. But the closest most of us ever get to a proper chat about personal finances is when we lie to each other over coffee about how much our new clothes cost. We have to get over this passivity. And, given how important financial security is to our long-term contentment, we have to do it soon. We have to give managing our money the same level of attention as we give our diets, our houses, our health and our jobs, because no one else is going to do it for us.

You can do it

The good news is that you can both live well and prepare for the future, and much more easily than you think, as long as you are prepared to put a bit of work into it. There are two things to note here. First, the financial world is much simpler than the financial professionals would like you to think it is – this book explains everything you need to know to sort out a whole lifetime of money in three hundred straightforward pages. Second, and more importantly, there is little doubt that once they put their minds to it, women are just as good with money as men and in some ways often better.

There is evidence that women who do invest are better at it than men, for example: research from Digital Look shows that over more or less every time period, female investors have outperformed male investors. In 2003, for example, the average woman's portfolio rose by 10% a year. The FTSE index (which measures the performance of the UK stock market as a whole) rose by 7% and the average man's portfolio by 6%. And even in the year to the end of October 2002 when the FTSE fell by 22% the average female portfolio rose by 2%. So much for the idea that women are useless with money; in fact once we overcome our passivity and get started we are actually pretty good with it.

All this makes complete sense to me. Not everyone likes to admit it but in lots of ways the very nature of women makes us better suited to long-term money management. Thanks to social and biological roles as nurturers and carers, women are in general more cautious, patient and questioning than men. They don't mind admitting ignorance and asking for things to be explained. They know that money doesn't grow overnight and that investing and saving, like bringing up children, is a long-term job that requires substantial amounts of planning. And they know that when it comes to money the small things matter as much as the big things. All in all (and this is a huge generalization but not an unfair one), we have a much better temperament for dealing with money than many men. What we need is the knowledge and the will to take advantage of it and this is where we too often fall down.

Taking charge

I've been through a lot of the financial journey this book travels myself. I've been a student, I've done years of unpaid or underpaid work experience, I've had and left badly paid jobs in television and journalism as well as a few highly paid jobs in the City, I've worked full-time, part-time and freelance as well as in London and in Tokyo, I've participated in the setting up of a new business and most recently, in rather quicker succession than I initially intended, I've married and had a baby. I've been grossly financially irresponsible during a lot of this but I've also now managed to pull myself together and emerge in a relatively stable position.

A few years ago I realized that while I liked to think I had my finances under control, I simply didn't. I had no pension arrangements and no plan in place for paying off my mortgage. I had various bits and bobs of savings but no real plan as to how they worked together. Then something happened to jolt me into action. I met my husband and he moved into my flat and took over half the mortgage. He was interested to see that it was an interest-only mortgage. How are you saving to pay it off at the end of the term? he asked. I confessed I wasn't. He was horrified and I was embarrassed. But I was also prompted by his surprise, as well as his unwillingness to sort it all out for me (as he says, if he has to do half the housework, I can sort out my own bank accounts), to take charge of my own money. So I've sorted out my pension arrangements, I've started saving regularly and doing so in a tax-efficient way, I've switched the mortgage to the cheapest repayment mortgage I could find, I've reviewed my income and made sure it matches my skills and the work I put in, I've made sure we are paying the lowest possible prices for all our utilities and I've put a check on some (not all) of my unnecessary spending. It's taken some time and been a reasonable amount of effort, but it feels very good indeed.

The point of this book is to show you that you too can use your natural skills to take control of your finances at every stage of your life. The first section looks at how to increase the amount of money you have every month. Your income is the most important factor when it comes to controlling your finances. Once you know that you are getting paid as much as you can for what you do you can settle down to working out how to turn that income into wealth. So the fact that most of us aren't maximizing our incomes, aren't paid what we are really worth, or as much as the man at the next desk, is a fundamental problem that we need to sort out as fast as we can. The section then considers spending (which isn't all bad) and at debt (which also isn't all bad).

The second section looks at how you can grow your assets – at saving, investing, pensions and property. Here we'll go through the financial options on the market and explain which ones offer value and which ones are simply complicated vehicles invented by the financial industry to rip you off. I want to be the richest pensioner on my road when I retire and I want the same for you (as long as you live on a different road).

The next section considers what happens when you need to share your money. How will you pay for a wedding and how will you organize your finances within your marriage? How does the money work if you don't marry but live with a long-term partner? What about children? How much will they cost and how will you pay for them to get what you want them to have? How can you possibly maintain your financial independence if you stop working to look after children? What are your legal rights as a working mother? And what if your marriage doesn't work out? We look at how to deal with the financial shocks divorce throws at women.

Finally, in the last section we look at how money can make you happy – and how it can't. Happiness isn't all about money but financial clarity in your life will bring you a peace of mind that is hard to beat. I hope that by the time you get to the end of the book your finances will no longer be a source of blushes or stress but a source of that peace of mind.

Section 1:
Finding the Money

"Make your money and buy your freedom."
Tamara Mellon, owner of Jimmy Choo

1
Maximizing Your Income
How to Get Paid What You Are Worth

A few years ago Linda Babcock, a professor at Carnegie Mellon University in the US, noticed that year after year the starting salaries of the men who graduated from her classes were higher than those of the women – to the tune of around 7%. This confused her – they all left with similar qualifications and went into similar jobs. So she investigated. It turned out that the majority of the women, thrilled to be offered jobs, had accepted the starting salaries they had been offered. The men had not. They had negotiated the salary up – by an average of 7%. The employers were not discriminating against the women; the women were discriminating against themselves.

My mother always told me life wasn't going to be fair. But for much of my childhood I wasn't really convinced. It seemed to me that most of the time you got what you deserved. At school if you were nice to people they were generally nice back. If you worked hard you did well in exams and were praised accordingly. And if you didn't you weren't. It was the same at university: if you followed the rules and worked hard you got a good degree. If you didn't you didn't. Simple and perfectly fair.

Then I entered the world of work and found that my mother was completely right. In the office things aren't fair at all: working hard and being nice in no way guarantees you a fair wage. Instead, if you are a woman, it very often condemns you to an unfair one.

According to the Women and Work Commission, women who work full-time are paid on average 13% less than men who work full-time and women who work part-time are paid a horrible 40% less than men. This gap has not closed significantly for going on 30 years and has barely budged in the last 10: in 1997 New Labour came to power full of heart-warming promises about their female-friendly policies but since then the pay gap between men and women for full-time work has fallen by only 3.6% and for part-time work by a mere 2.5%. If it keeps moving at this snail-like speed, says the Commission, it will be 140 years before male and female part-time workers earn the same wage for similar work.

The difference this makes is important. The average full-time salary for a man is around £31,000. The average for a woman is more like £23,000. Look at something like the banking sector and the difference is even more extreme: the average salary of a woman is £31,600 a year and that of a man £53,700. And even female company directors are paid less than their male counterparts: a survey from the Institute of Directors in 2005 showed that the pay gap here, in an area where one would think women would be tough enough to get what they wanted, was still 24%.

So what's going on? There are all sorts of explanations doing the rounds. The main one is the fact that women tend to leave the workforce for long periods of time to have and to bring up babies, something that stops them moving into senior positions as often and as fast as men. It is also true that women tend to go into traditionally low-paid jobs such as those in childcare, in cleaning and behind cash registers (the three 'c's) and where the hours are more flexible than elsewhere. But there is more to it than just this. According to the Equal Opportunities Commission (EOC) 40% of the pay gap between the genders comes down to pure discrimination: women are paid less because they are women. For proof look no further than the fact that even before the baby thing kicks in women are paid less than men: research by the EOC tells us that five years after graduation the difference between the wages of equally educated men and women is, on average, 15%.

This depressing statistic is backed up by a study done by the London School of Economics (LSE) in 2003. The LSE tracked down 10,000 recent graduates and found that after three years of working (and before having children) the female graduates were earning 12% less than the male graduates. And according to the DTI, overall, single childless women make only 93% of what single childless men make.

Do you need a degree?

Education in itself is no guarantee of a high income. Consider the case of the average university degree. Today around 40% of young people go into some form of higher education. This means that having a degree isn't special any more – everyone who wants one is now getting one so you aren't going to get paid much of a premium for having one too. In fact, according to the Higher Education Statistics Agency, a good 25% of graduates now go into jobs that didn't require them to have degrees in the first place: more are working in low-paid office administration jobs and customer service jobs (27%) than in 'professional occupations' (25%). Recent research also shows that the average graduate (male or female) now has to wait until they are 33 – that's after 12 years of full-time work – for their earnings to overtake those of someone who skipped university and began work at 18. I'm not sure this should particularly surprise us. After all, most of us learn little of vocational use at university and the traits that employers value most are rarely teachable. When the Council for Industry and Higher Education last year asked 45 top businesses what they were looking for in employees the most common answers were 'innovation' and 'the ability to think creatively'.

I once interviewed a charming young man with a good degree from a top university for a writing job at *Moneyweek*, the magazine I edit. A lot of what we do at the magazine is précising material from other publications so I asked him to précis a piece for me in order to check both his comprehension and his writing style. When I got his effort back I found it quite confusing: his article seemed to tell only half the story and came to no real conclusion. I dug out the original to check what had gone wrong. It soon became clear. The article I had given him to summarize was on two sides of one piece of paper. He hadn't turned the piece of paper over. University not only didn't teach him to think creatively. It didn't teach him to think at all. In contrast, a year or two later I hired as my deputy editor a young woman who had not been to university. She was several years younger than most people I would have considered for the position (having three years more experience than most people her age) but I could see no difference between her skills and those of the many others (all graduates) who I interviewed for the job.

Given all this, it's worth thinking very seriously about whether university is really for you, particularly with tuition fees now coming in at £3,000 a year and most students leaving university with upwards of £15,000 worth of debt (you don't pay the fees until you graduate). If you can go to a top university and get a top degree odds are it will turn out to have been worth the effort, but if you are going to a low-grade university and expecting to get a third is it really worth the bother?

If you decide the answer is yes one of your main priorities (only just behind making sure you get at least a 2:1) is to get through the whole thing with as high an income as possible in order to run up as little debt as possible. Students from particularly needy families (annual income

£17,500 or less) can get grants worth up to £2,700 a year in 2006–7, while everyone is entitled to cheap student loans of up to £4,405. These are far and away the best way to borrow, given that the rate is well below that on any other kind of debt and you don't have to start paying the money back until your income hits £15,000 (see www.slc.co.uk for details of student loans). Otherwise there are hundreds of different grants, bursaries and scholarships about. A full listing of all the bursaries and scholarships on offer can be found at www.ucas.com, the website for the Universities and Colleges Admission Service. Note that a survey last year showed that 95% of students about to head for university knew nothing of the money on offer. This is excellent news for those who bother to find out: the fewer people who know the less competition there will be for the funds and the more there will be for those who have done some research.

Finally, you might need to think about working while you are at university. However this does need to be kept to a minimum. If you think you are working too much to study enough to get your 2:1 stop working: you don't want to end your three years with nothing to show for it other than a skilled pint-pulling technique.

This sounds outrageous and it is. But the really nasty thing about it is that to a large degree it is our fault. Study after study shows that women are paid less not because their bosses are actively discriminating against them, but because they never ask for more. In 2006 *Grazia* magazine surveyed 5,000 working men and women, asking them about their pay and their thoughts on their pay. Two-thirds of the women who took part said that they had

never asked for more money, despite the fact that 80% of them also said that they thought they were underpaid and to a degree overworked (50% of the men surveyed said they took a full lunch hour every day whereas 25% of the women said that they never took a lunch break at all and 61% said they never took full lunch breaks). Only 29% of the women surveyed said they had ever plucked up the courage to ask for a rise and of those, said *Grazia*, half claimed it was one of the most 'stressful and embarrassing things' they'd ever done.

Linda Babcock and Sara Laschever, the US authors of *Women Don't Ask*, point to research showing that men initiate negotiations four times as often as women and that, unlike the women surveyed, who said negotiating was like 'going to the dentist', the men said they found it to be like a 'wrestling match'. Men find negotiating exhilarating. Women find it humiliating. So much so that when they do force themselves into asking for a rise, say Babcock and Laschever, they do it so badly they end up with 30% less than men in the same circumstances.

So why do we find asking for money so hard? It seems to come down to a different method of self-measurement. Women assume that if they were worth more than they are paid, their boss would pay them more automatically, so they don't ask. To do so would be embarrassing; it would be to suggest that work and the relationships formed at work are not satisfying in themselves but that they have a set monetary value. We also think it might somehow be rude and adversely affect our relationship with our boss – it's an emotional thing for us. We think that pay levels should automatically be fair (just like A-level grades) and if they aren't we are too nice to demand that they should be made so.

I'm guilty of this myself. Like many other women, I think a part of me feels I'm somehow lucky to have my job (rather than that my employers are lucky to have me) and that if I ask for more money anyone employing me would be entirely justified in telling me that I can empty my desk and be off – they can find someone else who would be thrilled to have my job on any salary with no trouble.

Men are different. They internalize their confidence more. They don't need to be loved by their colleagues or their bosses and in general they don't feel lucky to be allowed to work. Most of them are clear about the fact that they work mainly for money (and the status that brings) so they take a view on what they are worth and insist on having it. They can separate their view of themselves as a person from their idea of how they do their job and what they deserve as a result. Women think about their weaknesses when they negotiate. Men think about their abilities. Women self-deprecate. Men demand and then revel in praise and the status it brings. They ask more so they get more.

"Remember Ginger Rogers did everything Fred Astaire did, only backwards and in high heels."
Ann Richards, governor of Texas 1991-1995

Those in any doubt that those people who ask for more get more should take note of a survey out from Woolworth's just before Christmas the year before last. It pointed out that on average parents spend just under £100 more on Christmas presents for their sons than for their daughters. Why? The answers from the parents surveyed should give every woman in the country something to think about: boys ask for more presents, and the presents they ask for tend to be more expensive (the most expensive toy in the top five for girls that Christmas was the Amazing Amanda doll at £69.99, for boys it was the PlayStation Portable at £179.99). Girls also asked for smaller presents that they can 'love, care for and collect' said the Woolworth's spokesman. They 'keep their toys for longer and are not so demanding for the latest craze'. Boys, on the other hand, 'always ask for the new toys as soon as they are released'.

And, just to ram the point home, the parents surveyed said that if they didn't get what they wanted their boys got nastier than their girls.

The point is that self-discrimination starts young. Women don't ask for enough often enough. The result? They get stuck with cheap dolls when they are 9 and then rubbish salaries when they are 29.

This kind of thing matters. Imagine that a man and a woman are both offered a job at the same time at the same place. The offer includes a starting salary of £25,000. The woman takes it. The man negotiates it up to £28,000. Thereafter they both get 5% pay rises every year over the next 30 years or so. How much more do you think he will earn over his career than she does?

The answer is a shocking £285,000. And that's a minimum number: if the woman accepts the 5% every year but the man pushes it up a little more at each annual review (don't forget men initiate negotiations four times more often than women) he will end up with even more. A quarter of a million pounds is many times more than the average person's net worth will ever be but women throw that kind of money away every day simply by being too embarrassed, too shy and, let's face it, too foolish to ask to be paid what they are worth. So next time you think that you're lucky to have your job remember that, if you aren't paid the market rate, you aren't nearly as lucky as the employer who has managed to get you to do the same work as the man at the next desk for less money.

All this means that you must have your wits about you in the workplace. There are many ways to make yourself better off – and we'll be looking at many of them later in the book – but the simplest way to get richer in a hurry is to make sure you are getting paid what you are really worth. Once you've done that you can start working to turn that stream of income into long-term wealth. But first you have to ask for more money and the sooner you do it the better.

Here's how to go about it.

Eleven ways to get paid what you are really worth

1 **Get the knowledge.** Find out how much other people in your line of work get paid. When I started in journalism I made a point of asking a friend senior to me in the business how much she earned and how much she thought I should earn. Now she always tells me everything she knows about pay standards in our industry and I tell her. Also visit recruitment websites or call a recruitment consultant. If you feel able to ask colleagues what they make go ahead (a few drinks might help here). Next visit **www.paywizard.co.uk** (it doesn't give much detail but it will help you to see the range of pay on offer for jobs similar to yours). Finally, get your personnel department to show you the firm's pay data. You can't ask to see what individuals are paid but you can see a breakdown of pay by sex, which might help your case a little. Knowledge is power – no one can argue with you if you have the right facts to hand and you have a good case.

2 **Do your own PR.** Women aren't programmed to shout about their achievements in the same way that men are but the more you let people know both that you exist and how well you are doing the more they will remember you. Perhaps you can keep your boss aware of your progress on a weekly basis. I don't mean going into their office at the same time every Friday to bore them with the details of how special you are, I just mean that you should make sure that every week they are copied in on an email that makes you look good or that you regularly mention any positive feedback from colleagues or customers. You also want to be sure that you aren't overlooked. You need to speak up in meetings whenever you get the chance (even if you aren't

convinced your contribution will be an exceptionally good one – when did that ever stop a man?). When the time comes to ask for a rise collect evidence to show that you do your job adequately. It's nice if you do your job particularly well but you only need to do it averagely to get paid the going rate for it. Also make a list of any achievements, especially if you can show that they have affected the firm's bottom line (in a good way) and get together any comments or letters of praise or thanks from suppliers or clients. Then take them all in with you. Remember that a key part of doing well – of being promoted and of being paid more – is self-promotion. Don't ever be too modest. When you were at school if you worked hard you automatically got As. But this isn't school and there is no exam that tells people what you should be paid. You have to tell them yourself.

3 **Be objective.** Forget how much you feel you are worth. This isn't about your self-esteem; it's about an objective assessment of your market worth. And asking for more money isn't rude. It's perfectly normal.

4 **Don't wait too long.** There's no need to wait for an annual pay review. You can ask for more money at any time. The worst that can happen is that the answer will be no.

5 **Begin as you mean to go on.** When you start a job don't accept the first salary offered. Immediately try to bump it up a bit. The higher a base you start from the faster your salary will rise.

6 **Start high and expect to be argued down.** Know what the minimum you will accept is before you start negotiating.

7 **Never threaten to resign unless you really mean it.** If you don't

get what you want and you then don't resign your position will be permanently undermined.

8 **Don't assume no means no.** Ask for another review in six months. Also consider asking for non-cash options – perhaps more training or more flexible hours, time off to study, or a day working at home. Ask if you can be sure of a pay rise if you hit particular targets; ask to have set objectives you will be judged against.

9 **Ask on a Wednesday afternoon.** A recent survey from Office Angels found that four out of five employers are at their most receptive to pay demands in the middle of the week and in the afternoon.

10 **Use the law.** If you really think you are paid less than a man for broadly similar work and none of the above has worked you will need to take it further via the legal system. Under the Equal Pay Act you can write to your employer asking for information to help to establish if you are getting equal pay and if not why not. Download a list of the questions you can ask from the EOC website on **www.eoc.org.uk**. If you remain convinced you are being discriminated against but your employer still refuses you a rise, write a letter of grievance to them. Wait 28 days for a reply. They should then set up a meeting to discuss the situation. You can take a union representative or colleague with you. If your grievance is not upheld you can and should then appeal against the decision. If this too doesn't work you can, as a last resort, go to a tribunal. Get advice on it from the EOC and the independent Advisory Conciliation and Arbitration Service (**www.acas.org**), which tries to settle claims. In 2002–3, 17,000 women took their employers to a tribunal. There is one final thing to say on pay and

discrimination. Do not ever go to a tribunal or threaten your employer with a tribunal if you don't have a good case but just hope you might get a cash payout. It isn't good for any of us.

11 **Never be afraid of being called a feminist.** Too many people think that being 'pushy' in the office will end up with them being labelled a 'feminist'. And too many people think there is something wrong with that. According to a poll commissioned by the women's rights organization Womankind Worldwide in 2006, only 29% of UK women are happy to be called feminist these days. This is an outrage. If you agree with women having the vote, having equal rights in the workplace and at home, getting as much say over the family car as a husband, being free from domestic violence and rape and so on then you are a feminist. Anyone who says they are not should take a step back and remember that the world of opportunity they live in was created for them by the women who invented the word – and suffered for it. We do them a great disrespect to deny their label. I'd be horrified if anyone suggested that I was not a feminist.

Being worth more

So far we've just been looking at how to get paid what you are really worth. But you can also look at this the other way around: if you want to get paid more perhaps you should make yourself worth more. You are selling yourself in the labour market. Within that market there are a lot of ordinary people. They can all type, can all do basic administration, can all answer phones and so on – they can all do low-paid commodity-style jobs. So if you want to get paid more than them you have to have skills they don't have. You can do this formally. It is generally accepted that the better educated you are the more you will get paid and in the case of professional qualifications that is absolutely true. As a doctor or a lawyer, an architect or a web designer the better your qualifications and the more of them you have the more likely you are to be able to find the best and the best-paid jobs in your sector. You also need to be sure that you keep upgrading your skills – don't be the last person in your office to learn new IT skills; be the first, for example.

But if you like your job you will also accrue value as an employee informally – being engaged and enthusiastic makes you of more worth to your employers than being bored and disengaged from your work. So ask yourself this. Do you like your job? Does it make you happy? Do you actually want to do it? Too many of us just drift into our first jobs and then end up stuck in them or variations of them for ever whether we like them or not and whether we are particularly good at them or not. This makes us disconnected, something that stops us learning or moving ahead – who wants to promote someone who is clearly bored with her career? If you take a job you are genuinely interested in, however, you should find that you are excited by it, that you learn and grow on the job, that you understand how the company you work for operates and what it needs from you. This makes you valuable and it makes you promotable. The upshot? If you do something you enjoy you are more likely to become good at it and hence to be paid more for doing it. So think about the bits of your job that you really like, do more of them, do them better and make sure everyone knows you've done them better. A rising salary should be the reward for that time and effort.

Three other ways to make more money

Changing career

What if you've done everything you can to get paid the going rate in your current job and you still don't feel that your income is high enough? The obvious thing to do is to change jobs. When someone offers you a new job they usually offer you 5–10% more than you are currently earning (otherwise, unless you were deeply unhappy in your old job for non-financial reasons, why would you bother moving?), which not only bumps up your current salary but bumps up the base from which it will be increased in future pay rounds. But more promising as a long-term tactic than moving jobs within your industry might be to consider changing the kind of job you do.

For all the wrong reasons much work remains effectively divided into women's work and men's work. Women are nurses, child carers, beauticians, primary school teachers and shop assistants. Men are plumbers, train drivers and construction workers. And guess what? Yes, all the traditional male jobs pay significantly more than the traditional female jobs despite the fact that the skill levels required can't be considered that different. Do you need more skills to drive a train than to teach a class full of 30 five-year-olds? To build a wall than to take blood from an elderly cancer sufferer? I don't think so. None the less this kind of pay discrimination exists right up to the top of the career tree: an article in the *Financial Times* recently pointed out that the work of (mostly female) clinical psychologists and (mostly male) psychiatrists overlaps significantly, yet the former are generally paid less than the latter.

What they earn

Cherie Blair (lawyer): £200,000

Lily Cole (supermodel): £2 million

Anna Wintour (editor of *Vogue*): $1 million

Stella McCartney (fashion designer): £669,000

Davina McCall (TV presenter): £1 million

Kirsty Young (newsreader): £500,000

Laura King (beauty therapist): £11,000

Louise Hitch (personal trainer): £20,000

Inge Mecke (trainee solicitor): £29,000

Alessandra Sartore (executive PA): £35,000

Rachel Dodd (care assistant): £13,000

Zoe Baglin (occupational therapist): £18,500

Helen Pike (teacher): £37,000

SOURCE: *Grazia*

You'll clearly be fighting a losing battle if you are a beautician (paid around £18,000) and want your employer to pay you a construction worker's salary (more like £35,000), so the best way to earn more is simply to switch over. There is currently a huge shortage of skilled labour – bricklayers, decorators and carpenters, for example – in central London, yet there are so few women in the business (around 1% nationwide) that when an all-women team turned up working in the capital the story merited a full-page article in London's *Evening Standard* (headline: 'CHICKS AND MORTAR'). I'm not suggesting that we all take plumbing courses, just that we look around us and wonder if the industry we are working in is the best one for us over the long term.

Getting a second job

The other obvious way to boost your income in a hurry is to get a second job. Second jobs are usually low paid and boring – waitressing, Saturday shop assisting, cleaning and the like – but if you pick them right they can also occasionally offer you experience that can take your career to another level. One of my first jobs was working as a researcher at a Japanese television station. My fellow researcher (Riko) had a second job doing the same at MTV in the evening. She ended up becoming an MTV video jockey specializing in hip-hop music and then a bigwig at a large record company. Still, that kind of thing doesn't happen very often and for most of us the main problems with a second job are not, as they were with Riko, hoping that our main employers don't see us on TV and fending off fans when out for dinner, but getting enough sleep and making sure our tax affairs are in order.

The tax thing is boring but important. You will need to tell both your current employer and the Inland Revenue that you have a second job so that both your income tax and your national insurance can be correctly calculated. There is, for example, a limit on how much national insurance anyone has to pay on their salary so with two jobs – and two employers deducting it on behalf of the government – you could find yourself paying too much and then having to claim it back by filling in your own tax return. You also need to make sure you are paying the right amount of income tax. You get a personal allowance (an amount of income you don't have to pay tax on) every year (£5,035 in 2006/7) but if you don't let your employers know about each other you may find that they both give you the allowance, leaving you with a large bill to pay to the Inland Revenue later. If your second job means your total income is high enough to make you a higher rate income tax payer yet both your employers are only collecting lower rate payments the same could also be true. Make sure your employers know about each other and get you the right tax codes if you want to avoid any difficulties (see the Inland Revenue's website, **www.hmrc.gov.uk**, for more on this).

Finally, before you take on a second job do make sure it is both possible and really worth it. Working two jobs isn't easy so ask yourself a few things before you commit yourself to it. Will your main employer allow it? Many companies explicitly say in their contracts that employees are not allowed to take on any outside work at all, so, while you may think you can get away with it simply by not telling your main employer, taking on a second job might put your first one at risk. Do the sums really add up? You may need childcare, which could eat up much of the extra income, and if you are on any benefits you will find that as your income rises they fall. Making your own money rather than relying on the state (and effectively the largesse of other tax payers) sounds good in theory, but in practice it can be a tad exhausting. So check what will happen to any benefits or tax credits before you head out to work a second job.

Then you might think about whether you could look at your income equation the other way around. A study from Liverpool Victoria last year showed that over 40% of those with second jobs had taken them not to pay off debts or save for something special but just to meet their living expenses. However, perhaps instead of boosting your income to meet those expenses you could simply reduce the expenses. You probably think you can't cut down, but most of us overspend, be it on shoes or insurance. A little time spent concentrating on cutting our costs can improve life immeasurably more than spending Friday and Saturday nights stuck behind a bar – and usually a lot faster too. See the next chapter for more on this.

Start your own business

All the things we've discussed in this chapter so far have been about how to increase your income in a marginal sort of a way – about adding 20% rather than about multiplying it by ten. But most of us secretly hope for a great deal more than that: we dream that one day we'll be rich. Ideally, we'd like this to happen without us having to make much in the way of effort. That's why every week 14 million of us buy tickets for the National Lottery. Sadly, playing the lottery is an absolutely hopeless way to get rich: every week about 13,999,999 of us don't win a penny. So what's a better way? A more realistic answer is to start your own business. One million women in the UK are self-employed and women now own a third of our small businesses. Following their lead isn't easy and it certainly isn't foolproof: a large percentage of small businesses fail in the first year and another large percentage struggle on for a few more years without ever making real money. But some will hit the big time.

Remember the story of the Body Shop? Thanks to having the right idea at the right time and working relentlessly to make her dream a reality Anita Roddick is now a millionaire many times over. The same is true of Julia Pankhurst, founder of Friends Reunited, a social networking website valued at many millions of pounds. And these extreme examples of success aside, there are thousands of other women around the country making good livings from their businesses.

One is my sister Tabitha. She has always found working for other people tricky and long had dreams of running her own company. So three years ago, at the age of 28, she started doing just that and launched her own accessories firm called Tabitha. She designed a collection of handbags, got them made up at a factory in east London and then spent the next few months schlepping from trade show to trade show selling them. Selling is one of the things she does best and within months she was deluged with orders. Today her bags are on the arms of many a celebrity (Danni Minogue is a big fan!), she manufactures her products in China and Brazil and her turnover in 2005 was nearly £750,000. She's done extremely well and done it very quickly but, as she says, it really hasn't been easy and it still isn't – she seems to hit a new business-related crisis of some kind every week. For the last two years she has worked every hour possible; she has barely seen her friends and family; she hasn't had time to have a proper boyfriend; and she has had to cede custody of her cats to an old flame as she has no time to look after them. Starting and running a small business is, she says, the hardest thing she has ever done and no one who isn't 'truly passionate' about their product or idea should even consider following in her footsteps.

Her words are echoed by Caroline Bennett. Twelve years ago, Caroline, now 40, raised £90,000 and opened a sushi bar called Moshi Moshi in Liverpool Street in London. Years of hard slog later she has two more restaurants. Moshi Moshi turns over nearly £3 million a year and produces profits of several hundred thousand pounds a year. Smaller scale, but getting there, is the firm launched in 2001 by Australian Ashe Peacock. Antipodium is dedicated to Australian fashion with a shop in Soho but Ashe also does PR for Australian brands in the UK and wholesales their products into other retail outlets here. She now has eight staff in London and turns over a few hundred thousand pounds a year.

So how can you have a go at following in their footsteps? I've asked Caroline, Tabitha and Ashe for their top tips and summarized them below.

1 **Don't start a business unless you really want to do it.** If you don't want it enough you won't be able to cope with the long hours, the financial difficulties and the utter lack of time for anything not related to your work. It just isn't enough to like handbags to start a handbag business and liking sushi isn't enough to give you the drive to launch a restaurant chain.

2 **Research, research, research.** Your idea may sound good to you but is there really a gap in the market? Make a proper business

plan showing exactly how you imagine your project will develop. How big is the market? Who are the competitors? How big can you grow? What are the potential weaknesses? What are the costs likely to be? 'I didn't do a proper business plan,' says Tabitha. 'I thought I'd just figure it out as I went along. Big mistake. Without set targets and proper pre-planning the business was a huge mess by the end of the first year.' NatWest has a free online advice programme to teach entrepreneurs about planning and conducting market research. See **www.natwest.com/newbusiness**.

3 **Get all the advice you can.** If you go it alone you have a 40% chance of succeeding but if you join a mentoring scheme of some kind those odds improve to 50%. But never forget it's your business. Everyone has an opinion and likes to offer advice, says Tabitha. 'Listen but stay focused on what you want and go with your gut instinct.' You're the one who will end up dealing with the consequences of your actions so all the final decisions have to be yours.

4 **'Take full responsibility for everything,' says Ashe.** If you start a fashion business 'you don't just get to play around with dresses'. You have to understand all the boring bits too. If you don't do your own book-keeping you won't make it. 'I've learned the hard way that no one else will do things as carefully as you, so you have to be qualified to supervise everyone who works for you on every level.'

5 **Understand that employees and friends are different things.** However much you convince yourself that having friends working with you or for you will work, says Tabitha, 'it just won't – ever'. Managing staff isn't something you think about when you first start up but if you have any success at all you won't be working

on your own for long. Then hire very carefully. Once hired, staff are hard to get rid of, 'and in a small company politics can be so destructive'. 'Business is about the people you employ,' says Ashe and it is hugely challenging learning 'how to be a leader while being fair and allowing people the freedom to make their jobs as interesting as they want them to be'. Remember too that you have to support them but they won't support you: 'The boss gets no support from anywhere: people assume you don't need it.'

6 **Be nice to your bank.** An understanding bank manager will make all the difference when you have cash-flow problems. And you will have cash-flow problems, says Tabitha. Lots of businesses look great on paper but go bust anyway when they run out of the cash they need to deal with day-to-day expenses. Small fashion businesses collapse every day thanks to department stores not paying them for months after their wares have been sold, for example. See **www.payontime.co.uk** for advice on making the big boys pay you what they owe you.

7 **Use the Internet.** Web-based businesses can start smaller and use less capital than others. Eighty per cent of the businesses in the UK run by women have a website and it's essential that you too have an online presence. A good website doesn't come cheap, says Tabitha, but it is the most important part of your branding: get it right and it will be the best investment in yourself you ever make.

8 **Remember size isn't everything, says Caroline.** If you have started the business looking for the status and recognition that come with having a well-known brand that's one thing, but if it's financial freedom you want you may find that you are better off expanding slowly, or if you are doing well being small just staying

small. A small company offering a good regular income is better than a large one making losses.

9 **Don't get too hung up on looking for grants.** There are around 3,000 different types of grant available to small businesses – from the government, the EU and various other support bodies (see **www.businesslink.gov.uk**) – but most small business owners say that the red tape and form filling take up so much time and energy that it simply isn't worth bothering to apply for them.

10 **Remember that you will have to take risks.** Being an entrepreneur is uncomfortable and working hard alone won't guarantee success. You'll need creative thinking and luck too. 'You can't assume that the people you do business with will be honourable,' says Ashe. 'Anything that can go wrong will.' 'You are always the last to get paid,' says Tabitha, 'so if you need routine and security, don't do it – entrepreneurship isn't for you.'

11 **Don't let yourself be discriminated against.** A recent study by Warwick University showed that women starting a business pay up to 1% more a year for their start-up loans than men. They also borrow much less: an average of £6,100 against £18,500 for men, says the Association of Chartered Certified Accountants. There are many perfectly rational explanations for this (perhaps women tend to start riskier businesses) but it's worth bearing in mind – most bank managers are, after all, men.

Scams: the ways you won't make money

When you need money badly it's tempting to fall for one of the many get-rich-quick schemes about, particularly as so many of them sound so very plausible. But like most things when it comes

The Avon Lady and Ebay: Selling in your spare time

I remember the Avon Lady coming round when I was a little girl. She had cases and cases full of wonderful coloured smelly goodies and my mother, after a good rummage through and a bit of a gossip, would occasionally buy a lipstick or two from her. But who would have thought that in today's Internet age the Avon Lady would still exist? Well, amazingly, she does. Christianne Randolfi became an Avon Lady by default. She used and wanted to keep using the products (Avon aren't just about lipstick these days – you can buy anything from foundation to knickers to jewellery from your local representative) so she signed herself up as a sales rep. Now she sells to her friends and local acquaintances in a small way, putting in an order for around £70 and making roughly £10 for herself each time. Could she make more? Easily, she says. A few very elite Avon Ladies are said to make six-figure incomes from the firm, but she's happy to earn enough just to pay for her own cosmetics. Contact **www.avoncompany.com** for more information.

Still, something tells me that Avon Ladies aren't the wave of the future. If I were looking for a way to make a bit of extra income out of a few hours a day I think I would turn to eBay, the auction site where anything can be bought and sold to anyone. For inspiration take the case of Caroline Brown, an eBay trader who specializes in clothes. At 61 years old she has a lifetime of knowledge about fashion and fabrics behind her, so she visits charity shops all over the place, buys the good stuff and then auctions it on eBay. Does she make any money? You bet she does. As an accomplished dressmaker in her own right Caroline can separate the good stuff from the dross in seconds ('it's all about the cut and the fabric') and while it is true that vintage clothes are all the rage and the pickings are thinner than they were even five years ago she says there are still plenty of bargains about: a piece of quality high street clothing that retails at £75 will probably sell for a tenner in a charity shop and £20 or so on eBay. That means that if you have a good eye, says Caroline, and you can shift ten or so items a week you could make £100–£150 a week relatively easily; she's sold her wares to people in the US and in Japan as well as to residents of the Outer Hebrides (who haven't much access to high street shops) and to a pub landlady in Wales. Caroline suggests looking in particular for the labels everyone knows – French Connection, for example – when you start out, as they are easiest to sell.

But eBay isn't just about fashion: if you want to do well on it you have to work with what you know. Suzette is very knowledgeable about books. She spends her spare time combing car boot sales, markets and country auctions looking for deals that she then sells on eBay. Sometimes she makes only £5 on a trade but sometimes she strikes it lucky too: she once sold a Kylie Minogue magazine supplement to a man in Florida for £85 and a rummage through a skip in Finchley provided her with £1,000 worth of sales in rare classical music books and RAF memorabilia. Overall, she has found that with a little concentration she can make up to £1,000 a month trading books. Suzette is a single mother so this is a very useful extra income for her. Carlotta isn't a very active trader, but everything she needs for her two children is bought and sold on eBay: when she needs a new pram she saves money by getting it second-hand on eBay and when she doesn't need it any more she claws the cash back by reselling it on eBay too. Below are Carlotta, Suzette and Caroline's five top tips for doing well on eBay.

✳ **Get all the relevant information about your product into the descriptive title. People won't search under the words 'stunning' or 'fabulous' but under 'skirt, green, size 12'. Suzette says she's even made money buying things on eBay that had been badly listed and then reselling them.**

✳ **Try to have all your auctions end at the weekend, preferably on Sunday evening as that is when eBay is busiest and people have time to watch the items they want properly.**

✳ **Always overestimate rather than underestimate the postage costs – losing out here can be very irritating.**

✳ **Try to have everything sent by recorded next-day delivery. Most people are prepared to pay the extra for it and it means that you can keep track of your items and keep your feedback 100% good (everyone you deal with can rate you on eBay and if your feedback is less than around 98% good you'll have trouble selling stuff).**

✳ **Be nice, be efficient and be scrupulously honest. On the Internet your feedback ratings (a proxy for your reputation) are the most important thing you have.**

to money, dealing with scams is a matter of common sense. All you have to do is remember this: when it comes to money, when something sounds too good to be true it always is. There are no exceptions.

"A large income is the best recipe for happiness I ever heard of."
Jane Austen

The most common scams often have something to do with pyramid selling. These are effectively schemes that have as their sole purpose signing up other people to the scheme. You may be told that it is a sales company and that once signed up you will be making your money by selling cosmetics or drinks or some such but once you have handed over your 'membership fee' you will find that making money from the sales is no easy business. Instead the money is in signing up others. And you won't be able to do that – it takes a particular kind of high-pressure sales personality to get other people in and most of us don't have it. When I was in my early twenties I was persuaded to join a skincare products 'multi-level marketing' company (MLM is a polite term for pyramid selling) but I never made a single sale; in my heart of hearts I knew the stuff I was supposedly selling wasn't much good and I just wasn't up to the job of selling it and I certainly wasn't up to the job of signing up anyone new to the scheme. Anyway all these schemes eventually collapse: they rely on an endless number of people being available to be signed up and the supply of people is, of course, never endless. When the supply of recruits dries up the pyramid collapses.

What to watch out for in particular in the UK is so-called 'gifting schemes'. The last well-known one was Women Empowering Women (WEW), which began in 2001 on the Isle of Wight. This was a pure cash pyramid – there was no pretence about there being any products of any kind involved. Women were asked to buy one of eight 'hearts' on a sheet; above that were four more, then two and finally one – the receiver – at the top. When new 'gifters' joined, the original members moved up the pile. When they reached the top they got the £3,000 contributions from the eight new hearts and took home £24,000. There was a lot of talk about helping other women and yourself at the same time and about making money outside the male capitalist society. It was all nonsense – WEW was as much a scam as any other pyramid scheme and like any other pyramid scheme it eventually collapsed. This was a shock to the women who lost money (remember, for every woman who was paid £24,000 eight had to lose their £3,000 stake) but if they had stopped to think about it for just a minute it really shouldn't have been. Even to move one pyramid down six stages needed a quarter of a million people (8x8x8x8x8x8). To move it down twelve would have required the entire population of the world to be involved. This kind of pyramid still pops up periodically; they call themselves Hearts or Circles. Don't fall for their stories of sisterly solidarity.

The next money-losing scam to look out for is the lottery or prize draw scam. You'll get a notification that you have won a huge prize, usually in a US or European lottery. You're then asked for a registration fee or an admin fee, probably of a few thousand pounds. Don't pay it – you'll never hear from them again and you'll never see your money again. This kind of thing often looks tempting but remember this: if you didn't buy a ticket you can't have won the lottery.

Then there are the Nigerian 419 scams. These are called after the section of the Nigerian penal code that legislates against them. They've been going for years – first in letter form, then as faxes, now as emails. The idea is simple. They tell you that due to some bizarre quirk of fate they have millions of pounds to hand but they need to get it out of Afghanistan, Nigeria or some other distant country. They want you to help them by letting them use your bank account to receive the cash in the UK. In return they will give you a couple of million to keep. The catch? You have to send them some cash first so that they can pay miscellaneous expenses at the other end. You also need to give them all your personal and account details. If you send the cash you will only hear from them again to demand more and if you send your personal details you leave yourself vulnerable in many ways (never give out your personal details: sounds obvious but people do it all the time). The stories told in 419 emails are always topical and often quite convincing (after the tsunami in 2004, for example, I got an email purporting to be from a newly orphaned teenager who needed help getting his parents' fortune out of Indonesia – see **www.419eater.com** for many more fantastic examples). But however good these letters sound you should never respond to them: not only is doing so both greedy and illegal but the authors of the letters are criminals.

Similar fraudsters are involved in the increasingly common eBay/Western Union scam, which works like this. You are selling something online – perhaps a piece of furniture on eBay or a special car on a car sales website such as **www.autotrader.co.uk**.

You get a response from someone who wants to buy your goods, say for £5,000. They say they will send you a cheque not for £5,000 but for £7,000. The £5,000 is for you but they then ask that you forward the extra £2,000 on to a friend of theirs via money transfer firm Western Union (the story you are spun is that the friend is to arrange shipping or some such for them). You get the cheque. You deposit it and send on the £2,000. Then you get a call from your bank. What's happened? You guessed it. The cheque has bounced and you are down £2,000. It's simple but it works brilliantly. One to be aware of whenever you are dealing online.

Finally a word on working-from-home scams. You will often see adverts telling you that you can make money addressing and stuffing envelopes at home. But you can't. If you reply to the ad you'll be asked for a registration fee. Then you'll be advised to make money by placing the same ads you replied to around the place. There is no real job – it's just a way to con you out of your registration fee. Other similar scams involve adverts that offer work assembling things at home. If you respond you'll be asked to pay upfront for the assembly kit or whatever materials you might be using. You'll never get it back and you won't ever get paid for the assembly – your work will be returned as 'substandard'. The result? They get to keep your deposit. See **www.homeworking.com** for more detail on how to avoid falling prey to this kind of con, but most of all remember that you should never have to pay to get work. If you do something's wrong.

Redundancy

Losing your job is horrible, however much you hated it, however much you kept wishing on a Monday morning that you would lose it and never have to go again. The fact is that being told you are surplus to requirements is a huge blow to your self-esteem. You'll be shocked, you'll be angry and you'll be hurt. But above all you'll be dealing with the fact that you no longer have an income.

Statutory redundancy pay is pathetic. Between the ages of 18 and 21 you get half a week's pay for every year of service. From 22 to 41 you get a week's pay and from 42 on one and a half weeks' pay. But this is subject to a maximum of a few hundred pounds a week and you can't claim for more than 20 years of service. This means that the absolute maximum the law can make your firm give you at the moment is less than £6,000.

But there is some good news too. The first £30,000 of redundancy pay comes tax free and you are likely to get more than the very basic amount. This means that redundancy does give you an opportunity to rethink your career and even your life. You could take a few months off to retrain and change direction, for example; now might actually be the time to set up your own business! However, the first thing you will need to do is to get your finances in order to make sure you can weather a few months with no income and to rebuild your confidence. Remember that redundancy usually isn't personal (if you think it is get a lawyer).

1 **Budget.** Hopefully you'll have six months' worth of money saved up (see Chapter 4) but if not you'll need to work out how many months you think you could be out of work and budget with your redundancy payment accordingly.

2 **Don't delay in claiming benefits.** You should be able to get a job seeker's allowance, although this will depend on you having paid

enough national insurance over the previous two years. If you haven't paid enough and are in a bad way you may still be able to get a means-tested allowance. You may also be able to get support for rent, council tax and mortgage costs. See **www.dwp.gov.uk**, the website of the Department for Work and Pensions, for more detail.

3 **Don't rush into the first job you get offered.** Being without work is frightening but you spend all day every day at work so you need to be sure you end up with something that is at worst bearable and at best actually enjoyable.

4 **Work on your confidence.** Make a list of all your skills – not just the ones you have used in your work but all your skills. This will help you to figure out what you have to offer a new employer.

5 **Keep going.** Set yourself a few targets every day so you don't just end up staying in bed.

WHAT Do I Do Now?

✳ **Find out if you are paid correctly.**

✳ **Demand more if you are not.**

✳ **Take action if you don't get it.**

✳ **Consider changing jobs or even careers to move yourself up the salary ladder.**

✳ Consider alternative, non-salaried routes to bumping up your income.

✳ Have the right mindset. If you work hard you do deserve to be paid well.

✳ Make an effort: it isn't fair but study after study shows that the well-groomed and slim make more money than the poorly groomed and overweight.

✳ Read the chapter on investing; this explains how to make your money create more income for you without you having to lift a finger.

2
Spend Less, Have More

Why is it that you never seem to have quite enough cash? Where does all your money go? The answer isn't that far away. Look in every cupboard in the house and rummage around under the bed. Then take out and collect together every piece of clothing you've worn once or never, every pair of shoes you have ever bought in the sales that doesn't quite fit, every kitchen utensil you've never used or used just once (this includes the juicer and the sandwich toaster) and every piece of specialist equipment that has been gathering dust since you decided your new hobby wasn't much fun after all. Get out your calculator and add up how much you think they all cost. Now you can probably see where a lot of the money went.

£ 851 : the value of the possessions the average British woman carries with her. This includes clothes, mobile phones, MP3 players and so on (Zurich Insurance).

£ 13,000 : the average value of the clothes the average UK woman has bought but never worn (Prudential).

£ 2,900 : the value of the average student's electronic goods (Direct Line).

£ 36.6 billion : total sales of clothing in the UK in 2004.

What's the point in making all the effort we do to make money if, instead of making it work for us properly, we then just waste it?

Because that's exactly what most of us do. Sixty-three per cent of women confess that they have often bought clothes on sale that they have never worn; 56% say they have bought shoes and 42% toiletries they have never used. They also say that on average they wear only about half the clothes in their wardrobe regularly and, worst of all, nearly 8% of them say that they have never worn the most expensive thing they have bought. On average we buy £13,000 worth of clothes that we never wear over a lifetime, something that makes a hefty contribution to the £69,000 that research from the Pru says we all waste in the average 40-year working life. That's enough to pay council tax for each household in Britain four times over every year or to pay for a really substantial asset each (£69,000 would buy you a perfectly nice holiday home in Croatia, for example).

A third of us have bought books we have never read or kitchen equipment we have never used, a quarter of us have bought DVDs we have never watched or CDs we have never listened to. And it doesn't seem to matter what stage of life we are at, we all buy endless amounts of stuff. It wasn't very long ago that students who owned their own toasters thought themselves pretty well off. Today, according to a survey from Direct Line, the average student owns nearly £3,000 worth of electrical goods. Two-thirds have a laptop (which is probably fair enough) and one in eight has a widescreen TV of their own (which probably isn't). In August 2006 a magazine survey showed that young women were some of the worst binge spenders of all: four out of five said they spent more than they earned every month and those between 21 and 24 had an average of nearly £4,000 in credit card debt. All this spending leads us into a terrible trap. The more we spend the more we need to earn to maintain our lifestyles, particularly if we are using debt to spend. This eats away at our freedom: we have to stay in jobs we hate just to keep the income coming in to pay for the clothes and TVs that, truth be told, we never needed in the first place.

"I love shopping. It's like a little present to me."

Lisa Snowdon

The obvious question – and the one our grandmothers always ask – is why on earth do we buy all this stuff? The answer isn't a good one. We do it because we have allowed ourselves to be conned into believing both that we need it and that it will make us happier. For most of human history the average person hasn't had enough of anything. Until very recently our main problems centred on getting enough to eat and drink and not getting too wet or cold. But in the last 100 years things have changed so much that in the West at least we now have too much of everything. The corporate and public sectors between them have provided us with housing, clothing, healthcare, food and entertainment. We don't actually need anything else.

But companies still have to make profits and the only way they can do so is to persuade us that we need more – in the fashion world they can't just shut up shop because you already have ten dresses. So every 'season' manufacturers change things. They produce new styles, new colours, new combinations and new materials. Then they spend millions advertising, marketing and sucking up to fashion journalists to get the details of their new 'must-have' look out there. Marketeers know we aren't entirely happy (who is?) and that leaves a huge opening for them to push goods that appeal to our emotional needs. These days they separate us from our money by promising us that if we improve our 'lifestyles' – by buying the stuff they are offering us – we will somehow improve our lives too: that having a pair of £100 jeans will make us happier than a £4 pair; that carrying a £500 handbag as seen on Sienna Miller will provide more life enhancement than a £20 one from Oasis; that spa breaks and £50 bottles of body lotion will make us more beautiful; and that buying brand-new skis will make us better at skiing, and expensive DIY tools make our houses significantly more attractive. In 2005 there was even the launch of a magazine called *Happy*, devoted entirely to shopping, with a cover line '300 great buys to make everyone love you'. The magazine – which is still being published –

represented the propagation of the great marketing lie: that owning things, and particularly expensive things, will in itself bring you a sense of well-being.

All this works. Fifty per cent of those asked by a *Vogue* survey in 2005 said that the brand image was one of their major shopping influences when it comes to clothes and 60% said the same of beauty products; 85% said they bought not ordinary skincare products but 'premium skincare products', while 64% agreed that *Vogue* had the 'ability to make products more desirable'.' And just look at the reaction of *Style* magazine to the news that the average woman spends nearly £100,000 on clothes in a lifetime. 'Who cares,' wrote one of their regular columnists, it's worth it. 'When it comes to shopping ... the normal rules don't apply.' She's not alone in thinking this. *Glamour* magazine last year ran a little piece about a woman looking for a boyfriend. The journalist asked her how she was going to go about it. Her answer? She's going to splash out on a Caribbean holiday so she has an all-over tan, have her hair done at Nicky Clarke, buy all her cosmetics at Carita, her lingerie from upmarket underwear shop Myla and her clothes (£500 worth a month despite the fact that she takes home pay of only around £1,300 a month) from upmarket designer Paul and Joe. This makes no sense. Most men have never heard of Paul and Joe and while the label makes lovely clothes they aren't going to make her look much nicer than Topshop stuff. Nor will knickers from Myla. Oh, and the sun shines in places other than the Caribbean. This woman might end up with a boyfriend (although he'd have to be a very tolerant one) but it won't be because of her Carita face cream. And she'd better hope he's a generous boyfriend because she's always going to be broke.

The fact is that normal rules do apply. They always apply. Spending money should not be thought of as an emotional experience. Falling in love is an emotional experience; having a baby is an emotional experience; attending your best friend's wedding is an emotional experience; buying a handbag simply is not.

"I like my money right where I can see it – hanging in my closet." Carrie Bradshaw, Sex and the City

If you aren't happy with your weight, with your job or with your relationship, no number of dresses will cheer you up for long; a £1,000 weekend at a spa will do you no more good than a lie-in and a walk in the park, and if you're getting old a £100 pot of wrinkle cream will no more make you young again than a jar of cold cream. Instead it will just make you feel slightly disappointed, pushing you back to the shops to search for something new to cheer yourself up. Women often say that they feel moments of 'joy' as they make new purchases. Why? Because for that moment they genuinely believe that what they have bought will make their lives better. But they quickly see that it has not and the joy goes – it is a very fleeting feeling, to say nothing of an expensive one. The moment you have something you start getting used to having it and the joy you find in it starts declining. New shoes make you happy for a few days but after several wearings they're not all that new any more. To be happy you find that you need another pair. It is the same for handbags and jeans.

It's also worth pointing out that it's not just expensive stuff we've been conned into buying too much of. When advertisers aren't using the 'improve your life' line to sell us stuff, they're using the 'it's so cheap you'd be mad not to' line instead. Over the last decade the big business success story has been the rise and rise of the discount store – the likes of Matalan and Primark for clothes and Lidl and Aldi for food. I've nothing against discount stores – low prices are obviously a good thing – but when prices are cheap we tend to buy more than we would have otherwise and end up spending more money in total. We think we are saving when we buy jeans at £4 and if we needed jeans anyway we probably are. But if we didn't intend to buy jeans and only did so because they were so cheap and then bought three pairs for ourselves and one pair each for our sisters as well, we are not saving, we are spending: £4 spent is £4 not saved.

We now buy twice as many clothes as we did a decade ago for the simple reason that they are cheap. In 2004 clothing sales in the UK were worth a total of £36.6 billion, 19% more than in 2000. Around £9.5 billion went on men's clothes and £6.6 billion on children's clothes. The rest – a massive £20.5 billion – was spent on women's clothes. We also travel at least twice as much as we used to. Back when it cost £400 to go to Paris people didn't go very often. Now it costs £29.99 to fly there on a discount airline we go at the drop of a hat. Then when we get there we stay in a hotel, go out for dinner and buy souvenirs. The same is true of electronic goods. We don't buy just one television or DVD player. No, at £29.99 each we don't see why we shouldn't have one in

Shoes and handbags

My friend Nick once asked me why on earth it is that women spend so much money on handbags and shoes. A man, he said, only needs three pairs of shoes – one for wearing with work clothes, one for wearing with casual clothes and one for playing sport. Yet every woman he had ever known appeared to need upwards of 20 pairs. Indeed a survey from *Harper's Bazaar* in 2006 interviewed 1,000 women and found that half of them owned over 30 pairs of shoes and one in ten owned 100 pairs. One in ten also admitted to spending £1,000-plus a year on shoes. The right shoes, said the editor of the magazine, 'can turn you from the girl next door into a sex goddess in seconds'. Nick found handbags even more bemusing. Men, he said, don't need them at all; they just carry money and door keys in their pockets. So why do women need to have so many bags? Indeed why do they need them at all?

A few days later he came back to me. He'd figured it out, he said. They are the only two things that look the same on everyone regardless of their weight or body shape: the average woman may not be able to fit into the same jeans as Kate Moss and would feel miserable even having a go in the changing room but a pair of Prada shoes looks much the same on everyone. He's right of course. The runaway sales of shoes and handbags are nothing but a function of our insecurities about our figures. How sad is that?

every room and a digital radio or two thrown in for good measure. It all adds up to a lot of money being spent that would never have been spent a decade ago. How much have you bought in the last six months that you don't need? Find a credit card statement from a few months ago and have a look at it. How many of the things you paid for with your card can you remember ever having or do you still have? Were they really worth buying or would you now rather have the cash in hand?

"I'm always buying new shoes and I might spend as much as $1,500 on a really great pair, but I don't splurge on clothes"
　　　　　　　　　　　　　　　　　Shania Twain

And it isn't just clothes, cosmetics, CDs, TVs and face cream you've been conned into buying when you don't need to. It's new cars, insurance, overpriced credit card debt, and expensive mortgages, phone tariffs and utilities. Financial services firms are just like fashion firms in many ways: they know that many of us have all we need when it comes to money (a mortgage, a current account, a savings account or two and a pension) so to keep their profits growing they have to continue to invent new products and persuade us we need them. So once again we find ourselves paying too much for useless tat (insurances against things that really won't ever happen, for example) only this time it's usually useless tat we don't even understand. This doesn't make any sense: you work hard for every penny you earn so why let it slip through your fingers so easily? Distinguishing between the products you really need for yourself and those that the corporate world wants you to think you need (so it can make ever higher profits for itself) is absolutely vital.

So next time you think you might need a new pair of shoes, another credit card, some clever kind of insurance, or any other financial product stop and think. Do you really need it? Or does someone else need you to think you need it? Nine times out of ten you will find it is the latter.

I have a simple self-help method I use when I have to bring reality into my spending. When I see something I want in a shop I look at the price and see how many work hours it will take me to pay for it. Then I decide if it is really worth buying. Take a £200 handbag. If you earn £30,000 a year and work 8 hours a day, you are clearing around £10 an hour after tax. So that handbag is going to cost you 20 hours, or two and a half days of solid work. Do you want it that much? Sometimes the item in question might be so perfect that you do want it that much. Spending – even if unnecessary – is not all bad. I happen to think that having a coffee in Starbucks every morning *is* worth it, for example – I like the coffee and I like to sit by myself in one of their armchairs for a few minutes before I go to work. I also think that going to a spa with my sisters for the occasional weekend is worth it, not because I have the faintest faith in the treatments (I've had a great many massages in my life and I still have cellulite) but because it gets us away from our work, husbands and boyfriends and gives us time to talk. And very occasionally a handbag is worth it too. Think of spending in terms of how much happiness you are buying yourself for the money you are spending. Is it enough? Very often it is not.

My friend Caroline has a good anti-spending wheeze too. It works like this, she says: 'Read high-end catalogues in the bath, and as you wallow, imagine the whole consumer process: choosing the lovely new chrome coffee maker, the thrill of arrival, the excitement of first use, the novelty wearing off, the putting away in the cupboard, and, finally, the sullen realization that it hasn't changed your life. By the time the water gets cold, you don't want any of it after all. Sting's been quoted as saying he wishes his wife would get into tantric shopping and that's exactly what this is – you look and look and look but never buy.'

The good news is that shifting your behaviour so that you spend less shouldn't be too hard if you concentrate: the scientists tell us that it takes about three weeks to create a new habit or break an old one. And when you're vacillating, it's worth bearing in mind a phrase that the Texans have for those who spend stupid amounts of money on ostentatious consumer goods they neither need nor can really afford. They call them 'big hat, no cattle' people – people who consume for the sake of it and as a result have lots of rubbish stuff but not much in the way of real assets. Look at it like this and I think you'll find it easy enough to cut your spending on 'big hat' style things.

There are a thousand ways to cut your spending on the smaller things in life. We all know that if we took our lunch to work and never visited Starbucks we'd save a great deal – we can all cut at least £50 out of our monthly spending with a little concentration and most of us can cut out a great deal more. The easiest way to do this is simply to make yourself keep a spending diary for a while. Just as keeping a food diary is a splendid way to lose weight (everyone hates to look at a list that proves overeating at the end of every day), keeping a money diary is a great way to cut spending (looking at a list of wasted cash is also a nasty way to end a day). A survey in 2006 showed that the average member of the British public cannot account for £1 out of every £8 that they spend –

Bartering for books

If you really want something you may not actually have to buy it to get your hands on it. Instead you could swap an item you have already but don't need for it. **www.ReadItSwapIt.co.uk** is a book-swapping site – it has around 8,000 members with 40,000-odd books available to swap. The founders estimate that the swaps done in the site's first three years saved the members £350,000 they would otherwise have spent buying books.

www.Mybookyourbook.com is similar but charges you to join. Swopex.co.uk is another swapping site that allows users to trade DVDs and computer games. **www.Iswap.co.uk** and **www.eSwapit.co.uk** allow you to swap pretty much anything. Another site worth looking at is **www.Freecycle.co.uk**. The idea of this one is to find free homes for unwanted possessions of any kind. If you find what you want you just arrange to go and get it, no payment involved. Finally you might look at new site **www.swapaskill.com** which allows people living in the same community to exchange skills.

making a total of over £80 billion every year. Where does that money go? A Diet Coke while you wait for the train, a packet of crisps when you suddenly feel a bit peckish at eleven, a few bits and bobs when you are passing Boots on your way to the post office and so on. The details may be hazy but the money's gone.

I don't want to spend all of this chapter on the small stuff so I've put in an appendix at the back of the book offering 53 ways to make many small savings which I hope you'll read (they all add up). Many are obvious (turn your heating down a few degrees) and some are not, but I hope that once you realize how you are constantly allowing yourself to be conned by consumerism and its corporate cheerleaders, and start looking at your purchases rationally, you'll find you buy less unnecessary stuff and that your spending will automatically fall. I also hope that when this happens it feels very good indeed.

You may find that as you stop wasting hours in the shops, your obsession with consumer culture diminishes, the burden of desire lifts from your shoulders and you are suddenly much happier (see Chapter 11 for more on why consumption alone can't make you really happy). You may be able to see beyond your needs as a consumer (i.e. those implanted in your brain by the corporate world) to your real needs as a person (time spent with your mother as opposed to time spent racing round Ikea at the weekend, perhaps). And as your spending falls you will also find that you have given yourself more choices. The less you spend the less you need to earn and the more you can look for work that fulfils you rather than just fills your bank account. Remind yourself as you go that while you don't want to be living entirely in the future, everything you buy now that you don't need or that doesn't bring you pleasure is effectively money stolen from your future.

In the rest of this chapter I want to go beyond the small things and look at the big things we pay too much for on a regular basis, such as cars, furniture, utilities and insurance. Houses are another area where we waste vast amounts of money, so much so that I've left them out of this chapter and given them a chapter of their own. See p.221.

New cars: why you don't need them

Every time the petrol price goes up we hear endless moaning about how much it costs drivers. The pressure groups looking for the government to 'do something' about the high oil price add up how much every penny on a litre costs the average driver and splash the results over the front pages of the papers and the nation gets itself in a tizzy calling for windfall taxes on the oil companies. But a penny on a litre of petrol adds up to well under £100 for the average driver. And that's absolutely nothing compared to the money most people are chucking down the drain every day just by owning their cars.

A new car loses 20% of its value as soon as it leaves the forecourt and will be worth 30% less than its list price within three months. A few examples. If you had bought a Citroën Xsara Picasso 1.6 SX in 2004 it would have cost you £14,100. Try to sell it eighteen months later and you'd have got (according to *What Car?*) around £6,000 for it. That's a loss of over £8,000 or 57%. You'd have lost a similar amount on a Ford Kaa 1.3 hatchback (£5,000 or 52% of your cash) or a Saab 9-3 1.8 four-door (£9,250 or 45%). On the Saab you're losing about £17 a day. On a really expensive luxury car you could be losing £100-plus a day.

This doesn't make any sense at all. Why would anyone throw that kind of money around just to drive a brand-new car? Particularly as a new car turns into a second-hand car as soon as you drive it off the forecourt. None of the answers to this question is a good one. Some say they just like to have a car that no one else has ever driven. But there's no such thing. How do you think your new car got to the showroom? It didn't just drive itself off the lorry – someone else's bottom has always sat on the driver's seat at some point. Some say they like that 'new car smell'. And maybe they do (although given that it is a smell of plastics, metals and various not particularly desirable chemicals I can't think why) but if that's the case they could amuse themselves by putting a plastic bag over their heads and ripping up £50 notes. The final effect would be roughly the same as that of buying a new car.

"I just ordered the new Bentley convertible. How much was it? I don't know - I didn't ask." Paris Hilton

Some say that with a new car they know that nothing is likely to go wrong. They also know that if it does they have a guarantee to ensure peace of mind. This too is nonsensical. If a car has been on the road for five years and been properly serviced there's no more reason why it should break down than a new car. And if you buy a second-hand car from a reputable dealer of any kind you can get the same kind of guarantee you'd get with a new car anyway. As for the often voiced concern that if you buy a second-hand car you could end up with one that has been in an accident and been reconditioned, this really isn't a big deal either – you can get any car checked any time by your own mechanic or by the AA before you buy it for a matter of £100 or so.

The final reason people give (when pushed) for buying a new car is that it shows off their relative wealth and status. I'm not going to start on the stupidity of this except to point out that anyone who really thinks that driving a new Picasso gives them more status than driving a year-old one probably has bigger problems than I can address here. If you are very rich and status is very important to you then go ahead, buy all the new cars you like (there's nothing wrong with it as a hobby if you can afford it), but if you aren't and it isn't (and it shouldn't be) take yourself down to your nearest car supermarket next time you need a change of car. Then put the ten grand you save in a pension. You'll thank yourself later (see Chapter 6).

While I'm on the subject of money wasted on cars I want to go back to petrol. Why do people insist on buying super unleaded petrol at about 10p a litre more than ordinary unleaded? The AA says it makes no difference whatsoever to the performance of a car or to its petrol consumption, so if our average driver uses super instead of normal on a regular basis, they're throwing away another few pounds every time they fill the tank. And that's not the end of the car-related waste. Even more comes in the form of the dealer network garages that so many drivers take their cars to. A recent survey showed that these dealer garages charge up to £140 an hour for their labour compared to £35–£40 for an ordinary garage. So let's say you get your car serviced once a year and it takes four hours. That's another couple of hundred pounds down the drain. The whole thing is beyond me.

If you must buy a new car you might want to think about buying it at the end rather than the beginning of the month. Why? Because that's when dealers are most desperate to hit their monthly sales targets and so most likely to give you a proper discount. Last year *What Car?* sent undercover buyers to car showrooms at the end of March and then again at the beginning of April. On average they were offered the same cars at £525 less at the end of the month than at the beginning and in some cases the price difference ran into the thousands. And when you do go in to start your negotiations make sure you are tough about it whatever time of the month it is. You may think you live in an equal sort of a world but car salesmen think nothing of the sort: they think women are a bit of a soft touch and so save up all their big discounts for men. *What Car?* sent both a man and a woman into 45 dealerships around the country last year and discovered that on average women are asked to pay up to £1,800 more for exactly the same car as men (the problem also exists in the US where women are charged on average $1,300 more than men for the same new car). Four out of five of the salesmen approached by *What Car?* were prepared to cut prices for men but less than half offered any deal for women. If you can't face fighting this kind of inbuilt prejudice (life is too short to fight every battle) send a man in to do the bargaining bit for you.

Finally, before you shell out consider if you need a car of your own at all. According to Sainsbury's Bank the average motorist spends about £2,000 a year on car expenses – insurance, fuel, parking, tax, servicing and repairs. Include depreciation, says the RAC, and that number goes up to around £5,000 a year and higher for real gas-guzzlers (a Porsche Cayenne will cost its owners going on £19,000 a year, according to the RAC's figures). That's a whopping amount of money particularly if (like me) you live in a city and don't use your car that much. So why not consider a sharing scheme of some kind? Join a car club and you can order up whatever kind of car you want whenever you want it, without the bother of tax or maintenance and for a fraction of the price of owning your own car. You pay a monthly fee to the club and are then charged based on how long you have the car for on each outing and on how far you drive. Carplus suggests that driving this way will save you around £1,000–£15,000 a year as long as you drive less than 6,000 miles a year. Carplus is a charity set up to promote car clubs so its numbers aren't exactly unbiased, but I don't think they are that far out either. Car clubs aren't a perfect replacement for owning your own car (there is the inconvenience of having to walk to a nearby parking bay to pick up your car rather than having it waiting for you directly outside your door) but, given the savings on offer, they're a pretty good one. Car clubs include **www.citycarclub.co.uk** and **www.mystreetcar.co.uk**.

Cutting utility bills

These, like many money-related things, are boring but very important. Unlike many of our expenses utility bills are not optional. We all have to pay for our water, electricity and gas. Worse, the cost of making these payments has been soaring for three years as water shortages have kicked in and energy prices have been rising: gas bills have jumped an average of 39% since 2003 and electricity bills are up nearly 30% over the same time period. All this makes it very important to use the cheapest possible supplier. To find out if you are doing so visit one of the price comparison websites such as **www.uswitch.com**, **www.energyhelpline.co.uk** or **www.simplyswitch.co.uk**. Uswitch claims that the average household can save £140 a year on its energy bills by switching supplier. One of my friends, on a saving binge after the birth of her first baby, estimates that she has cut £250 off her family's annual utility bills since she spent an hour on uswitch.com changing all her suppliers.

You should also take a look at your water bills. If you live alone or don't use much water (perhaps you don't have a garden) you are probably paying too much and may find it worth your while to ask your water company to fit your house with a meter so instead of paying an average tariff you simply pay for the water you use. If you live in a block of flats or somewhere else where it is not possible to get a meter fitted ask to start paying the Average Household Charge instead of the usual charge based on the rateable value of your house. This can often provide hundreds of pounds of savings a year. I moved on to it a few years ago when I was living alone and using very little water (I was showering at the gym and was hardly ever home) yet paying the same water bills as the four people living in the flat above who appeared to do nothing but play in the bathroom. My bills were immediately halved.

You might also consider going green to save money on energy. Switching off everything in the house that is on standby will save you considerable amounts (at the moment the government estimates that appliances left on standby cost a total of £740 million a year), but you might save even more by switching to a renewable energy provider such as Ecotricity. Check this on **www.uswitch.com**.

Ensuring that you are paying as little as possible for your phone is another way to cut your spending easily. More than a third of UK fixed telephone lines are now with a non-BT supplier and the tough competition in the market means that prices have tumbled. Again, visit the price comparison websites to see if you can change suppliers and cut your costs. You should do the same with your mobile phone. Altogether we spend  £25 billion a year on our phones but we could probably spend rather less if we shopped around a bit before we signed up to our contracts. According to another comparison website, Onecompare.com, the average person could shave £210 off the cost of their mobile by switching firms. More than half of mobile users have never switched firms and are therefore on uncompetitive deals or on the wrong deal for them: the mobile phone companies have a splendid racket going whereby they create very cheap packages that include a certain number of texts or call minutes, persuade us they are good value and then once we've taken them out (without reading the small print) charge us a fortune for making more calls or sending more texts than we are allowed to under the contract. Finally, you might consider signing up to Internet telephony with one of the many firms that now offer it such as Tesco, BT or Skype. They all offer prices significantly lower than landline or mobile prices.

Flashy furniture at a discount

The sofa market is an extraordinary thing. There seems to be a sofa shop on every corner of every street in every town in the UK and half the advertising time on evening television appears to be taken up with adverts for various unattractive sofas from dfs. An alien landing on the average high street would think we were nothing but a nation of sofa addicts, a people who just can't walk

20 yards in an urban environment without popping into a shop for a new piece of furniture to lounge about on. I don't get this (there is only one sofa in my – admittedly small – house and I've had it for seven years), but more than that I don't get why, if you must buy sofas and the like, you would pay the full list price for them on the high street when you can buy at an out-of-town warehouse at a 50% discount. Sofas (like cars) become second-hand and hence verging on worthless as soon as you take them out of the showroom, so it makes sense to pay as little as possible for them.

Good news, then, that warehouses have been springing up all over the country selling end-of-line pieces, oversupply and bits of furniture no longer needed in show homes. The Showroom Warehouse, about an hour and a half up the M1 from London (**www.showhomewarehouse.co.uk**), is one good place to look. It contains the entire contents from show homes around the country priced at a half to a quarter of their original price. This is a great place to buy almost-new furniture at major discounts, although you should always bear in mind that to make the rooms look bigger ex-show-home furniture is often designed to be smaller than normal furniture (take this into account if you are thinking of buying a new-build house or flat too). This is particularly the case with beds so test before you buy. Trade Secret (**www.trade-secret.co.uk**) is another place to try (it specializes in discounted brand-name furniture at around 50%) as is You're Furnished in Essex (01279 870036), which specializes in selling top-quality bathrooms and kitchens at major discounts.

It isn't that much hassle to seek out this kind of place and the savings can be huge; if you are looking at the sort of kitchen

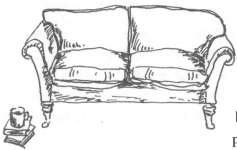

that might usually come in at £10,000 but get it for £5,000 at a warehouse, any research and travelling you might have to do along the way is going to be well worth the effort. Another plus point of these outlets is that at most of them what you see is what you leave with – there is none of the absurd nonsense you get in high street shops of having to wait 6–8 weeks for your new piece of furniture to be delivered to you. See **www.homesandbargains.co.uk** for more places to pick up discounted furniture.

Big designers at small prices

There's no more reason to pay retail prices for designer clothes than there is for sofas. In fact these days you shouldn't ever have to pay retail. There are a hundred ways to buy the same clothes the uninformed and lazy are paying fortunes for in department stores and boutiques for a fraction of the price. You can, for example, visit a branch of TK Maxx (I go to the one in Hammersmith, London but there are branches everywhere – see **www.tkmaxx.co.uk** for locations). TK Maxx fills its stores by buying in stock at cost from designers who have cash-flow problems or who have ended the season stuck with too much inventory and then adds a small margin. The result is prices that end up more than 50% less than they might be elsewhere. I do much of my Christmas shopping at TK Maxx every year. The only problem I have is maintaining a degree of discipline so I don't end up spending hundreds of pounds on things that weren't on my list in the first place.

Otherwise you can visit designer warehouse sales where and when you can (see **www.dwslondon.co.uk** for details of sales in London where you can get up to 80% off clothes and **www.bdbinvite.com** for an invitation to the Billion Dollar Babes designer sample sales), or apply for tickets for the sales after fashion week when designers sell off their samples cheap to the general public after the fashion press and department store buyers have seen them (see **www.londonfashionweekend.co.uk**). Finally, you might consider combining a bit of bargain fashion shopping with a holiday: Outlet Firenze (**www.outlet-firenze.com**) near Florence offers discounts on labels from Gucci to Armani and is also pleasantly close to the Prada factory in Montevarchi.

Current accounts: get them cheap

Most people have a current account. We all get our salaries paid into them and then pay our mortgages, rents and bills from them. But very few people have given much thought to why they have the one they have and what they want from it. As a result 70% of people still bank with the UK's four big high street banks – Lloyds, HSBC, Barclays and NatWest – despite the fact that they offer some of the worst accounts on the market. Even I had a current account at Lloyds until last year. Why? Because my mother was with Lloyds so when I opened my first bank account we automatically opened mine there too. I then, like most of the population, never thought about it again. I kept that account for 20 years.

Then suddenly my cashpoint card stopped working while my husband and I were on honeymoon. I didn't do anything about it at the time on the basis that no one should have to speak to a call centre when they are on honeymoon. But when I got back I called to complain. The reason my card didn't work, I was told, was because I had ordered a new pin number. I hadn't. It says here, said the woman at the call centre, that you have, so we have blocked your old one and sent you a new one. But you can't have blocked it, I said, because I can still use it as a chip and pin card in shops and restaurants. No you can't, she said. Yes I can, I said. And so on. This absurd saga went on for some days (getting more and more complicated with each phone call). We never established how the problem had come about but the final result was that I had no access to my accounts for well over a month and that I suddenly realized that having an account at Lloyds was a very expensive way to be inconvenienced.

Why an expensive way? Three reasons. The first is that, like the other big high street banks, Lloyds pays practically no interest on current accounts (the average current account pays just 1.2% on your money). This is important because if it isn't earning interest your money loses its purchasing power fast: if inflation is rising at 3% (i.e. prices are going up at an average rate of 3% a year) you need to make 3% interest on your money to be able to buy the same amount of stuff at the end of the year as at the beginning. If you aren't making 3% you are effectively losing money. The second is that while I didn't often get overdrawn it did sometimes happen, and Lloyds, again like the other high street names, charges interest of 17–18% on overdrafts. Other banks pay proper amounts of interest on their current accounts and charge as little

The sales: one big scam?

We all love the sales. We think we are getting fabulous bargains. But we probably aren't. The retailers think of sales as just a way to get you into their shops so they can flog you more overpriced rubbish than they can at non-sale times: there are so many loopholes in the laws covering the sales that whatever they say in their windows they can get away with not producing much in the way of discounts inside. For example, by law any goods marked with a reduction must have been for sale at the full price displayed for 28 days at some point in the previous six months. However, the stores are also allowed to put up a disclaimer in little letters somewhere in the premises saying that hasn't actually been the case (that it has only been for sale at that price for one day, for instance) so you can never be sure whether you are paying a properly discounted price or not. Shops are also guilty of occasionally putting things out at stupidly high prices for 28 days so they can slash them to an OK price but call it 80% off a few days later.

But that's just the beginning of the tricks they'll use to draw you in to the shops and get your wallet open. Rails of substandard items are often brought in just before the sales so they can be marked at very cheap prices near the door. Retailers will also put up signs all over their windows saying 'up to 70% off' when in fact almost nothing inside is that cheap. The law says 10% of goods on sale should be at

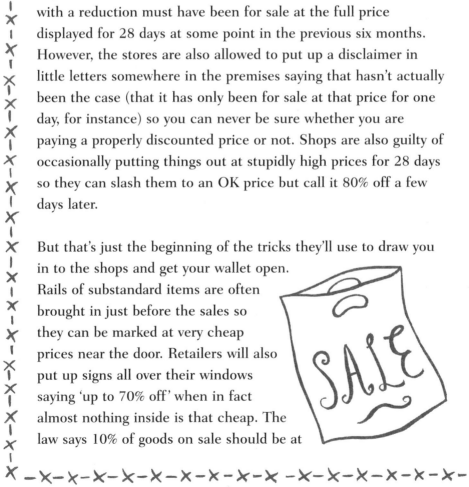

75

the maximum stated discount but who checks? No one. The fact is that sales are a great time for shops to shift their old, substandard, out-of-fashion or obsolete stock. So before you succumb to bargain fever check whether the frock you are feverishly fingering is really a bargain (and a bargain that you need) or simply another con. Never forget that just because something is cheaper than it was doesn't mean it offers any value to you: some things are expensive at £100 and still expensive at £10. Before you pay the sale price always ask yourself if you would have paid that price for it if you weren't at a sale and as you do so remind yourself that over two-thirds of women admit to buying things in the sales that they have never worn.

If you do end up buying rubbish in the sales remember you have the same consumer rights as you do if you buy that rubbish before the sales. Many stores will tell you that you are not entitled to a refund if you buy something at a reduced price. This is not true. If you have simply changed your mind about wanting something you are not entitled to your money back (although many stores will let you exchange things out of goodwill), but if something is broken or faulty (this includes everything from TVs that break to shirts that lose their buttons after only one wearing) you are entitled to a refund or a replacement even if you have lost your receipt. Don't let the retailer fob you off by telling you that you have to complain to the manufacturer not to them. That's not true either. You have three rights under the Sale of Goods Act 1979 as well: the goods you buy must be as described; they must be of satisfactory quality (which suggests that they must last for a reasonable time); and must be fit for a particular purpose. On top of this you have the right to claim against them for 'consequential loss', so if your discounted freezer breaks and food gets damaged you can ask to be reimbursed for the food as well as the useless freezer.

I am endlessly determined to get value from retailers: when I recently found that a bit of fish I had got from grocery delivery firm Ocado was off I insisted on being reimbursed by them for not just the fish but the leeks and mushrooms I had started cooking it with too. It sounds petty, I know, but why should I be out of pocket because Ocado delivered substandard goods to me? (Ocado, by the way, reimbursed me immediately and have done so every time I have complained to them about any of the products they have delivered).

as 7–8% on overdrafts. Finally, I had a 'premium' account at Lloyds, meaning that I paid an extra fee every year for a variety of perks I never used (most current accounts are free of annual fees). Lloyds sent me a nice bunch of flowers to make up for all the confusion – something which made me feel a bit warmer towards them but wasn't quite enough to compensate for all the other downsides to banking with them. I closed the account.

My current account is now with First Direct. If you are as lazy as I was for 20 years and are still with the same high street bank where your mother opened your first savings account, it might be time for you to think about cutting your expenses by making a change too: to find the account that will pay you the most interest when you are in credit, charge you the least when you are not and won't charge you any annual or monthly fees, see **www.moneysupermarket.com** or **www.uswitch.com**. You will probably find that the Internet accounts offer the best deals. If you do decide to switch it shouldn't be hard: once you have made the request your old bank has three days to provide all your details to your new one which should then set everything up. When I switched from Lloyds to First Direct this all appeared to work perfectly.

Beyond current accounts we'll look at the many ways that banks work to remove your money from you in the next few chapters, but for now it's worth remembering that when it comes to bank charges of any kind you need to be endlessly vigilant: *Which?* claims that the major banks effectively overcharge customers by £400 a year each thanks to their range of rotten savings and loans products and their high fee structures, while **www.moneysupermarket.com** claims that bank small print contains a staggering 110 fees and charges for basic financial transactions.

Insurance: mostly it's overpriced rubbish you don't need

Reading the personal finance sections of the newspapers can be a terrifying business. Every week they are packed full of stories about terrible things that have happened to people or that could happen to people. There are stories of people breaking their legs in seven places on skiing holidays and having to be airlifted back to Britain; stories of families having to spend their whole holidays in the same clothes because their suitcases have been lost; stories of wretched cat owners who can't afford the bills for pet surgery after a car accident; stories of brides spilling red ink all over their

Bad banks

Banks are businesses. Their job is to make money out of you. That's fine except for when they do it unfairly. Which they do. They market products in a deliberately confusing way so that you open accounts without realizing that you will be penalized for withdrawals or without understanding that their special bonus interest rates last for only six months. They charge you very little when you are in credit but then go bananas charging you for every tiny slip they can when you are not in credit: going 10p overdrawn can cost you £25, as can paying a credit card bill a day late – the high street banks are said to generate about £1 billion of their annual profits from penalty charges alone. They hide behind technology, stating that they need up to five working days to transfer your money for you when in reality it takes about two seconds (this works for them because they then don't have to pay you interest on the money during the five days they categorize it as in transit). They try to scam you into thinking you have to foot the bill when your bank account is used fraudulently when you don't: you only have to pay the first £50 unless they can actually prove that you were negligent with your details. And of course when you complain they think that if they ignore you you will go away. You probably can't change much of this (though you should keep complaining wherever appropriate – when pushed, banks often refund penalty charges for example) but you can take away a few lessons from it: first, always read the small print, and second, never ever trust a bank.

£3,000 dresses; stories of people mugged in the street and losing £400 worth of items from their handbags and so on and so on. It's miserable stuff. But there is a common thread in all these tales of woe: the people in question have apparently not had enough insurance to 'protect' them financially from calamity. Had they had the correct travel insurance, pet insurance, wedding insurance or contents insurance, we are told, things would have been so much better. All these stories, as you will probably have guessed, are placed in the press by insurance companies with one aim – to scare you into thinking you need to buy more and more insurance. If they had their way we wouldn't leave the house without being insured against everything from the front door shutting on our fingers and dropping our lipsticks down the drain at pedestrian crossings to being abducted by aliens outside Tesco on a Saturday morning.

Insurance should be a simple business. Basically it works by offering you cover against injury or loss in pretty much any situation, in return for an annual or monthly payment (the premium). The insurer works out your premium by assessing the risk of something nasty happening (you crashing your car, for instance) and what it will cost to pay for the damage. In some cases having this kind of protection makes sense but it all depends on the premiums you have to pay (i.e. the cost of the insurance), the flexibility of the policy and how likely it is ever to pay out. You need some insurance – some of it is compulsory anyway – but most of it is overpriced and underused. Buying it is often simply no better a use of your hard-earned cash than buying a coat in the January sales that you never wear. You would, in the main, be better off opening a savings account (call it your Calamity Account) and putting all the money you might have spent on insurance into it. Then, if you have a disaster of the kind we are so often warned about, you will have the cash to cover it and if you do not you will soon find you have a tidy – and growing – sum of money to keep. My bet is that your account will rarely be empty.

Below I've made a list of some of the insurances the financial services business thinks you should have (it's not a comprehensive list – they're always coming up with more) and looked at whether it's a good idea to have them or if they are just another clever wheeze to part you from your money. Basically, you should only be buying insurance for things you cannot replace, pay for, or forgo without suffering real pain.

Do you need it?

Life insurance? *Sometimes*

Very often it makes sense to insure against the really big calamities. Small disasters you can swallow from your income; really big ones you probably can't. However, that doesn't automatically mean you need life insurance. Yes, if you have a non-working partner and children you need to provide for, but if you have no dependants you just don't: if you die a lot of people will probably be very upset but as it won't make a financial difference to anyone why spend your money on insurance now? What difference will it make whether your mortgage is paid or not when you are dead? Put the money in a savings account instead. If you do have dependants it is different – you will probably feel that you want to have some insurance to cover them if something awful does happen. However, you may not need to take out a life insurance policy. Insurance salesmen are big on emotional blackmail. You need to be stuffed up to the eyeballs with life insurance, they will tell you, to 'protect your family' ('How would your family cope without you and your income?' 'What happens if the unthinkable happens?' 'How much do you matter?'), but don't be scared into giving them your money when you don't need to. Don't forget they get hefty commissions on every policy they sell.

If you check your contract at work carefully you will probably find, if you are a white-collar worker, that you have life cover at three to four times your salary as standard and that a pension may be paid to your dependants. If so, and you have other savings, that may well be enough. If you are not the main breadwinner in the family you also won't need much insurance, and if you are at or near retirement you shouldn't need it either. By then you should be free financially (mortgage paid, pension sorted, children independent): your death will not bring financial hardship to those around you so you don't need to insure against it.

If you are the main breadwinner, are not near retirement and have neither work-related insurance nor sufficient savings what should you do? The answer, I think, is to get the simplest and cheapest form of insurance possible. This is term assurance, which works like this. You choose how long the policy runs for (it can be anything from 1 to 30 years but you should probably time it to run until your retirement or the date your mortgage will be paid off). You then pay annual premiums and if you die within the time specified the insurer will pay out a lump sum to your dependants. The alternative is to buy whole of life insurance, which pays out whenever you die rather than just within a set term. This is much more expensive and I think probably pointless: the idea of the term is that you are covered for as long as you need to be (during the 20–30-year period when other people would really suffer financially if you died) so why pay more to be covered when you no longer need to be?

Car insurance? *Yes*

Some insurances you have to have and if you drive car insurance
is one of them, so all you have to worry about is finding the
cheapest policy you possibly can. This is much easier than it used
to be. Before the days of the Internet comparing prices meant
calling ten different insurers and then choosing the cheapest.
Most people never bothered – it was just too boring – and that
meant that insurers got into the habit of charging you pretty
much what they fancied. Not any more. Today you can log on to a
variety of websites such as **www.moneyfacts.co.uk**, or
www.insuresupermarket.com and **www.confused.com** and
compare prices in a matter of minutes. Make sure you do: if you
buy without comparing you'll just be throwing money away. The
same goes for every insurance I mention here.

There are distracting gimmicks aplenty in the insurance industry
and a new entry to the car insurance market is women-only car
insurance. This is an idea based on the fact that women are less
dangerous drivers than men and should therefore be able to get
cheaper car insurance than men. Both these things are true
(Home Office figures show that 96% of dangerous driving
offences are committed by men) but that doesn't mean that
buying your insurance from a women-only outfit such as Sheila's
Wheels or Diamond will get you a better deal. All insurers base
their premiums on the same calculations of the various risk
factors involved in taking on a policy and they all include in their
calculations the fact that women are in general
safer drivers than men so they all charge them
less accordingly. The all-women insurers may
offer a variety of amusing perks (Sheila's
Wheels offers handbag insurance and a
counselling line you can call after an

accident) but don't be distracted by this. They are just as much businesses out to make maximum profits as the other insurers (Sheila's is no female-friendly small company, but part of banking and insurance giant HBOS). So whatever you get from them you'll end up paying the market price for. The same is true when buying insurance for older people: some firms claim to specialize in them but again that doesn't mean they'll offer a better deal. So don't go for the ladies' policy or the special old people's policy, just go for the cheapest one.

Wedding insurance? *No*

This is the insurance I hate most of all. What is the point? If the photographer doesn't turn up how will getting a cheque for £200 help you to remember your big day? And if the food gives all your guests food poisoning what are you going to do? Claim on insurance and get them all back to eat it again? Of course not. The fact is that the only thing you could really do with insurance against is the wedding not taking place but that would only happen if you or your groom-to-be changed your mind. And no one will insure you against that. So take the £200 you might have spent on wedding insurance and put it in a special account to earn interest and pay for a weekend away on your first anniversary.

Health insurance? *Probably not*

We hear so often these days that the NHS is dreadful that most of us are slowly becoming convinced that, if we can afford it, we should take out medical insurance. But is it really true? I don't think so. For starters note that medical insurance doesn't cover the conditions most of us need treatment for. It doesn't cover childbirth (not even emergency Caesareans), it often doesn't cover depression and it also very often doesn't cover chronic or incurable illnesses such as diabetes, asthma or multiple sclerosis. It is also utterly useless in an emergency: private hospitals don't have emergency rooms and anyway the NHS never makes you wait more than an hour or two to have a broken leg sorted out. Medical insurance isn't cheap – the cheapest I could find for myself when I looked was nearly £30 a month and it came with so many exemptions that I would have had to be almost dead before I was able to claim on it.

The alternative is simply to save all the cash you might have spent on insurance into your Calamity Account and then to pay for any treatment you might need that you don't want to have or to wait to have on the NHS. This sounds frightening but it shouldn't be. For starters let's not forget that you've already paid for the NHS via your taxes and that it really isn't that bad. I've had nothing but good experiences with the NHS over the last four or five years and it is generally accepted that in emergencies and in the care of people with serious or terminal illnesses the organization does an excellent job of providing comprehensive medical care. It's also worth remembering that the doctors you see privately will be the same ones you would have seen on the NHS – they're just bumping up their incomes by going private – and that NHS consultants are usually the ones at the cutting edge of healthcare.

Where the NHS sometimes (but far from always) falls down is on the treatment of acute but curable conditions, but if you are saving correctly into your Calamity Account you should be able to pay for this yourself if you feel you need to. Note that 80% of these treatments are dealt with on an outpatient basis (blood tests, consultations, x-rays, scans and the like). These aren't particularly expensive. What are pricey, on the other hand, are mainly procedures that you won't need until you are heading for your fifties and sixties (hip replacements, for example) by which time your Calamity Account should be looking pretty healthy if you have regularly put £50–£100 a month into it in lieu of paying for insurance. A private hip replacement comes in at about £7,000, cataract removal at about £2,000 and a coronary artery bypass graft between £2,000 and £15,000. Note, too, that only 4% of private health care claims are for sums over £5,000.

If you aren't convinced on this one and still want health insurance, one way to cut the costs is to get it from a firm that will allow you to pay for your own treatment up to an agreed level (the excess – usually anything up to £5,000) and then it will pay any costs beyond that itself. This can more than halve the cost of premiums yet still leave you covered should something horrible happen to you. See **www.insuresupermarket.co.uk** to find a cheap policy.

Critical illness insurance? *No*

The idea of critical illness insurance is that it pays you out a lump cash sum if a long-term illness makes you unfit to work. Advisers are very keen to sell this to everyone as it pays them massive commissions (they can pocket 120% plus of the first year's premiums as a reward for selling you the policy, so if your premiums come to £800 a year they can walk off with well over £1,000 for a couple of hours' work). However, this kind of insurance doesn't make sense for many of us. If you are young and single you probably don't need it, for example. I took out my first mortgage when I was single and living alone but my mortgage adviser still insisted that I needed critical illness insurance at £50 a month. I believed him for a few minutes until I remembered that I was in my twenties with no dependants. If I had suddenly found myself with a critical illness I would have sold the flat and gone home to my mother. No insurance necessary.

But even if I had thought I might need critical illness insurance it might not have done me much good had I actually got a critical illness. One of the reasons insurers can afford to pay advisers such huge commissions to sell critical illness insurance is because they rarely pay out on it so they get to keep most of the premiums (for every 100 policies sold only 3 claims were made in 2005). This is because it only pays out if you suffer from one on a very specific list of ailments (mainly cancer, heart attacks and strokes) before your mortgage is paid off (most policies stop either at 65 or when the mortgage is paid off), which most of us are pretty unlikely to get in that time frame. And one in five claims fails anyway, often thanks to some minor legal detail. *Which?* magazine points out that the application forms for critical illness insurance are so full of medical jargon and demands for detail that they make the average consumer vulnerable to oversights that could (and do) invalidate their claims. You often have to list every appointment you have had with your doctor in the last five years. Who can do that accurately? There have also been cases where a claim has been refused because people have put their height down incorrectly on forms.

Generally you are probably best to ignore critical illness insurance and get something called permanent health insurance (or income-protection insurance), which is much cheaper to buy and pays out not a lump sum but a monthly income until you are ready to go back to work or you retire. That said, this is often just as hard to claim on as critical illness insurance. Insurers will do their utmost to invalidate any claims – finding inconsistencies on your application and in your medical records just as they do with critical illness, for example. Many policies are also written on an 'any occupation' basis so even if you can't do your old job, if you can do any job at all despite your illness (envelope stuffing and so on) you will not be eligible for a payout. Only get a policy like this if you have read the small print and it is on an 'own occupation basis'. And if you have a reasonable amount saved or your company provides excellent sick pay or long-term sickness benefits don't get it at all. Consider saving into your Calamity Account instead.

Payment protection insurance? *No*

Payment protection insurance (PPI) is a favourite of the high street banks. Why? Because it is overpriced and hard to claim on, with the result that they make an absolute fortune from selling it to you. Paymentcare estimates that of the £4 billion spent by borrowers on PPI every year a massive £2.5 billion is stripped out immediately by the banks in commission payments, for example. So what is this shocker of a product? You'll be offered it every time you take out a mortgage, a credit card or a loan of any kind, the idea being that if your circumstances change such that you are unable to repay your debt the insurance will do it for you. The sales pitch will be that buying it is the sensible thing to do, that if you are made redundant, get very ill or have a serious accident you will need it.

But will you really? Probably not. You should have a good six months' worth of income in a savings account to provide for such an emergency anyway and most employers (85%) offer more than the statutory sick pay: many pay your salary for six months or so before reassessing things. PPI tends to come with a great many get-out clauses included to the benefit of the insurer too: you won't be able to get a payout if you have a part-time not a full-time job, if you are self-employed, if you find you can't work as a result of a health condition that was pre-existing or if you are working on a short-term contract. So even if you think you might need some kind of income insurance this is not a good one to have. Only 4% of people who take out PPI ever claim on it and 25% of those claims end up being rejected.

PPI is also outrageously expensive, particularly if you get it from one of the high street banks which can charge up to five times the level of premiums of the discount insurance groups such as **www.Britishinsurance.com** or **www.Paymentcare.co.uk** (note that PPI is always optional and if you do decide you want it you are under no obligation to buy it from the same people who are providing you with your loan). The banks often have a nasty habit of 'frontloading' the cost of PPI. They calculate the cost of the insurance but instead of demanding a monthly premium they simply add the full amount to the value of your loan and have you pay interest on the whole lot over the term of the loan. There's no logical reason for this. It is just a way to get more money out of you. The *Mail on Sunday* last year pointed to a case where someone had borrowed £16,000 from HSBC. The insurance was calculated at £5,150 (about a third of the value of the loan!) making a total of £21,150. The borrower paid off about £6,000 of the debt in instalments and then came up with the cash to pay off the rest early, only to find that she was to get no refund on the insurance at all. Over £5,000 had disappeared for nothing. *Which?* magazine has warned very strongly against PPI, pointing out that it can double the cost of a £5,000 loan. The authorities are aware of all these issues and are investigating PPI sales but you still need to have your wits about you when you take out a loan.

UK banks are dead set on what they call cross-selling, which means always trying to sell you more than one product: open a current account and they'll try to sell you a credit card, take out a mortgage and they'll have a go at pushing critical illness insurance on you, pay a bill over the phone and they'll be selling you contents insurance. The drive to sell PPI is just one example of this. But as long as you are aware of this passion to find ever new ways to separate you and your cash you should be OK. Just say no.

Extended warranties? *No*

It isn't just the banks that make a killing out of insurance. The retailers have been having a go too. When you buy white goods or electrical products these days you will invariably be offered an extended warranty of some kind. But you just don't need them. For starters, most things come with a one-year guarantee so if there is a fault of any kind in the first year the manufacturer has to repair it for you. You are also protected under the Sale of Goods Act 1979 (as discussed earlier in this chapter) whereby goods must be 'fit for purpose'. Still, the sales blah that you get when someone is trying to make you buy an extended guarantee suggests that, regardless of the fact that it is pointless in the first year, having one will save you money in the long term. But will it? Again the answer is probably not. Most modern appliances just don't break down. *Which?* magazine pointed out a few years ago that 81% of washing machines don't break down at all in the first six years after you buy them, for example. But if you pay £150 for a five-year extended warranty on a machine it would need to break down four times in years 2–5 for

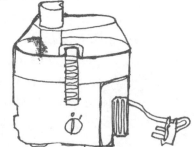

Silly celebrity spending

£110,000: the price Cheryl Tweedy is said to have paid for her wedding dress.

£1,000: the price of a jar of the Crème de la Mer face cream that J-Lo apparently uses all over her body.

$1,000: the cost of Jessica Simpson's bed sheets.

£5,500: what Camilla Parker Bowles spends on her hairdressing every month. Still, Mariah Carey beats that hands down. She has a hairdresser and make-up artist who she keeps on a regular daily basis. Cost? $7,200 a day.

£200,000: the price of the Phantom Rolls-Royce Victoria Beckham bought for her husband as a Christmas present in 2005. At the time he already owned several other cars. He bought her a £1.2 million diamond and ruby necklace in exchange.

$44,000: the amount Victoria Beckham is said to have spent on having her teeth whitened. That's over $4,000 per tooth.

£55,000: the amount the wives and girlfriends of the English football team spent in one hour in the shops of Baden-Baden during the 2006 World Cup.

$600,000: what Mariah Carey paid for a piano formerly owned by Marilyn Monroe. According to **www.eonline.com** no one is allowed to touch it.

£75,000: what J.K. Rowling is said to have spent on one week's holiday in the Hamptons in 2006.

you to gain anything (assuming that it costs about £50 to get a washing machine fixed). The odds are working very heavily against you – which, of course, is the way the insurers like it.

Buildings insurance? *Yes*
If you own a home this is compulsory so again it is just a matter of finding the cheapest policy you can. Use the usual websites.

Pet insurance? *No*
Pet insurance isn't cheap and you really won't need it that often. It does not cover the routine costs you have with animals such as immunizations, worming and the like. The insurers are great at pulling the heartstrings for pet insurance. They add on little extras such as pet theft insurance (if your cat is stolen they pay for the cost of advertising for its return as well as for a reward) to draw you in. But try to stay rational: these extras are rarely claimed on. This is one where you would be much better off just contributing to your Calamity Account instead.

Mobile phone insurance? *No*
You don't need mobile phone insurance. It is much too expensive at £8–£10 a month given that a new handset costs as little as £20. Do you really expect your phone to be stolen every two months? Because that's how often it would have to happen to make it worth buying insurance. The policies are also supposed to cover calls made when the phone is stolen but they won't pay out if the phone vanishes as a result of being left unattended and otherwise will only pay out if the loss is reported within 24 hours. This makes it extremely hard to claim. If

the phone was stolen from you and you noticed you'd report it right away so there would be no call costs involved. If you didn't notice you might well not notice for another 24 hours. Another for the Calamity Account.

ID theft insurance? *No*

The financial services companies are brilliant at putting the frighteners on us. Over the last few years they have managed to make us all absolutely paranoid about identity theft, for example (sales of shredders have gone through the roof). Now they are trying to sell us insurance against it. But we don't need it. The policies cost around £7 a month and consist mainly of the company making regular credit checks under your name to be sure there are no unexplained borrowings that might suggest someone was using your name to take out loans. But you can do this yourself for £2 a go (from **www.callcredit.co.uk** **www.experian.co.uk** or **www.equifax.co.uk**). And if someone does steal your identity you shouldn't lose any money – you're not liable for the debts if you didn't take them out. The same is true of debt anyone else runs up on your credit card. You aren't liable for the debt so you don't need insurance against it.

Travel insurance? *Yes*

Travel insurance is one of the few non-compulsory insurances that I think you probably do need as much for your peace of mind as anything else. Britons make around 70 million overseas trips every year. Most of them make it home unscathed but some do not and if something terrible does happen to you, you really don't want to have to worry about either money (it can cost £10,000 to be airlifted off Europe's ski slopes and repatriated to the UK) or how to organize medical care. If you are properly insured your insurer should take care of both for you. However, if you are getting travel insurance make sure you get it for as low a premium as you can. Do not buy insurance from a travel agent. Instead head straight for the Internet and use the comparison sites to find the cheapest deal you can.

You might also look at **www.insureandgo.com**, a website that allows you to put together your own policy. You can increase your excess or strip out all but the bare essentials to cut the price of the deal. Do you, for example, really need delayed baggage insurance? I can't see why – if your baggage doesn't turn up (and this really isn't particularly likely) it won't cost you much to buy the bare essentials to cover you until it does. So why not cut that out of your policy and cut its cost? Also make sure that if you have more than one holiday a year you look at a multiple trip policy rather than taking new cover for each trip. This comes in much cheaper. Finally, if you are travelling in Europe take an EHIC (European Health Insurance Card – available from the post office) with you. This entitles you to free or reduced-payment medical care and is very necessary, as your insurance will not cover any routine treatments. However, it isn't enough in itself, as it won't pay for eventualities such as the cost of flying you home if things are truly calamitous). The more serious and complicated your injury or illness the more likely you are to need insurance on top of your EHIC.

Contents insurance? *Yes (but not as much as you might think)*

Floods, fires (and more often) burglaries do happen and it's as well to be insured against the loss of all your possessions. You can make it cheaper by lowering your risk – fitting window locks and the like. But you also want to be sure you aren't over-insuring. If your house gets broken into you might want to replace your television and your camera but what about less easily replaced things? Items that have sentimental value – say your grandmother's jewelry – might be worth a lot of money too but that's not why you have them. You keep them for the memories and that isn't something you can pop out and buy on the high street. If something isn't repaceable – and you weren't ever going to sell it anyway – why insure it?

WHAT Do I Do Now?

- Figure out your hourly wage and never buy anything unless you reckon it's worth the hours of work you are putting in to pay for it.

- Before you buy anything ask yourself a few questions. Do I need it? Do I already have something similar? Could I borrow it from someone instead or swap something I have already for it? Could I get it cheaper elsewhere?

- Review all your insurances and dump the ones you don't need.

- Run through all the direct debits on your bank accounts to see if you really need them – gym memberships, magazine subscriptions and so on renew automatically if you don't cancel them.

- Check to see if you can save money by remortgaging (see Chapters 3 and 7) or changing any of your utility providers.

- Never accept a product or service that doesn't offer you value for money ever again.

- Stop thinking about buying new cars. In fact don't buy anything new if you can get it second-hand for less.

- Read the 53 money-saving tips at the back of the book.

- Try living only in cash for a few weeks – never buy anything with a card. Instead go to the cashpoint and get out the money you need to pay. More often than not by the time your card has gone into the slot you'll find you no longer think you need whatever you were about to buy anyway.

- Kick-start your new spending habits by keeping a spending diary for three weeks.

3
Debt
Getting Rid of It and Keeping Out Of It

A few months ago an already deeply indebted friend bought a sofa. 'How much was it?' I asked her.

'Two and a half thousand pounds,' she said.

'That's insane,' I said. 'How can you possibly pay so much for a sofa?'

'You don't have to worry,' she said, 'I don't have to pay for it all at once so it really isn't a problem.'

I don't think this friend understands debt. Not only is she going to be paying for the sofa for many more years than she will like it for (she's a fickle girl) but, add in the interest from her 'great financing deal' and it's going to cost her much more than the £2,500 she thinks she is paying.

How do the rich get rich? They routinely spend less than they make and save or invest the rest. It follows, then, that the poor stay poor because they routinely spend more than they make and that the moderately well off can soon make themselves poor by doing exactly the same – by living on debt.

Debt is not always a bad thing. Borrowing to buy a house is often (but not always) a good thing to do, borrowing to set up a new business can be an excellent thing to do, debt taken out to go to medical school can't be considered all bad and nor, on a smaller scale, can borrowing to buy an interview suit when you need a new job. All these things should provide you with the kind of return that makes the effort of paying off the debt worth while. But even if you take out this kind of 'good debt' you need to know that you have a strategy for repaying it. Even mortgages can be counted as bad debt if you haven't thought carefully enough about the house purchase and you aren't sure how you are ever going to repay the capital – as is the case with many of the Britons who currently hold interest-only mortgages (each month they pay the bank interest on the capital they have borrowed but none of the capital itself).

In fact any kind of debt can be detrimental if it takes over your financial life: most people go through much of their lives under the cosh of some kind of debt, usually taken out for the best of reasons (to buy a house, to pay university fees, to finance a wedding, for example) but all of it faintly exhausting. An entire working life spent trying to repay debt leaves little time for the risk-taking needed to gain real wealth or for finding true happiness.

Your credit rating

How often do you think about your credit file? If you are anything like me the answer is almost never. It is simply too boring to give any brain space to. Unfortunately this is the wrong approach: as well as being very boring credit ratings are extremely important. Your credit file is held by the credit reference agencies such as Equifax (**www.equifax.co.uk**), Callcredit (**www.callcredit.co.uk**) and Experian (**www.experian.co.uk**). It contains a terrifying amount of financial information on you – everything from any loans you have ever had, any late payments you have ever made, and what your credit limits are on any cards you have, to any county court judgements ever made against you. A final point to remember on credit files is that every time you apply for credit, whether you end up taking it out or not, a 'footprint' is recorded on your file. Too many of these footprints don't make you look good.

Every time you apply for a loan, a credit card or a mortgage the lender you are dealing with will check your credit file. If it finds anything it doesn't like (a history of late payments perhaps) you will find that the interest rate you are offered will start rising – the advertised APR you were hoping to pay will suddenly no longer apply to you. Because the impact can be so huge, it is worth keeping an eye on your credit rating even if you think your record is spotless, just to make sure that no mistakes are being made. You can get copies from any of the agencies.

But the worst kind of debt of all is the debt we take out simply to satisfy our consumer needs – future income pledged to pay for stuff we feel like having now. It's the money we owe on our credit cards for hordes of small purchases that have added up and added up, the money we owe on store cards, taken out for an instantaneous 10% discount on a purchase but never paid off, the money we owe because we bought an expensive new sofa or TV despite having a perfectly good one already and the money we spent on new handbags and dresses in the sales because we thought they were bargains. For most of us all this happens quite slowly. We spend a trivial few pounds here and a few pounds there on a card, we buy a few things to pay back at £20 or £30 a month but then suddenly we find that all those little things add up to a lot and that we owe a great deal of money for items that we don't have any more (caffe lattes and muffins), are already useless (those clothes we don't wear) or are falling in value fast (you can't sell a TV to pay off the debt you took out to buy it, whereas you can usually sell a house to pay off a mortgage). This kind of debt drags you down: not only do you have to keep paying the original price for the goods you bought long after they aren't worth that any more, but to add insult to injury you have to pay interest on the price too.

"What can I say? I spent too much. I drank champagne, I flew club class. I had a blast.... I'm gloriously bankrupt."
Wendy Turner

For every £1 we save we borrow £1.20. UK consumer debt has more than tripled in the last decade and is still rising at around £1 million every five minutes. Total consumer debt is now well over £1.3 trillion (a trillion is a 1 followed by 12 zeros) and credit card debt alone is over £30 billion (12 million women in the UK have at least one credit card). The average household debt per head (excluding mortgages) is nearly £8,000. More than half of all adults in the UK have non-mortgage debt; 8% of us owe more than £10,000, according to a survey last year from YouGov, and 5% of us owe more than £20,000. Even worse, 61% of those with debts between £10,000 and £30,000 are under 25 and according to the Financial Services Authority almost half of 20–29-year-olds have debt that eats up more than half of their monthly earnings. That's not a nice way to start adult life.

The strain of all this is starting to tell. In 2005 one in ten people admitted in a Bank of England survey to having unsecured debts (i.e. non-mortgage debt) that they found 'a heavy burden'. The Citizens Advice Bureau sees more than a million people every year with debts averaging more than their annual income, and the number of people in what they call 'extreme' debt (i.e. they owe more than £100,000) doubled between 2004 and 2005. The Consumer Credit Counselling Service (CCCS) now hears from one person a week with that much debt. The CCCS also says it has seen a huge rise in calls from the under-25s and in particular from women under 25. The trouble is showing up in the courts too: in 2005 county court judgements served on those with unsecured loans rose by a quarter. The recipients of these judgements and the people calling the CCCS in desperation aren't necessarily the people you think they are. They aren't always low earners or the unemployed. Instead they are young women working in white-collar jobs and middle-aged married people. The average client of the CCCS is in their mid-thirties with children and owes nearly £31,000. And

18–29-year-olds now account for nearly 20% of all bankrupts in England and Wales. In the first six months of 2006 one person was made insolvent by our courts every minute and the number of home repossessions rose by over 70%. An awful lot of people are in financial trouble.

This is a terrible thing. Debt erases freedom more surely than anything else. Once you are in real debt your quality of life disappears. Life becomes devoted not to living but to paying back debt. You can't go on holiday. You can't change jobs (you can't not have a salary even for a week), you can't go on a course, take a sabbatical or stop to think. You can't actually do anything to fulfil yourself at all. Instead you just have to play it safe to keep the income coming in and pay your bills. To survive on a monthly basis you have to squash yourself on to a tube train or bus every morning, be nice to your boss and stay on a treadmill you might never have meant to get on in the first place. You aren't really living, just surviving from month to month. Your choices are gone. Borrowing to consume too much means you end up achieving too little in life. That's not how it is supposed to be. The fact is that debt isn't just about owing money, it's about being trapped and it isn't a nice feeling.

In May 2006 Frances Embleton disappeared in Australia. The 24-year-old law graduate never appeared at a farewell party her friends had organized on her last night in the country as a backpacker. She never caught her flight back to the UK and when her family called her mobile to find out why it was switched off and not taking messages.

They panicked and a huge search got under way. Then a week or so later Frances walked into a police station. She wasn't hurt, she hadn't been held against her will and she hadn't got lost. The problem was something else altogether – her debts. She owed a total of £25,000 (£16,000 to Barclays Bank for a professional studies loan and the maximum £9,000 in student loans) which she couldn't see herself being able to pay back. The pressure of having £25,000 worth of debt was too much so she just ran away.

She's not alone in feeling the strain. A third of those questioned in the survey mentioned above said that their debt had had an adverse effect on their relationships and it had actually made 8% of them clinically depressed.

How did this happen to us? Just a few decades ago debt was seen by almost everyone as a very bad thing (it was even seen as a sin by many of the religions) but now no one thinks twice about it. We are desensitized to debt and there is no longer any hint of

Debt denial

A survey from ClearDebt showed just how complacent people can be about debt. It asked what they might or might not give up to get out of debt. Smoking, second holidays and second cars were all considered to be worth being in debt for. Of those who said they were worried about being in debt 53% said they would not give up a second holiday to cut it down; 48% said the same of their cigarettes. So what would they give up? Children's ballet and football lessons apparently: half of the smoking parents interviewed said they would give up paying for their children's activities before they gave up their fags. Nice.

stigma attached to buying things on the never-never. Whose fault is it? The financial services companies have to take some of the responsibility for this huge transformation. In the last chapter we talked about how often we let ourselves be conned into spending money by the marketing men. Well, the banks and credit card companies are in on the separating-us-from-our-money game too: their plan is to get us to borrow to spend, to pay overly high interest rates for the privilege of doing so, and then to stay in debt indefinitely. To this end the financial services industry spends £1.4 billion a year advertising its services. It does this very well. It has trained us to stop calling debt 'debt' but to refer to it as 'credit' instead (sounds more friendly, doesn't it?). And it has tempted us mercilessly. One ad for Amex cards a few years back arrived with a little gift box for you to wrap up the first thing you bought with the new card.

A while ago an Egg email went out telling the indebted to say 'to hell with it', have a night out on their credit card and worry about paying for it later. A few months later Visa started telling us to 'Love Every Day' by putting all our 'simple pleasures' on our Visa cards. And almost every 'pre-approved' card application you get in the post will aim to draw you in with soothing words about how nice it would be to have a kitchen extension, a holiday or a brand-new car. Early in 2006 MasterCard even introduced a credit card aimed specifically at teenagers. The cards were prepaid so you couldn't actually build up debt on them but they were still a nasty way to get children hooked on plastic and used to the idea of getting fleeced by credit card firms, targeting, as they did, little girls via *Smash Hits* and *Bliss* magazines ('Shop till you drop with your very own exclusive *Bliss* Platinum Card').

Along with the marketing blitz has come a variety of incentives to help you get deeper and deeper into debt: minimum repayments on credit cards have been slashed from around 5% of the outstanding debt a few years ago to below 2%, lending criteria have been cut so that you can borrow many times your income on a credit card and mortgages have been redefined so you don't need deposits or even the wherewithal to pay back any of the capital to take them out. At the same time bank staff have been transformed from advisers into sales people, there solely to hit loan and credit card sales targets and paid on commission for doing so. If they want to make a living they can't think about your needs or about how too much debt is going to ravage your life, they've got their own needs to consider. Your debt is their livelihood.

However, we can't just blame the banks for misleading us with this blurring of the boundaries between debt and spending. We're culpable too. Much of the debt we have allowed ourselves to be persuaded to run up is lifestyle debt – built up to maintain a lifestyle that we see on television and in magazines and that we think we deserve. We buy things we don't need and can't afford (in 2005 75% of us replaced a big-ticket item such as a TV despite the old one being in perfectly good working order). We don't wait to buy the things we want; we just shove them on our plastic without thinking. Walk around even the lowest income areas of Britain and you'll see children being pushed around in prams that cost hundreds of pounds and teenagers dressed head to foot in designer gear. Go into any office in London and you can be sure there'll be a receptionist in there earning £16,000 a year but carrying a Gucci handbag. All this stuff is paid for on credit. Egged on in our shop-a-thons by credit card issuers, celebrities on the make, retailers and magazines, we've become a nation of buy-now-pay-later debt junkies. If we see it and we want it we get it.

"Nothing in life comes easy. You have to earn everything. So you have to know the difference between what you want and what you need." Sarah Jessica Parker

The final responsibility for this can't be laid at the door of the marketing geniuses of the financial services industry. No, it rests with us. We don't have to spend and we don't have to borrow: we fall for the exploitative marketing of the financial services industry because we don't think about debt or the consequences of it properly. We don't look for the best interest rates, we don't have proper repayment plans and we very rarely stop to work out the figures before we borrow. The number of people made bankrupt not because of terrible changes in their circumstances but because of 'reckless spending' rose by over 3,000% in 2006.

If we stopped to think we would borrow a great deal less, if anything. Consider the case of the average store card charging almost 30% a year in interest. If you borrowed £1,000 and made only the minimum payment each month it would take you 10 years to pay off the debt, according to figures from comparison website **www.uswitch.com**, and by then you'd have paid around another £1,000 in interest. If you ran up a debt of £20,000 and took 3 years to pay it off at a rate of 17%, it would cost you around £3,300 in interest. Make that 5 years and the interest will come in at over £8,000. Make only the minimum monthly payments and it will take you 27 years to pay off the debt and cost you £15,000 in interest, according to **www.uswitch.com** (see the box below for more on how interest works). No wonder the Competition Commission says that store card holders are ripped off to the tune of £100 million a year by their issuers.

We make similar mistakes with all kinds of debt. We just don't calculate how much they are going to cost us. Note that 70% of those who owed more than £10,000 last year told research company Mintel that they weren't worried about it and a significant proportion also said that they would consider borrowing more. Idiots! Anyone who stopped to think about being £10,000 in debt and how long it would take to pay back (on the average wage, a good five years and that's only if you lived on baked beans and never went out) would be very worried indeed.

When you are the one paying it out, interest is the biggest killer of wealth there is.

We also waste vast amounts of money by not managing our debt well. Back in 2004 Barclays caused outrage across the country when it said that it had made a record £722 million in profits from its credit card holders. That's £68 each. But the card holders could have cut their costs at least in half had they behaved a little more sensibly – making their payments on time, swapping their debt to a low-cost personal loan or taking advantage of the many 0% deals available on other credit cards at the time.

So what do you do if you are in debt? The first thing is to face up to it cleanly. Most of us have levels of debt that are just about manageable if we focus but the longer we wait to take control of

Understanding interest

Understanding how interest works is vital to taking control of your finances. Why? Because, if you don't manage your money properly, the interest you end up paying on your debts will be the greatest killer of wealth you will ever come across. Say you borrow £10,000 at an interest rate of 5% with the intention of paying it back as a lump sum at the end of 5 years. At the end of the first year you will owe 5% (£500) of the original sum in interest – a total of £10,500. The next year things will get rather worse – the 5% interest will be charged not just on the original £10,000 but on £10,500. You'll be paying interest on interest and will owe £11,025. This interest on interest accumulates every year and by the end of the five years you will owe a nasty £12,762.81. That's bad enough but then imagine that instead of taking out the loan at 5% you had done it at 10%. Then at the end of the five years you would owe £16,105.10. See the difference the interest rate makes?

Time makes a huge difference to how much you end up paying back in total as well – clearly the longer you keep the money the more interest you pay. Borrow £10,000 at 10% and pay it back in monthly instalments (which will include a bit of interest and a bit of the original capital every month) over 5 years and the total you pay back will come to £13,189.80 (this is less than the number above because you are paying back a little of the capital every month rather than all at the end so your total interest bill is lower). Do the same over 10 years and, thanks to the fact that you will be paying interest on the money for much longer, you will end up paying back £16,274.40. The lesson? Borrow on as low an interest rate as you possibly can and pay it back over the shortest time frame you possibly can. Remember too that the level of monthly payments is not the figure to look at – the total paid back is. See the chart below.

Amount	Years	Rate	Mthly Paymt	Total Paid
£10,000	5	10%	£219.83	£13,189.80
£10,000	5	15%	£248.59	£14,915.40
£10,000	10	10%	£135.62	£16,274.40
£10,000	10	15%	£166.04	£19,924.80

it the more likely we are to find ourselves at crisis point. You are already in trouble if you end every month in the red, if you more often have an overdraft than a credit balance, if you have ever taken out a loan to pay off other debts, if you have more than two credit cards, and have ever used credit cards to pay household bills or day to day expenses, or if more than 15–20% of the income you have left after paying your taxes and your mortgage is spent on debt repayments.

For women, keeping out of debt is even more important than it is for men. Most men at least know that they will have an income for most of their lives and so can keep making repayments if need be. That's not the case for us: we take maternity leave and constant children-related career breaks when we have no personal incomes at all. That's tough at the best of times but it gets a lot tougher if you have debt at the same time as you have no income: it's one thing to expect the father of your child to provide you with an income while you are at home with children, but it's quite another to expect him to make repayments on personal debts you ran up before you met him too.

The good news is that if you are in debt you can change things. There is no quick fix – you borrowed the money and you have to pay it back. That said, there is cheap debt and expensive debt, good debt and bad debt and if you really have overstretched yourself you may well find that your creditors are prepared to help you out a bit. I'm not going to go into great detail about how to pay back your debt (it's obvious: spend less and use the surplus to pay it back, starting with the most expensive debt) but I hope that once you understand the many ways in which all the providers of debt are fleecing you the world of debt may look rather less attractive to you than it has in the past.

Below we are going to look at all kinds of debt from overdrafts to credit cards, personal loans and mortgages, and discuss how to use them and how not to use them. The key is to stop ourselves having to use the money we earn today to pay interest on items we bought months or years ago and probably never needed in the first place. We'll also look at the options for those of us who have completely lost control of our financial situations.

Credit cards: horrible things

When credit cards were first introduced in the 1950s in the US (in the form of the Diners Card) they were an exotic novelty. Now they are a part of everyday life. The average American has eight cards in their wallet and we are fast catching up: there are 1,500 different cards available to us, the average UK credit card holder has 2.4 cards (adding up to a total of more cards than there are people in the country), and altogether we spend over £120 billion a year on them. That's £120 billion we probably shouldn't spend. Credit cards are a terrible way to borrow money (and we know it – one woman in three says she lies to her partner about credit card debt). The interest rates on them are insanely high, the credit limits offered to most of us are far beyond the level of debt our incomes can support and the fees charged for minor infringements such as being a day late with a payment are outrageous.

The main problem with credit cards is their interest rates. Quite apart from the fact that they are in general far too high, they are also impossible to figure out. And I don't just mean impossible for the financially illiterate, I mean impossible for everyone. Most people use the APR (annual percentage rate) to compare credit cards but different companies calculate it in different ways (there are at least 14 calculation methods according to *Which?* magazine), so knowing the APR often isn't much help. Some cards start charging you interest as soon as you buy an item, some when the money leaves their accounts; some charge interest on interest accrued in previous months, some do not and so on. The result? Two cards that appear to charge the same rate of interest could cost you completely different amounts even if used in the same way. In some cases one with a higher advertised APR (say 16%) could end up costing you less than one with a lower APR (of, say, 13%). It all adds up to the most extraordinary lack of transparency.

Next up, however, is the fact that credit card companies have set minimum repayment levels so low that if you pay only what they require you to pay you will be in debt pretty much for ever. Uswitch recently published research showing that if someone with an average credit card debt of £3,138 paying the average APR available in the market (15.2% at the time) made only the minimum payment each month (i.e. 2% of the balance) it would take them a shocking 32 years to pay it off. If you paid not 2% but 3% it would take 16 years and 11 months, assuming an interest rate of 15.10%. In the first example the total amount of interest you would pay would be £4,275 (significantly more than the original debt) and in the second it would be £1,969.50. See how much money the banks make out of letting you get away with paying your debt off so slowly? Low minimum payments make debt seem more affordable to you but to the credit card company executives they just spell pure profit.

The third reason to chop up your credit cards is the many non-interest charges that credit card companies have invented. They charge you up to £12 if you pay your minimum payment late regardless of the size of your balance. So if you owe them £70 for a dress you picked up in the sales you could end up paying out almost 20% of the price again in late payment fees if you aren't careful. You'll also very often pay a 2% charge if you use your card to withdraw cash and another 2.5% 'loading charge' if you use your card abroad. It all adds up: according to **moneysupermarket.com** credit card customers pay a huge £116 each a year in penalty fees. Credit card companies go to great lengths to persuade you that being a card holder is somehow a privilege but once you add up all the charges it doesn't seem so much like one, does it?

I'm not suggesting that you cut up all your cards. I keep one for emergencies – just in case something awful happens to me when I am abroad or somewhere else where I don't have immediate access to my savings account. There is also a case for having one with a very low credit limit to use when you shop on the Internet (a low credit limit reduces the level of mischief anyone can get up to with your card if they manage to steal the details and hence the level of stress you will have to deal with when sorting it out). The other plus point of credit cards is that they offer valuable consumer protection. Buy something worth more than £100 and the card company is as liable as the retailer if anything goes wrong. If the retailer goes bust or you have problems with non-delivery, for example, you can go straight to your credit card provider to complain, whether you bought the goods abroad or at home.

So if you are going to have a card which of the 1,500 on the market should you have? The answer, as with all financial products, is the cheapest one available. If you already have credit card debt you should immediately think about switching to one offering 0% on balance transfers (debt transferred from one credit card to another). But remember as you do so that 0% on transfers doesn't necessarily make a card cheap. If you are not going to build up any more debt and intend to pay off your balance before the 0% period ends 0% cards are great. Nothing else matters – just move to any one of them and get on with it.

If, however, you are still borrowing (which you shouldn't be) or not paying down the debt fast enough to have it gone before your introductory period ends you might need to think a bit harder about which card to have. Why? Because 0% doesn't mean 0% on everything: any new purchases you make with that card will generally be charged at the card's usual APR (think anywhere from 15% up), while anything you pay back comes out of the debt on which you are not paying interest, not the more recent high-interest debt: until you've paid off all the low-interest debt you won't be able to make a start on the high-interest debt. That makes finding a cheap APR important because interest will be compounding on the expensive debt all the time and the higher the rate, the worse things will get (see the box on understanding interest).

It might be better to find a card you can transfer your balance to that has a permanent low interest rate for the duration of the balance you transfer. These are called 'life of balance' cards however if you get one you don't want to put any more cash on it – the banks always find a way of clawing their cash back.

One thing you must not do when looking for a credit card is go for a prestige card of any kind. These cards come with high annual fees (sometimes hundreds of pounds) and offer various perks (travel insurance and the like). However, you can usually get most of the same perks elsewhere. That said, I admit you can't get them all elsewhere. I once saw a woman march to the front of a long queue in the Joseph sale, plonk a pile of clothes and a black American Express card down on the counter in front of an assistant and say, 'Wrap it all, I'll be back in 20 minutes.' The assistant stopped serving everyone else and did as she was told. Still, not many cards will give you that kind of power, making most of them no more than expensive status signifiers. And why would you need a credit card to explain your status to other people?

I also wouldn't be drawn in by cards that offer cash back. You might get 0.5% or 1% of the money you spend rebated to your card but if you then have to pay interest of 16% what's the good in it? The same is true of reward points and air miles. There is absolutely no such thing as a free lunch when it comes to credit cards: credit companies wouldn't offer incentives if they didn't have every intention of clawing back any costs to them many times over in interest and in charges. I wouldn't bother with charity cards either. They say they give 0.25% or so of your monthly balance to charity but if you want to give your money to charity why not just do it yourself?

Finally, whatever card you choose, keep yourself in check by insisting on a low credit limit. If yours is too high for comfort (leaving you at risk of temptation) ring and insist it is reduced. Call centre staff find this completely bemusing but it is worth persisting until they get it done.

To find the cheapest cards visit **www.uswitch.com**, **www.moneysupermarket.com** or **www.moneyfacts.co.uk**.

Store cards: even worse than credit cards

Six per cent of us have outstanding debt on store cards. But absolutely none of us should have any at all. Store cards are nothing more than very expensive credit cards offering a shocking lack of value to anyone stupid enough to use them: the majority of them charge interest rates in the region of 25–30%. There is

LOVE IS NOT ENOUGH

absolutely no reason to have them. You usually get offered a hefty discount on your purchases on the day if you agree to take out a card there and then but why do you think the store is prepared to offer you 10% off a pair of shoes? Because they know that as likely as not you'll either forget or you won't be able to pay off the balance at the end of the month and they'll get to start charging you obscene amounts of interest. And that, they know, will soon make up for the couple of quid they lost on the discount. If you can't afford to pay for something out of your current account don't buy it.

Note that the regulators, who are generally pretty slow about this kind of thing, have had a go at reining in store card providers. They now have to put a 'wealth warning' on application forms if they charge more than 25% a year in interest, something that brought to the surface the twisted logic of the credit card promoters. The wealth warning could, said a spokesman for the group that represents the store card providers, 'harm less well-off shoppers'. How exactly would that work, I wonder. Don't touch these things. It's just too dangerous.

Credit card cheques: a scam pure and simple

These are a scam pure and simple. That might not be how the banks see it but it is how it looks to me and how it should look to you. Credit card cheques work like this. They arrive in the post whether you asked for them or not. According to the marketing blurb you can use them just like ordinary cheques. You can write them out to utility companies to pay your bills, to other credit card companies to write off your debts with them and transfer

your balance to the cheque issuer instead or even, best of all, to yourself to buy a nice new kitchen (the sellers of debt in the UK are obsessed with kitchens) or a holiday of a lifetime. 'Make life easy' said one lot of marketing material I got last year.
And how do you do that? Use your unsolicited credit card cheques to 'transfer money into your bank account to pay off your overdraft'.

What the blurb only tells you in the small print, however, is that credit card cheques are an even more expensive way to borrow money than using credit cards in the usual way. If you use them any money spent is whacked on to your credit card bill but at a higher interest rate than the rest of your debt (lenders that charge 15–16% on other card debt tend to put it up to 20% plus for money spent with a cheque). You also get charged interest from the day the cheque is used rather than having the normal interest-free period you get when you use your card (this can be as long as 52 days) and there are a slew of other charges too: you will often be charged 2% of the amount you have written the cheque out for as a one-off fee (this is referred to as a 'handling fee'). Finally, note that the main advantage of credit cards – the extra consumer protection you get when you buy things with them – doesn't apply to credit card cheques.

If you get credit card cheques in the post rip them up and throw them away immediately. They are designed by the banks for one purpose and one purpose only: to lure you deeper and deeper into long-term and very expensive debt. Don't be fooled – there's no value here.

Consolidating:
paying more to be in debt for longer

Watch daytime TV for more than half an hour and you'll see an endless stream of cheerful adverts from financial services firms that appear to suggest that debt is not a problem at all. Why? Because give them a call and they'll help you to consolidate all your pesky loans into one big loan with one 'simple monthly payment' much lower than the combined payments you are currently making. And that's not all. When you consolidate your loans like this you also get the chance – again – to borrow more at the same time (to pay for that new kitchen, new car or 'holiday of a lifetime') and best of all you can opt to take a payment holiday before you start handing over your simple monthly payment. Do this and you can make your dreams a reality!

Sounds great, doesn't it? Well it isn't, unless what you dream of is spending all your future income on interest payments. It is true that if you consolidate a loan with one of these companies you may find that you are paying a lower interest rate than you were on your credit cards. But there is good reason for this. The repayment of the loan is usually spread out over a much longer period, meaning that the total interest you pay is at least as much and very often more than you would have paid anyway despite the lower interest rate. The other reason the consolidators come cheaper than other creditors is that most of them offer their services to 'UK home owners only'. They can offer you a lower interest rate than you can get from a credit card company or reputable personal loan provider because by doing a deal with them you are swapping unsecured debt for debt secured against your home (most of the other debt we've looked at in this chapter is unsecured). This is a win-win situation for them: if you keep up your payments to them they get to make a killing on your interest payments and if you don't they get to force you to sell your house to pay them back.

And as for that payment holiday, don't forget that the interest is rolling up while you're sitting around admiring your shiny new car; the longer the payment holiday the longer it will take you to pay back the loan and the more money the consolidation firm makes from you. Still want them to pay for that holiday of a lifetime for you? The TV loan companies have long been promoted by a group of C-list celebrities, from Carol Vorderman down, but the association with celebrity doesn't make them any more reputable.

Most of us, I know, wouldn't dream of responding to the moronic TV ads offering consolidation but the interesting thing is that many of us are effectively following exactly the same path by remortgaging with the mainstream lenders to pay off our other debts. This seems at first glance to make sense (personal loans cost 10% plus and credit cards average over 15% but mortgage rates are only 5–6%) but the end result is not good: doing this simply means that short-term debt is converted into long-term debt and unsecured debt converted into debt secured against your home.

Figures from **www.moneysupermarket.com** show just how dangerous this can be. A family with a £25,000 personal loan at 6.9% to be paid back over 5 years would have to repay £492 a month and a total of £4,510 in interest. If they added the loan instead to a mortgage paying 4.85% the repayments would fall to a mere £150. But the total interest cost would rocket to more than £19,000 as they would take five times longer to pay the money back. The result? That flat-screen TV you paid for on a credit card and then remortgaged to pay for could, at best, cost you thousands more than you intended (despite the fact that within a few years it will be worthless) and at worst cost you your home. You aren't getting rid of the problem with remortaging, you are just stretching out the pain and the danger. Many Citizens Advice Bureaus are already reporting seeing people who have remortgaged or consolidated loans with their houses as security being threatened with repossession, as they can't make the repayments. Your property is not a safety valve and should not be seen as one.

You should only consider adding debt to your mortgage if you are sure you can pay it off quickly. If in the above example from **www.moneysupermarket.com** the borrower had continued to pay off £492 of their debt a month but at the lower rate the debt would be paid back in just 3? years and the total interest bill would be only £2,398. See Chapter 7 for more on mortgages.

Student loans: the best way to borrow

If you are a student you will probably have no choice but to borrow: 90% of students spent 2006 in debt and the average undergraduate lives on a mere £30 a week after paying rent. This means choosing a current account with the best overdraft deal you can. Banks love students: they hope they'll all grow up to be rich professionals and then use their money to buy expensive insurances and mortgages. As a result you should be able to find one that will give you a free overdraft of up to £2,000 both during your time as a student and for a year or so afterwards. Banks offer all sorts of gifts to students and even to new graduates to convince them to sign up with them not their competitors – from iPods to flight vouchers – but a big free overdraft is the best gift of all when it comes to student banking so make this the first thing you look for.

Being a student also means student loans. These are well worth taking out. The rates are low and the payback terms generous (see Chapter 1). However, when you take them out remember that while they are cheap they aren't free: if you borrow money you have to pay it back; while you may think of student loans as a debt to the government they aren't, they're a debt to the tax payer, something that makes it very important that you don't default. At the moment around 60,000 people are in arrears on their student debt and another 60,000-odd are getting behind with their payments. And do not imagine that you can get rid of your student loans by going bankrupt. Not only is bankruptcy an absolute last resort and a decision to be taken very seriously for all the reasons mentioned elsewhere but the government has specifically – and quite rightly – excluded student loans from bankruptcy regulations.

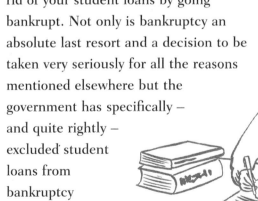

Personal loans:
a better way to borrow (if you must borrow)

I got a press release last year from Yorkshire Bank suggesting that everyone should take out a nice personal loan before the sales. Why? Because 'with a personal loan you're secure in the knowledge you can afford your spending spree'. What nonsense. If you have to take out a personal loan to buy stuff, you should know you can't afford the 'spree' in the first place. The answer is not to take out a personal loan but to stay at home. That said, there are going to be times when you might need to borrow money – perhaps you really must replace your car, for example. If so, a personal loan is probably the best way to borrow up to £25,000 over 2–5 years. They are relatively easy to arrange (you can now do it over the phone or on the Internet), the rate of interest and the payback time are normally fixed so you know where you are, and because you borrow a set amount of money you can't get into more trouble by dipping in and out as you can with a credit card or overdrafts and even with some modern mortgages.

As ever, make sure you get the cheapest loan possible. First, find the lowest APR you can (see all the usual websites to compare – you should be able to get a personal loan at about 1–2% above the cost of a mortgage). Next, consider how long you want to take to repay the money (what 'term' you want the loan to be). The key here is not to get hung up on looking at the monthly payments. The important number is the total you will end up paying back. The monthly payments for borrowing £5,000 over 5 years will be lower than those for borrowing the same amount over 3 years but the total amount you will have to pay back will be much higher thanks to the extra interest payments. Think about this carefully

before you take out a loan. If you
borrow £10,000 over 5 years to buy a
new car you will still be paying the
money back when the car is worth
only £5,000, despite the fact that,

including interest, you'll end up paying a great deal more for it
than £10,000. You might want to borrow less for a shorter time
and get a less flash car. Or not borrow at all and take the train.

Next you need to consider redemption penalties. Most borrowers
have no idea that if they repay their loan early they will get hit
with a whopping great penalty charge (known as an 'early
redemption charge') and are outraged when they find out about it.
They are right to be outraged, but if they'd read the small print
they could have avoided it in the first place by looking for a
flexible loan; there are a few about that allow you to make
overpayments when you can and to pay off the debt in its entirety
early without charge. The other thing to watch out for is the
'cross-selling' we looked at in the last chapter: it doesn't matter
how much the person arranging your personal loan tells you that
you need payment protection insurance, you probably don't.

Specialist loans:
complete nonsense

When you buy big expensive things – from double glazing and
kitchens to cars and even sofas – your sales person will be very
keen for you to sign up to their special financing packages too.
Almost a third of consumers surveyed told Alliance & Leicester
last year that they thought that most retailers' offers of credit were
reasonably priced. Big mistake. Take car finance. A typical loan
taken out via a car dealer will cost you around 12–15% in

interest. Yet a personal loan will cost only 6–7%. Double glazing deals are even worse, coming in at around 20% and most kitchen, bathroom and conservatory deals are equally awful at around 15%. Pushy sales people are excellent at finding ways to convince you their deal is the best (they'll chuck in interest-free periods and payment holidays at the drop of a hat) but that doesn't mean their deals aren't still rubbish.

A short interest-free period is by the by when the interest rate offered is double that of a personal loan and a payment holiday looks less good when you realize that all the time you aren't making payments your interest is rolling up. So when you next see a sign telling you that you can 'buy now with no deposit and nothing to pay for 12 months' remember that while you may have nothing to pay for the first year you'll have an awful lot to pay at the end of it: all the time you aren't paying, the interest is busy building up. You wouldn't buy a car or a kitchen from a bank so why would you get a loan from a car dealer or a kitchen salesman? You are much better off getting a personal loan from the bank if you need to borrow to pay for something. Not only will you pay less interest but you'll also be a cash buyer and hence in a better position to get a discount on whatever you are buying.

Overdrafts: a silly way to borrow

Using overdrafts is one of the easiest ways there is to borrow money. It is also one of the silliest. While a few banks charge reasonable rates on authorized overdrafts most charge well over 10% and practically no banks charge less than 20% if you haven't had your borrowing authorized first. Unauthorized overdrafts are also one of the banks' favourite ways to make themselves a little extra cash. For starters, as soon as you go over your overdraft limit they tend to charge you their higher rate on your entire overdraft not just the unauthorized part. Then they like to charge you daily amounts of cash too: perhaps £25 for every day you are overdrawn even if you've only gone over your limit by a pound or two. Next come item charges: a fee of, say, another £25 every time they pay a cheque or a direct debit from your overdrawn account. Finally, they start bouncing payments and charge you around £25 every time they do so: the average charge for a bounced cheque was £32.22 in 2006, according to **www.moneyexpert.com**. All this means that if you have an unauthorized overdraft for more than a few days you could end up paying charges of hundreds of pounds, something that will hardly help you out of the original situation: once all these charges start to bite, getting back into the black can

Bank charges hell

There is an argument that the huge penalty charges you get hit with by banks and by credit card lenders may be illegal under common law and that as a result they are unenforceable. This means that if you are very persistent in arguing against them you may find that they are either cut or disappear altogether. The banks insist that their charges are fair (though we know they know they aren't) but none the less they seem to cave in pretty often and so far haven't taken any of the campaigners to court, something that rather suggests they know they are in the wrong. For more on how to go about getting your penalty charges back see **www.bankchargeshell.co.uk**, a website devoted to the fightback against penalty charges. Other campaign groups include **www.bankactiongroup.co.uk** and **penaltycharges.co.uk**.

be tough going. On the plus side, the Office of Fair Trading suspects many of these fees may be 'excessive' and is looking into capping fees.

It is also true that authorized overdrafts can be a reasonable way of borrowing small amounts of money in the short term, particularly if you can find a bank that either has a low interest rate on them or that offers a small interest-free buffer. The only problem is one of discipline. If you allow yourself to borrow on overdraft can you be sure you can force yourself to pay it back even when no one is demanding that you do so? If you cannot you may find that it soon becomes a permanent part of your life.

What to do when you are desperate

Thirty years ago the stigma of bankruptcy was such that no one even considered it unless they really had no other choice – i.e. they were forced into it by creditors who saw it as the only way to get any money back. That's not the case any more. Well over 20,000 people applied for bankruptcy in the first three months of 2005 and more than half of those cases involved someone under

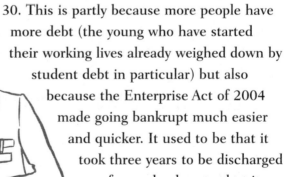

30. This is partly because more people have more debt (the young who have started their working lives already weighed down by student debt in particular) but also because the Enterprise Act of 2004 made going bankrupt much easier and quicker. It used to be that it took three years to be discharged from a bankruptcy but it now takes an average of only eight months, with the result

that many see it as a quick way to wipe their slates clean: once you are discharged all your debts are written off and you get to start afresh.

However, while this must sound like a dream come true to the heavily indebted there are huge downsides to bankruptcy. Once you have declared bankruptcy all your possessions pass into the hands of the Official Receiver who will then want to sell them. That means that if you have anything of any value – from investments to electronic goods and furniture – you will need to be prepared to lose it. Your car may go too unless you can prove you need it for your work and even then you may have to sell it and settle for a cheaper one. You will only get to keep the very basics – clothes, bedding and anything you must have for work. Your house may also end up being sold if it is worth more than your mortgage. But even if it isn't you won't be safe: the receiver can put a charge over your home, which means that they can still sell it if its value rises above the mortgage on it after you have been discharged from bankruptcy. While you are bankrupt you will not be allowed to have a cheque book or card so you won't be able to have a normal current account. At the same time utility companies will make you pay for their services in such a way that you never owe them anything: this could mean you have to use a cash key or metering system. You will also find, if you live in England and Wales, that news of your bankruptcy is announced in the *London Gazette*. None of this is very nice.

All these small indignities pale into insignificance compared to the way that a bankruptcy can blight your career and your finances even long after you are discharged. Many firms don't like to keep bankrupts on – check your contract, you may well find that you are out of a job. If you work in finance you will lose your licence; if you are a solicitor or an accountant you will probably be struck off; and after you are discharged you will find it tough to get a job handling money. Bad news if you have trained as a bank teller.

You will also find it hard to get credit for many years. Your bankruptcy order will be registered with credit agencies for at least six years so if you can get credit at all (which isn't a given) you will find you have to pay a great deal more for it than other people. And even after those six years are up you will often be asked whether you have ever been bankrupt when you apply for credit and charged more if you have. This is particularly the case with mortgages for which an ex-bankrupt may always be charged more than others: this means your bankruptcy could cost you a fortune. If you borrow £100,000 for 25 years at 5% the monthly bills will come in at £591.27, making a grand total of £177,381. If, however, you are forced to pay 1% more, those monthly payments go up to £651.88, making a total of £195,564. At 7% that total becomes £715 and £214,500. Bankruptcy doesn't come as cheap as you think.

Bankruptcy is also about more than money. It's about your reputation too. There is much talk about how bankruptcy shouldn't carry a stigma, that it isn't something to be ashamed of. But is this really true? Over 80% of today's insolvencies are not down to crisis but simply a result of people having regularly spent more than they have earned. I rather think that there is something shameful about running up debts for lifestyle reasons and then reneging on them – or at least that there should be something shameful about it. It just seems a bit – and here's an old-fashioned word for you – feckless.

A modern alternative to bankruptcy that doesn't leave your creditors quite so much in the lurch and which will protect your credit reputation to a degree is to take out an Individual Voluntary Arrangement (IVA) through the county courts. Most IVAs last for five years and involve you making regular payments of the maximum you can afford every month into a trust managed by an Insolvency Practitioner who then pays the money out to your creditors, all of whom are forced to go along with the plan as long as 75% of them agree to it. At the end of the five years you are free of debt regardless of how much of the original debt you have managed to pay down. This is good in that it doesn't affect your credit rating as much as a bankruptcy and in that your professional standing is less likely to be affected. It also beats bankruptcy in moral terms: at least you will be making an effort to pay your debts. Finally, it gives you a chance to get on top of your finances without losing all your stuff – unlike with a bankruptcy you get to keep your car, your home computer, and so on.

On the downside, arranging IVAs is a very lucrative business for the Insolvency Practitioners who you have to get to act for you. They take a fee from you upfront for arranging the IVA and then help themselves to around £75 a month on an ongoing basis. The problem? This gives companies an incentive to suggest IVAs even when they aren't suitable. Also anything they get is something your creditors aren't getting. For this reason it is also worth considering making your own informal arrangements with your creditors. You can negotiate with them yourself (download sample letters to send them from Nationaldebtline.co.uk or creditaction.org.uk) or get groups such as Citizens Advice to have a go for you. The idea is to get your creditors to stop charging interest and to give you a realistic amount of time to pay back your debt. Once creditors realize that you are in trouble but are trying to sort it out they are generally sympathetic; they know they are better off getting small payments from you than no payments at all. The Consumer Credit Counselling Service (CCCS) can help you with all this. If your creditors agree they will set up a scheme whereby you pay a set once-a-month payment to them and they distribute it among your creditors. You aren't charged for this (the CCCS is a charity and pays for itself on fees it gets from the lenders) and the CCCS will probably be able to negotiate much better terms than you can alone.

WHAT Do I Do Now?

* Figure out if you have a debt problem; if more than 20% of your income after paying tax and your mortgage is spent on debt repayments you are probably well on your way to having one.

* If you are in serious debt cut up all your credit cards and store cards.

* Cut your outgoings as much as you can.

* Assess what you have. Write down exactly what you owe and to whom and how much it costs you every month. List the interest rate of the debt next to it. Be honest.

* Make a list of all your incomings and necessary outgoings so you can see how much debt you can afford to pay off.

✳ Prioritize. Some debt is more important than others. You must not fall behind on your mortgage, for example. Beyond that, pay off the debt that charges the highest interest first (this usually means prioritizing credit card debt).

✳ Switch to cheaper debt if you can.

✳ Make sure you have the cheapest mortgage available – remember how much tiny-seeming differences in interest rates add up to over time.

✳ Get help from the Consumer Credit Counselling Service (**www.cccs.co.uk**); they will help you to assess things and set up a repayment plan for free. You can also contact the Citizens Advice Bureau (**www.citizensadvice.org.uk**), or National Debtline (**www.nationaldebtline.co.uk**), or the UK Insolvency Helpline (0800 074 6918).

✳ Never forget that the only real recipe for long-term financial happiness is to spend less than you have coming in.

Section 2: Using the Money

"Always buy a good pair of shoes and a good bed because if you are not in one you are in the other."   Joan Collins

4
Saving
Finding Your Freedom

One in five people in the UK surveyed by Sainsbury's said they didn't have enough savings to last them more than one month if they lost their jobs; 12% of the population have no cash savings at all and 30% have only £500 in savings. The average UK adult has only £3,000. It really isn't much. If this average adult loses her job and doesn't find another one immediately she's going to find herself in debt very fast indeed.

In the UK women just don't save enough, either in absolute terms or relative to men. Research from AXA Avenue shows that only 29 million of the UK's adults save at all and 1 million more of those are men than women. Women also save on average only £179 a month whereas male savers manage to put away a much healthier £304. After five years of saving, assuming an interest rate of 2.5%, the average woman will have over £7,700 less in her savings account than the man. All this is, of course, partly to do with the fact that women still earn less than men and that some women are in positions where they just can't get together the money to save at all (according to the Fawcett Society, which campaigns for equal rights for men and women, more than half of single mothers have no savings at all) but I wonder if there isn't sometimes more to it than that.

Most men instinctively know, even when young, that at some point there's a good chance they are going to be expected to provide for other people – a wife on maternity leave or not working while she looks after children and of course the children – so he has his mind on the financial future much of the time. Ask a 30-something man these days why he isn't married yet and more often than not his answer will have something to do with lack of money and a feeling that he still isn't well off enough to be a provider. I've met a great many men over the years who say that, given the cost of housing, education and healthcare, they won't consider marriage until their finances are properly sorted out. Women don't see it in the same way. We are more likely to see the perilous state of our finances as one of the top reasons to get married in a hurry. We, be it consciously or (more often) subconsciously, assume that when our children come we won't be the ones doing the main bit of the supporting. Instead, in our vision of the future, there'll be a man for that. I was long guilty of this. I've always been good at short-term saving – putting away money for holidays and so on – but hopeless at doing anything more long term, largely because despite considering myself to be a firm feminist it never really occurred to me that the long term would be my responsibility. This is a dangerous way for women to think – not only is there every chance these days that the right man will never turn up, but if he does who's to say he's going to be up to the job of being the main breadwinner?

We look at the impact not saving properly has on our old age in Chapter 6 (being poor when you're old really isn't nice) but there's a lot of life to live before you get old and you have to have your own savings for that too.

"Money is the root of all evil and yet it is such a useful root that we cannot get on without it any more than we can without potatoes."
Louisa May Alcott

Not everyone is ready to save. A lot of the women in the UK who do save are doing so despite the fact that they are in debt (5 million of us, says AXA). This is a mistake. I know it is tempting to want to have some cash set aside in an emergency fund or to start putting money away for your retirement but if you haven't paid off all you owe (mortgages aside) it really isn't worth it. Say you are paying 18% on your credit cards. A savings account is going to get you 6% tops, so if you save instead of paying off debt you'll be throwing away 12% a year even before you account for the tax you have to pay on the interest you earn. On AXA's figures the 5 million women both in debt and saving are paying out £5 in interest for every £1 they are earning on their savings. This makes no sense at all for most of us – it just makes the amount of time it will take us to get out of debt longer. If by any chance you have debt that is costing you less than the return you can earn on a savings account – a student loan perhaps – then if you really want you can start saving instead. My view, however, is that getting rid of debt makes you feel so much better, you might as well get rid of the lot as soon as you can.

Once you've done this you can start saving. This will be the greatest thing you ever do for yourself. Savings aren't just about survival. They're about choice. If you have none you can't leave your job. It doesn't matter how much you hate it. You're stuck with it. But if you have a year's worth of money in a savings account you can do pretty much whatever you like. Want six months off to consider your career options or go travelling? You can take it. Want to do a stint of volunteer or charity work? You can do it. Find yourself unexpectedly pregnant and hence with a few extra expenses on the way? It's OK. Whatever it is that you need to do, if you have savings you will have a financial cushion to support you through it, a breathing space. That's a nice feeling: when I look at my savings statements I don't see pounds and pence, I see freedom.

The first question to ask is how much you can save every month. To figure this out you need to make a list of your monthly incomings and outgoings. This will help you to work out how much you can realistically afford to save each month. The second question is more complicated. How many savings accounts do you

The miracle of compounding: how interest adds up

In the last chapter on debt we looked at how interest can destroy your wealth if you pay too much of it over too long a time. The exact opposite is true when it comes to savings: you want to get the highest rate you can over the longest time period you can. Why? Because every year you earn interest not just on the original sum you saved but on the interest you've accumulated too. If you save £100 at 5% you will have £105 at the end of the first year but in year 2 you will get interest on the whole £105, meaning that at the end of it you will have not £110 but £110.25. That might not sound like much but over time this 'compounding' really adds up and that means that both the interest rate you are getting and the length of time you save for are vital. If you save £1,000 in an account paying 2% for 5 years (as many silly people do) you'll have £1,104.08 at the end of it. If you do a bit of research and find an account paying 5% you'll have £1,276.28. At the end of 10 years the money in the 2% account will be worth £1,218 and the money in the 5% account £1,629. Or, to put it another way around, if your money earns interest at 2% it will take 36 years to double in value. At 5% it will take just over 14 years. That's a lot of extra money for very little extra effort.

There is a simple formula to help you to figure out how long it will take you to double your money at any given interest rate. It's called the rule of 72. All you do is divide 72 by the rate of return you are expecting. The result is the number of years it will take. So if you are making 10% a year it will take 7.2 years. The sooner you start saving and the higher the return you can get the more the miracle of compounding will work in your favour and the richer you will become. Time really is money.

need and what sort of accounts? I look at what sorts of accounts are on the market below but the answer to the first part, I think, is that – separate from your current account – you need three. The Calamity Account we discussed when we talked about insurance, a Freedom Account and finally a Future Account. The Freedom Account should have at least three months' worth of your salary, and eventually more like six months' worth in it to see you through any kind of emergency that might come up and to allow you to change big things in your life without panicking about how to finance them. The Future Account is the next step up from this. Once you have six months' worth of money you can afford to think about financing your long-term needs – getting together a house deposit, investing in the stock market, sorting out your pension and the like. All the money earmarked for this goes into your Future Account either to be kept in cash or to be dispersed into your investment accounts (we look at investing in the next chapter).

You could, of course, combine the three into one account but unless you are very disciplined this does put you in danger of not managing your money properly. One of the mistakes women make, says the Fawcett Society, is to use their savings inefficiently: even when they have enough put away to deal with any kind of rainy day, they still keep salting money away in an ordinary savings account.

Instead they should, as men more often do, move on to investing their money seriously. It's also worth noting that having a variety of accounts is no longer the admin hassle it used to be: if you open them all with an online bank you can look at them all together and shift money between them in a matter of minutes.

Getting started as a saver is simple. You just need to remember to pay your own savings accounts first every month. Have your salary and any other incomings paid directly into your Freedom Account. Then set up standing orders to pay money into your other accounts.

"The only way not to think about money is to have a great deal of it."
Edith Wharton

So, say you receive £2,000 a month in salary (after the taxman has deducted his increasingly enormous share) and you figure you can save £200 a month. The £200 stays in Freedom and the rest (£1,800) goes straight out again – into your current account, your Calamity Account and so on – leaving your savings behind. You've paid yourself first. The beauty of this is that if you get a rise or a bonus your savings automatically rise unless you change the amount that is debited out into your current account (which you should try not to do). A bonus that goes into your current account will soon find its way into the tills on your high street, making it instantly part of the past. A bonus that goes into Freedom becomes part of your long-term potential.

When you are ready to start saving into your Future Account you simply add another standing order to your list so you can pay into that too. Once your system is set up the whole thing becomes automatic – temptation is removed and before long you should find your accounts are filling up in a very satisfying sort of way.

Instant access accounts

Your Freedom and Calamity money needs to be where you can get to it swiftly: they're designed to deal with difficult situations and emergencies and both of these tend to emerge in a hurry. This means looking for an instant access account that allows you same-day access to your money but which also pays you a good rate of interest. Many of us who save do it badly, mainly by using rubbish savings accounts designed to make money not for us but for the banks. According to Capital One the level of general apathy among savers is such that £37.8 billion has been held in low-interest-paying accounts for over ten years. Overall, in mid-2006, the nation had a ridiculous £59 billion put away in accounts paying interest of less than 2%. When they could have got 5% with one phone call! Let's look at the effect of this over ten years. Say you invested £1,000 in an account paying 2% and left it untouched for a full decade. At the end of the period you would have £1,218.99 to play with. But had you invested the money at 5% you would have £1,628.89. That's a massive £420 difference, enough for a week away on the Costa Brava. If any of that £59 billion belongs to you rescue it right now.

One thing to look out for when you switch is bonuses. Banks and building societies very often add up to 1% in interest to attract savers to otherwise completely rubbish accounts. But the bonuses only last a few months, at which point the interest rate will drop back down to its previous lacklustre level. This trick makes the accounts look good in the best buy tables despite their rip-off rates of interest: don't go for them. The bonuses are also often removed if you withdraw any of your cash, something that you really don't want in any of your accounts; you may need to take money out of all of them for various things. You are after accounts that won't punish you for taking out your own cash.

Non-bonus accounts that look straightforward on the face of it also occasionally come with unexpected penalties. I was recently asked if I would like to apply for a First Direct savings account. It looked just the thing for me: it paid a good interest rate regardless of how much money you had in the account and appeared to be instant access. But when I looked a little closer I found a problem: no interest is paid on the account in any month during which you withdraw money. That means that even if I gave notice of wanting to make a withdrawal I'd still be penalized for taking out my own money (at the rate of about £40 a go if I had £10,000 in the account). That's no good for a Freedom Account or for a Future Account. In fact it's no good at all.

Notice accounts

Many of the accounts that offer better rates of interest make you give notice of anything up to 90 days if you want to take your money out. If you don't you tend to be penalized by the amount of interest you would have been paid during the notice period – so if your notice is three months and you need the money right away it will cost you the price of three months' worth of interest. Think quite carefully about these accounts. I'm not convinced that the rates are good enough to justify the risk of losing interest should you need the money. What if, for example, you were using a notice account to save for a house deposit and suddenly found the perfect house? You couldn't wait three months for your money then, could you?

Other accounts pay higher rates of interest if you don't touch your money for the first year. Again this is fine if you really think you won't but if you do you will – as ever – find that the penalties for withdrawal can be very high. You also often have to pay into them every month and lose the favourable interest rate if you miss a payment, and can only deposit a maximum of £3,000–£4,000 in total. Finally, when the year is up your interest rate falls to the provider's usual substandard level. The last bit here is the key: the bank hopes that your lethargy will mean that you keep the savings account regardless of the low rate you end up with, making them the usual stacks of cash and you nothing.

Inflation: the saver's enemy

Inflation eats away at the value of your money all the time. If prices are rising at, say, 3% a year you'll be able to buy 3% less with £100 at the end of a year than at the beginning. This means that you have to make at least 3% on your savings just to break even: if you get 2% you'll be losing money in 'real terms'. This makes it vital that you distinguish between the cash return you get and the real return you get on your savings account. If your account pays 5% and inflation is 3%, your real return is only 2%.

Fixed rate savings

A third kind of account is the fixed rate account. These usually (but not always) pay a slightly higher rate of interest than instant access accounts but as part of the deal you have to tie up your money for a fixed period of time – anywhere from 1 to 5 years. You aren't allowed to make any withdrawals during that time and you aren't allowed to add to your balance either. It's all a bit restrictive for me: the point of having cash is to be able to use it if and when you need it.

Tax-free accounts

The government provides the occasional incentive to help us save, the best of which is the Individual Savings Account (ISA). There are two types of ISA, the mini and the maxi. With a maxi you are allowed to invest up to £7,000 in shares. With a mini you can invest up to £3,000 in a savings account and £4,000 in shares with a different provider. The chancellor has said that changes are to be made to simplify the ISA rules (see p182 for details) but the £3,000 cash allowance will not change.

We'll look more at ISAs in the next chapter and explain exactly how they work (as is usually the case with government initiatives ISAs are much more complicated than they need to be), as they are a good way to invest. In general I think most of us are better off using our ISA allowance to invest in equities or bonds but in the early stages of your savings career a cash ISA isn't a bad way to start building up your resources given that the interest is tax free: online bank Intelligent Finance estimates that a basic rate tax

145

payer who saves £3,000 into a cash ISA every year for 10 years will end up saving £1,726 in income tax. Most banks and building societies offer mini cash ISA accounts.

Offset accounts

Offset accounts are relatively new to the market. They take account of the fact that many of us have both savings and a huge mortgage and that we are often paying more interest on our mortgage than we are making on our savings. If you merge the accounts together you can cut the interest you pay on your mortgage and hopefully end up paying it off earlier. If, for example, you have £10,000 worth of savings and a mortgage of £100,000 you combine the two so that while you receive no interest on your savings you pay interest on only £90,000 of your mortgage. You can also pay your salary into the offset account so that you pay interest on even less for a short time each month. This works because the interest on a mortgage is usually higher than that on a savings account and because it cuts your tax bill: if you aren't making interest on your savings you can't pay tax on them. However, it isn't always the best idea: offset mortgage rates are very often higher than standard mortgage rates, which cancels out the gains. If you are thinking about using one of these you will, I'm afraid, need to do some maths before you make a final decision.

One final point on savings accounts. If you are not a tax payer you do not have to pay tax on the interest on your savings. Your bank will provide you with a form to fill in verifying this and will then leave your money alone. Make sure you fill it in: £318 million is lost every year by people who never get around to it. If you've been entitled to save tax free in the past and not done so, you are also entitled to reclaim the money.

WHAT Do I Do Now?

- Set up your Freedom and Future savings accounts – online if you can. Find instant access accounts with the best rates via **www.moneysupermarket.com**, **www.find.co.uk**, **www.moneyfacts.co.uk**, or **www.moneyextra.com**. The higher the interest rate the harder your money will be working for you and the faster you will see your savings accumulate.

- Get your salary paid into your Freedom Account and arrange payments out of it into your other accounts as needed.

- Keep a very close eye on the interest rate on your accounts. If it falls move your money.

- When you have six months' worth of money in your Freedom Account start saving into your Future Account.

- Once your Future Account is under way start investing – see the next chapter.

5
Investing
Looking to the Long Term

*O*maha, Nebraska, isn't a very nice town. In fact to the casual eye it is less a town than a collection of highways, low-grade steak houses and nasty retail warehouses. Yet look a little closer and you will see it has something special about it. The retail warehouses don't sell the discounted Chinese-made clothes, fake leather furniture and general tat you'd expect to see. They sell incredibly rare matched red diamonds and European designer clothes. And everyone drives a Jaguar. Why? Because there are more millionaires living in Omaha than there are in any other town in America. Thirty years ago they invested money with a young man called Warren Buffett. Buffett is now considered to be the greatest investor ever: every $10,000 the residents of Omaha trusted him to invest for them is worth over $50 million today.

This is the chapter a lot of people will find frightening. It's also probably the most important in the book. Only by investing can you become genuinely financially secure and completely free as a result. The income from your job is not long term. It may go up over time as you become more skilled but to keep it coming in you have to keep working and that means that your time is not your own. It doesn't matter how much you have invested in your skill base and how good and valued an employee you may be, when you leave or are asked to leave your job your income will disappear. You may manage to have a certain amount of control over your work but the real decisions (where you would like to live, what time you want to get up in the morning, how you would really like to spend Friday afternoons and so on) are not yours to make. They remain firmly in the hands of your employer and of the market as a whole. In fact so does your whole future – from whether you'll be able to make next month's mortgage payment to which week in August you'll be able to go on holiday next year.

But if you own assets and those assets produce an income for you (as real assets should) you will suddenly find that your time becomes your own: the more non-salaried income you have the more of your own time you will own. Right now you are probably entirely dependent on your income (most of us remain so for most of our working lives), but your wealth is not about your income, it's about your assets – about the degree to which you are able to live without depending on the conventional world of work.

See all those bankers driving around in their Ferraris? Could they keep them if they stopped working and the cash stopped coming in as income? Unlikely. That means that they don't own their lifestyle, they're simply swapping short-term income for it – renting it, if you like. They can't leave; they don't have what they would call 'Fuck you money' – an amount that allows them to leave their jobs whenever they want. Invest properly and one day you might have. And the more control you have over your life the better your life will be and, importantly, the longer you will live. A study of civil servants in 1997 found that the higher up the tree people climbed the less likely they were to die of coronary heart disease: more control meant less stress and a longer life expectancy. This is one of the main reasons why the rich live longer than the poor.

"A full purse is not as good as an empty one is bad."
Yiddish proverb

Building asset-related income is particularly important for women. We're the ones who give up our work and hence our salary income for children and family and that can lead us into all sorts of trouble. If we have assets working for us when we aren't earning those troubles can be much reduced. If you want your money really to work for you, you have to invest properly. So once you have six months' worth of cash in your Freedom Account you need to start turning your surplus income into assets – into wealth. The money in your Freedom Account doesn't count as an investment – it's about giving you short-term freedom so you can leave a job you really hate without worrying too much or deal with the occasional hiccup, but as it is in cash you can never earn much more on it than the rate of inflation. Keeping money in savings accounts stops you getting poorer – which is a great thing – but it's hard for it to make you much richer. For that you have to invest. The good news is that there are millions of women in the UK in a position to start investing for their future freedom already.

According to Investec Private Bank 5 million of us have assets of over £25,000 excluding our properties and our pensions; 360,000 of those women have assets worth over £750,000 and over 100,000 of those are millionaires, and young millionaires at that: there are 47,350 female millionaires between the ages of 18 and 44 in the UK according to the Centre for Economic and Business Research; that's 24% more than there are male millionaires. By 2025 women are forecast to be controlling 60% of the nation's wealth (right now we hold just under 50%). Men will look at these numbers and immediately think widows (women live longer than men so there are a lot of well-off older women about) and divorcees, and while it is true that a great many women come by their wealth as a result of inheritance or divorce, large numbers of today's lady millionaires have earned every penny themselves: half the UK's doctors are women, 150,000 women a year start their own businesses and 30% of all corporate managers are women.

This is fantastic: it means that millions of us are making really good incomes, the kind of incomes that should make it relatively easy to push ourselves into positions where we aren't dependent on those incomes any more.

The bad news is that right now we aren't leveraging those incomes into wealth: despite the fact that we know we can't get rich keeping all our money in cash women on average have a quarter of their wealth held in cash, says Investec. Worse, 7% of us have all our money in cash: overall more than 2 million women have over £25,000 sitting in a bank account. Why? Two reasons. The first is that women are naturally risk-adverse (we're genetically programmed to see danger everywhere in order to be able to protect our children). We hate risk and we hate the idea of losing any of the money we've managed to save up. We think that by keeping it in cash we're doing the best thing, the lowest risk thing, for our futures. But we're wrong. The best thing for our futures would be to make our money work as hard for us after we've earned it as we worked to earn it in the first place.

The second reason why we hesitate to invest is that we have been brainwashed by the financial services industry into thinking that investing is complicated. But this isn't true either. Investing can be made complicated, as can anything if you give it a special language (as the City does for investing) and churn out endless material written in that special language so that only those conversant with it can understand. Women are particularly prone to fear of investing: a survey by Halifax a few years ago showed that about 25% of men claim to be interested in the market while only 11% of women say they are. The rest of us would just like to pretend it doesn't exist.

But you really don't need to know that much to manage your own money, nor do you need to be interested in investing – just in having more money. All you need to know is the basics about shares and bonds and a little about how the industry works so you don't get ripped off by it, and to understand that much of the stuff spoken of (endlessly) in the markets is utterly irrelevant to most of us. The City is, more than anything else, a talking shop designed to keep men in jobs and you in the dark. So, in this chapter I want to show you just how simple investing can be.

The special language of investing

One of the many things that makes us think that investing is complicated when it is not is the language that surrounds it. Yet most of the special words used in the markets mean nothing particularly difficult.

Equities: another word for shares.

Stocks: another word for shares.

Outperform: to do better than an index. If a fund is said to have outperformed it has returned more over a year than the relevant stock market index.

Underperform: to return less than an index.

Reduce: sell. Analysts hate to say the word sell. It's too absolute for them so they often say reduce instead.

Accumulate: the opposite of reduce.

Fundamentals: the actual state of a company's business.

Leverage: having debt.

Gearing: debt.

Volatility: fluctuations in price.

Beta: the returns a fund manager makes simply from being in the market when shares are rising anyway.

Alpha: the returns she makes additional to that by choosing good shares to hold.

Cyclical stocks: stocks of companies that tend to mirror the economy. When the economy turns up the stocks turn up, and when the economy falters the stocks fall.

First I'm going to explain what counts as an investment (shares, bonds, property and cash) and what does not (wine and snow shakers for example) and how those investments work. Then I'm going to look at exactly how I think you should invest in these asset classes. There are lots of highly complicated ways to invest but it is also entirely possible to do it very simply and without getting too bogged down in detail. Finally, I'm going to have a look at the financial advice industry and how it works.

This chapter is not going to be comprehensive – there are thousands and thousands of 'products' out there created by the financial services industry with the aim of making money out of investors. However, one of the main points I want to make is that you probably don't need them: anything that isn't mentioned here you don't, in my opinion, need to know about and you certainly don't need to buy. A word of warning. You may find much of this chapter boring. That's because much of the material in it is quite boring. But you should read it all: only by knowing about and understanding the basics of markets and investing can you stop yourself spending the rest of your life being income-dependent (and hence slightly scared all the time) to say nothing of constantly ripped off by the investment industry and start making yourself really wealthy.

What is an investment?

So here's the first question. What counts as an investment? You'll get all sorts of answers to this one. According to the many 'experts' all over the personal finance pages almost anything can be an investment – not just shares and bonds but classic cars, paintings, 1960s white leather corsets, vintage guitars (a banker favourite, apparently) and so on. But this isn't quite true. For our purposes an investment is something that offers you two things: an income and the possibility of a capital gain. You may be able to sell a classic car for more than you paid for it, assuming that other collectors still want it and that it remains in fashion but its value will depend entirely on supply and demand – as it produces no income it has no intrinsic value. That's not the case with a share that pays you a dividend. Yes, its resale value will depend on supply and demand but even if it is very out of favour it will still be offering you value in the form of an income and that will give it an intrinsic value. Everything that does not create this sort of income is not an investment but a collector's item. So what falls into my definition of an investment? Shares, bonds and property, I think.

Shares

When I first started as a stockbroker in my early twenties I had no idea what a share was. No one explained it to me in the very simple way I needed it explained – completely from scratch – and as a result it took me many months to figure out the basic point of my job and begin to understand how the markets worked. With that in mind I am going to assume that everyone else knows as little as I did then and start from the very beginning here – with a little history.

The concept behind shares and the stock exchanges on which they are bought and sold goes right back to the sixteenth century. Until then companies had usually been owned by small groups of private individuals: they put up the cash to get things started, they managed the business and they reaped the profits. But then came the huge opportunities offered by foreign exploration: it became clear that if you could get the money together to make a voyage to

Wine, fashion, cars and snow shakers

These days people seem to think that anything counts as an investment. I've seen articles in serious magazines announcing that everything from sneaker to snow dome collections are now to be considered serious investments, while pretty much everyone appears to think that wine and vintage fashion count as investments. In 2006 I even came across a fund that suggested you should invest in wine as a way to pay off your mortgage. This is just silly. It is absolutely true that the prices of various vintage wines and even vintage clothes often rise, but that doesn't make them investments. Why? Because they produce no income and have no intrinsic value – their price is based not on the income they can produce for you but on the vagaries of fashion.

Take the case of clothes. Right now vintage clothes are hot – even the big auction houses have regular sales of what we once knew as second-hand clothes with the best pieces going for thousands of pounds. But inside that market what's in vogue and what's not changes all the time. A few years ago 1960s fashion was selling very well. Now it isn't – people are more into 1970s gear from the likes of Ossie Clark and Biba. The 1960s stuff may come back in. But it may not. And if it doesn't not only will you not get much wear out of it yourself when you can't sell it on (we're all much fatter than our grandmothers) but it won't ever provide you with an income either. So why would you want it in your pension?

Then take snow domes. I love these so I was fascinated to see last year that there is now a huge market for them: collectors all covet one of Canberra and the Australian parliament house because it was withdrawn very fast after a sharp-eyed shopkeeper noticed it sported not an Australian flag over the main building but a Japanese one, while those sold in New York pre-2001 featuring the World Trade Center are also popular (see **www.snowdomes.com**). But again fashions might change: right now kitsch is in so snow domes are considered fun things to have but who's to say that won't change next year, leaving snow dome investors with nothing but worthless bits of plastic?

Much the same can be said of almost all the alternative 'investment opportunities' out there from classic cars to contemporary art and fancy watches (I know not everyone will appreciate art being compared to snow domes but the point stands). I'm not saying you shouldn't collect at all, just that if you do so you should remember that you are not investing but collecting things you love. They may go up in value if you keep them in pristine condition and the market goes your way but they may not: buy them for pleasure not for profit.

the East Indies, to India and Africa you could make yourself seriously rich. But these endeavours were far too expensive – and indeed far too risky – for one man or one partnership to finance alone. The answer? Getting the general public involved by creating the first real joint-stock companies.

The East India Company, launched on 31 December 1600, was a classic case in point. It needed vast amounts of money for voyages from which there was no guarantee of any return (but the possibility of a huge return). So it offered shares in the business to individuals in return for the cash to pay for the voyages. There would be no set return on the shares the investors would own in the new company, but if it did well its proceeds would be divvied up between all the shareholders and at the same time anyone who needed to get their money back before the proceeds (the dividends) were paid out was to be able to sell their shares on to someone else.

This worked a treat. As trade developed, the investors did extremely well: the tenth voyage (in 1611), for example, returned investors 148%. By the end of the seventeenth century, many more were getting in on the game: there were more than 100 'joint-stock' companies with tradable shares, and merchants and traders had started to gather in London coffee shops. This system was formalized in 1801 with the creation of the London Stock Exchange and since then – barring a few hiccups, such as the South Sea Bubble and the collapse of the railway boom, for example – it has barely looked back. Today, the London Stock Exchange (LSE) runs Britain's biggest exchange with nearly 2,000 companies making up what is referred to as the 'main market'. In addition, the LSE runs the Alternative Investment Market (Aim), a 'starter market' for smaller companies that also want to offer their shares to the general public.

You can of course start a business and sell shares in it to people without involving the Stock Exchange but if you want a large number of people to have access to your shares and a forum where they can easily trade in and out of them you need to be 'listed' on a stock exchange of some kind.

So why would you buy shares today? For the same reasons that investors did 400 years ago – for dividends and to make capital gains. Some investors buy shares purely to get a regular dividend income. Other investors are less interested in income and more in capital growth. However, it is crucial to understand that capital growth is intimately connected to dividends. A share rises in price mainly as a consequence of the expectation that a firm's profits will rise and that, as a result, the dividend payout will also rise in the future: the better a company's future profits (and hence dividends) are expected to be the more the shares will be thought to be worth. If you are investing for income, you buy shares that pay dividends already. If you are investing for capital growth, you buy shares that you expect to do well and to be able to pay a high dividend in the future, whether you intend to hold them for that long or not. The key is that the shares will either pay you an income now or have the potential to pay you or someone else one in the future.

The actual price of a share is, like everything, determined by supply and demand. Shares in companies that are judged to be unsound or overpriced will not attract investors and prices will fall. However, shares in firms that are successful – or are perceived as being likely to be successful – create demand and prices will rise. In the short term, press releases, newspaper stock tips, reports from professional analysts and sentiment drive share prices. This is what happened in the

1990s – euphoria pushed the prices of technology stocks to silly levels. In the long term, though, the truth always comes out in markets: shares that are too cheap rise in price and shares that are too expensive fall in price.

So here's the most important question of all: how do you know if a share is cheap or expensive? There is no absolute answer to this (successful share investing involves a large element of luck) but there are a few things that are good indicators of value.

The first is the **dividend yield**, which is the annual dividend paid to shareholders expressed as a percentage of the share price (if the share price is £1 and the annual dividend is 10p the dividend yield is 10%). The yield is the cash return on the share, so you can compare it with the returns you get on other investments – on bonds, savings accounts and other stocks.

A company with a yield higher than the interest on a savings account is worth a look for income investors. However, a high reported yield is not in itself a reason to buy a share. Yields are worked out on the basis of what a firm paid out last time. But until they announce it nobody knows what they will pay out next time – and, as we all know, the past is not necessarily an accurate guide to the future. A high yield can also suggest a rising perception of risk: if investors think a firm is no longer financially stable, they will sell its shares, forcing the price down and its yield (remember, this is the dividend divided by the share price) up.

The **price/earnings (p/e) ratio** is another good indicator of value. This is the company's current share price divided by the amount it makes in profit per share. So if the share price is £1 and the company made 5p in earnings for each share last year its p/e will be 20 times (100 divided by 5). This tells you how many years, at the given profit level, it will take the firm to make as much money as you are paying for each share – i.e. how long it will take it to double your money.

So what level of p/e suggests good value? Again there is no absolute answer to this. Shares with a p/e of 5 times may seem to be cheap – five years isn't long to double your money – but what if the profits of such a seemingly cheap company start to fall? If they halve you may suddenly find that the next year the p/e is 10 times and your doubling day is much further away than you thought. This works the other way around too. If you see a share with a p/e of 25 times you might think it looks pretty pricey, but what if it is doubling its earnings every year? The high p/e might just reflect the fact that investors expect profits to rise (and hence the p/e ratio to fall) very fast. Companies with a low p/e aren't always as cheap as they seem and those with a high p/e aren't always as expensive as they seem. Bear in mind too that just because a share looks cheap doesn't mean its price will rise: the numbers only tell you what should happen not when it will happen or if it will happen at all.

There is a school of thought that suggests that it doesn't really matter when you buy shares or at what price. Over the long term, it is said, shares are the best way to make money so if you are investing (which is a long-term strategy) you might as well just buy in and be done with it. I'm not convinced on this one. It is true that few people have ever lost money in the equity market if they have stayed in it for 20 years but a great many people have certainly lost money over 5 years, 10 years and 15 years: whether you think it doesn't matter when you buy or not rather depends on your definition of the long term!

On the plus side, if one market looks too expensive to buy into (you can judge this to a degree by looking at p/e ratios and growth rates for markets as a whole) there is usually another that is not. Remember that when it comes to buying shares you are not restricted to buying them on the London Stock Exchange. Everywhere from Canada to Uganda has a stock exchange and there is always value somewhere.

You can find all the information you need on dividend yields, p/e ratios and share prices on websites such as **www.bloomberg.com** and **www.iii.co.uk**, and on my magazine's website **www.moneyweek.com** you will find lots of introductory articles as well as share and fund recommendations.

Bonds

Bonds are very simple things. They are just IOUs issued by a government to raise money to cover expenditure that isn't covered by their tax revenues, or issued by a company to raise money to finance various business activities. As such, they represent a promise to pay the holder a set level of interest (known as the 'coupon') during the lifetime of the bond and to repay the money in full on a set date. In the UK government bonds are called gilts (short for gilt-edged securities), and in the US they're known as Treasuries (because they are issued by the US Treasury). So a debt certificate worth £100, with a coupon of 4.5%, set to mature in 2015, would mean that the bondholder has lent the government £100 (bonds are usually issued in £100 units), which he will get back in full when the bond 'matures' in 2015. In the meantime, he will get £4.50 – or 4.5% of the face value of the bond – every year.

Four basic investing rules

Listen to the jargon-filled mutterings of the nation's fund managers and you might think that there is some sort of secret to successful investing – one they know and you never will. But there isn't. Getting rich on the stock market isn't easy but there are a few simple rules to follow that should ensure that dabbling in it doesn't actually make you poorer.

1 **Keep your costs as low as possible.** If you regularly double your money overnight in penny shares you may not be too fussed about fees but for the rest of us they are the biggest drag there is on returns. Say you buy a unit trust (a type of fund – see below). You'll probably pay a 5% upfront fee just to be allowed to buy in and then 1.5% every year in management fees. That means the fund has to make you over 6% in year one just to get you back to square one. Pay this kind of fee too often and you will always be disappointed with your returns. Every time you buy or sell a share you will also incur costs – a fee for making the trade and stamp duty (another one of the government's stealth taxes currently charged at 0.5% of the value of your trade) – and these will eat into your returns. This means that you should only buy cheap investments and that you should then hold them until they are no longer cheap investments.

2 **Only buy if the price is right.** Just because a company is a good company doesn't mean it is a good investment. Take the case of Google in 2006. Was it a good company? Of course it was. The firm dominated the search engine market (I use it every time I look something up) and was growing at an extraordinary speed.

But was it a good investment? Absolutely not. The shares were trading on a p/e ratio of over 80 times: if you'd bought them it would have taken the company 80 years to earn the same amount of money per share as you paid for the share. Good company, rubbish investment. The same can be true of markets as a whole. Asia may be booming but if that is already reflected in the price of shares it may not be a good time to buy.

3 **Always sell when your investment is no longer a good one.** This could be because the price has gone up making it newly expensive or could be because something has gone wrong. The share price may not have changed but falling profits or expectations of profits could mean the shares no longer have potential. Either way, if you wouldn't buy the shares or fund at today's price you should probably sell them.

4 **Never invest in stocks for markets or products you don't understand.** This sounds simple but has been too often ignored at great cost to investors (remember the dot.com crash). If you are not sure why a firm is doing well in the first place you won't spot problems when they develop and you'll lose money.

The bond market is huge (in the UK the gilt market alone is worth around £350 billion) and government debt was publicly traded for years before equities really got a look in: back in the late eighteenth century, no one dabbled in the stock market – they just had a few thousand pounds in the 'four percents' (government debt that paid 4% a year; Elizabeth Bennet in Jane Austen's *Pride and Prejudice* had £1,000 worth). In fact, it wasn't until the 1970s that big investors started switching their investments out of bonds and into shares instead.

If you buy a bond when it is first issued it will generally cost you £100, which you will always get back at the end of the term. But between the start and end dates of the term you can sell the bond on and then you may get more than £100 for it or you may get less. Why? Because bond prices react to changes in interest rates. If general interest rates rise, the interest rate offered by your bond will start to look relatively less attractive and the price of your bond will fall as a result. If rates fall, your bond's offering will look more attractive so the value of the bond will rise. Imagine a government or firm sells 10-year 5% bonds at £100 each. This means you get £5 a year for every year you hold the bond: a yield of 5%. That may seem fair when general interest rates are around 5%. But what if general rates rise to around 7%, with savings rates offered by high street banks therefore paying out more than bonds? Who would want a bond paying just 5% then? No one. So the market price of the bond will fall until it is paying a yield of nearer 7% (to around £70). The price of bonds will also reflect what the market thinks will happen to interest rates in the future. If interest rates are expected to rise, investors will sell to lock in any capital gains and prices will fall. If they are expected to fall, they will buy to lock in higher yields and capture future capital gains so prices will rise. Therefore, anything that affects interest rates – inflation, economic growth and expectations about both – also affects bond prices.

When interest rates go up bond prices go down. When interest rates go down bond prices go up.

The main thing to note here is that bonds are not necessarily a safe investment. If you go to a financial adviser they will tell you that buying bonds is a low-risk purchase but while this is often the case it isn't always. If inflation rises fast and so do interest rates the value of any bonds you hold could plummet. It is also possible to lose a great deal of money on bonds bought from companies: corporate bonds are affected by interest rates as much as government bonds but while one assumes that the government will pay back its debts the same is not true of the corporate sector: if there is any suggestion that a firm may not be able to pay back its debts the value of any bonds it has issued will fall. If you buy bonds in a company that actually defaults on its debt, you could lose all your money. Bonds are not a risk-free investment.

Funds

Most of us can't be doing with buying individual shares and bonds so we look to other people to do the hard work for us by buying investment funds. These work like this: you and, say, 999 others stump up £100 each. The managers of what is to be the new fund collect the £100,000 and use it to buy other assets – shares or bonds, for example. With a bit of luck, the value of those assets rises. If in two years' time the £100,000 has grown to be worth £110,000, your unit of – or share in – the fund will be worth not

£100, but £110. You can now – or at any time – sell that share either in the market, or to the managers of the trust, who will sell it on to someone else.

The first of these schemes was set up in the UK by London-based solicitor Philip Rose in 1868. Back then, stock market investment was largely closed to all but the very wealthy. Rose wanted to provide a vehicle into which the ordinary investor could place his capital, have it invested for him and still sleep at night. So he did. Buying a holding in his fund meant buying a unit in a fully diversified portfolio. Rose's scheme is still going strong today, with 99,000 investors with money in what is now known as the Foreign & Colonial Investment Trust.

There are three basic kinds of investment fund available in the UK. The oldest are **investment trusts** (such as the Foreign & Colonial trust). These are listed companies with shares that trade on the stock market just like those of any other company. The difference is that their business is to invest in the shares of other companies. Investment trusts – known as closed-end mutual funds in the US – are referred to as 'closed end' because the number of shares or units into which the firm's portfolio is divided is limited: new money cannot be raised without a formal issue of new shares. To invest or exit, you have to buy or sell existing shares on the stock market.

More common today are the second kind of fund, open-ended funds. **Unit trusts** are open-ended funds. The amount of money in each of these is variable, rising and falling as investors buy and sell. If new investors want to buy into the fund, the manager will create new units to sell to them. They will then invest the money investors pay to increase the overall size of the fund's portfolio. To buy units of a unit trust you need to go via the fund manager, a financial adviser or a fund supermarket of some kind.

Given the choice between these first two types of fund I'd take an investment trust any day. Why? Because they offer more possibilities. For starters, as well as using the money that investors have given them they are allowed to borrow money to invest as well. Having more money to invest means they can make more money in good times (as long as the overall returns from investing the money are greater than the interest rate costs of borrowing it) – although it also means that you can lose more money in bad times. Investment trusts also often trade at a discount to their net asset value (the total market value of the shares in issue is less than the total value of the investment trust's portfolio of investments), which can, on occasion, provide clever investors the opportunity to buy good funds at prices below their real worth. On the downside, the fact that investment trusts can borrow money means that they can lose more money than they would otherwise when the market is falling.

However, the real reason I prefer investment trusts to unit trusts is because I can just buy them on the stock market. One of the good things about this is that it is easy but it has something else to recommend it too: it is a much cheaper way to invest and cheapness is very important. The more you spend buying and selling investments the less there is left in your money pot to provide for your future. When you buy a unit trust you will usually end up paying commission to whoever sells it to you: there'll be an entrance fee of anywhere up to 5% of the value of your investment (so if you invest £1,000 that's £50 gone right away) and you'll then pay a management fee as well as trail commission every year (I explain what this is when we look at financial advisers below). And when you sell you may even find that there is an exit fee to pay too. When you buy an investment trust all you have to pay upfront is the transaction fee to your broker (round £10) and, while you still have to pay a management fee to the fund manager who runs the fund for you, it will usually be much lower than the annual fees on a unit trust.

The odd 1% here and there may not seem like much but it makes a big difference over time. For example, £10,000 invested in a fund that grows at 7% a year would be worth £14,000 in 5 years if you were to pay no charges at all on the money. If you were to pay charges at 1% it would end up being worth £13,338 and if you were to pay charges at 2% it would end up being worth only just over £12,667. Over 10 years the gap widens. With no charges the money is worth £19,670. At 1% it is worth £17,790 and at 2% it is worth a mere £16,070 – over £3,000 will have been moved from your pocket to that of a financial services company. I'm not talking in extremes here. These are the kind of charges that most of us pay on our investments: the Total Expense Ratio or TER (annual fee plus expenses) on funds available in the UK averages about 1.5–1.7% and as a result the typical British investor putting a £10,000 lump sum into a UK equity fund would see about £1,300 removed from the fund over 5 years. Unit trust charges run at the high end of the range and investment trusts at the low end.

So how do you choose from the 1,500 investment trusts and unit trusts on offer in the UK? First you need to decide what you want from it. Do you want it mainly for income from the shares it invests in or mainly for growth? Do you want to invest in the UK, the US or further afield? To have money in just one sector, say oil exploration or mining? There's a fund for almost everything.

Morningstar.co.uk provides information on a fund's emphasis (growth or income and region) and tells you what shares it is invested in so that's a good place to start. One thing to bear in mind, however, is that funds are managed in two distinct ways: they are 'active' or they are 'passive'. The point of a 'passive' fund is that the fund manager does no actual share choosing (or 'stock picking' as they put it) but simply buys all the shares in any given index of shares (such as the FTSE 100 which is the 100 largest companies – in terms of their stock market value – listed in London). The fund therefore tracks the index and nothing else (they are also called tracker funds for this reason). An active fund works the other way around: instead of buying all the shares in an index the fund manager is supposed to use his stock-picking skills to choose the best of them and hence to make his fund rise more than the index (they call this 'outperforming').

So which kind should you get? The answer is usually trackers. Not only do they have the advantage of being cheap (computers do most of the work) but they tend to do better too. In the 1999 edition of financial bible *A Random Walk Down Wall Street*, Professor Burton Malkiel points out that, over the long term, trackers have outperformed actively managed funds by quite a margin. Had you put $10,000 in a US tracker in 1969, by the time Malkiel was writing it would have been worth $311,000. The same amount put in the average active fund would have been worth only $171,000. This doesn't say much for the so-called stock-picking skills of the City's overpaid fund managers (and is one of the main reasons why we shouldn't be intimidated by them!). The fact is that investment returns are much more random than investment managers would like you to think.

Not all active funds do badly – some fund managers do appear to be quite good at their jobs. But identifying which ones might do well in any given year is tricky. You will constantly see in magazines, newspapers and even on train platforms advertisements for funds run by star managers, but this hype always comes after not before they make good returns with the shares they have bought for their funds. As investors often find out to their cost, past performance is little indication of future performance: a fund that does well one year is in no way guaranteed to do well the next year too. The fact is that over the course of a 20-year career, most managers are going to have a good two- or three-year run at some stage. But this can have as much to do with luck or style as skill. All in all, my inclination, as it is with everything, is to ignore most of the noise about funds and their managers and to take the cheapest and simplest investing option instead.

What is an index?

An index is the average price of a group of shares. When we talk about the level of the FTSE we are simply talking about the average price of all the shares listed on the main Stock Exchange in the UK – have they gone up or down? The FTSE 100 is the average share price of the biggest 100 companies in the UK and the FTSE 250 is the average price of the 250 biggest shares listed in the UK. In the US people tend to refer to the Dow, which is the Dow Jones Index, the average of the prices of 40 big US companies. In Japan the index people look at most is the Nikkei. In France it is the CAC 40 and in Germany it's the DAX.

For me that means going with the third kind of fund available in the UK. These are effectively a kind of tracker fund called **Exchange Traded Funds** (ETF). They track either indices or groups of shares around the world but trade on the stock market just like shares. They are a bit like investment trusts but borrow no money and are not actively managed by their providers. You can buy an ETF that tracks the share prices of the biggest 100 shares in the UK, or perhaps one that tracks the biggest 250 shares in the UK, or you can go further afield and buy one that tracks shares in Taiwan, in the US, in Latin America or in Japan. You can also buy ETFs that track shares in particular sectors such as the oil sector or the water sector and ETFs that track the bond market (see **www.ishares.com** for all the ETFs you can buy on the UK market and **www.etfs.com** for those listed in the rest of the world). This means that you can invest perfectly easily in just about anything without the bother of looking at individual shares or of worrying about which of thousands of funds on offer you should or should not buy. Instead you simply make the big decisions – do you think the UK or Japan will do better over the next ten years, for example – and buy ETFs that reflect your choices. And if you can't be bothered even to make specific big decisions you can buy a selection of them; at least you'll be invested cheaply and you probably won't do much worse than you would if you entrusted your money to a random fund manager.

Products

So far I've just talked about bonds, shares and simple investment funds. But if you talk to an adviser or read any of the marketing literature that comes through your door you will find that you are being offered a great many more complicated things than this – investment bonds, guaranteed equity bonds, and so on. What are all these and do you need them? The answer to the first part is that they are what the investment industry likes to call 'products' and the answer to the second is that no, you don't. Products are the investment industry's way of confusing you into paying them more money than you need to. They know that we don't need that much in the way of financial products – we all need savings and simple investments but we don't need much more. But if we all just bought shares and ETFs directly through the market how would the nation's financial advisers and financial services firms ever make the money they need to keep themselves in Porsches and holiday homes in Marbella? They wouldn't, so they keep inventing new products and trying to bamboozle us into buying them. There are hundreds of financial products around and I can't possibly look at all of them and nor do I think I need to – once we've looked at one you'll get the general idea: people in the

Websites for funds

To look up the exchange traded funds (ETFs) available in the UK visit **www.ishares.com**. If you want to buy other kinds of funds **www.morningstar.co.uk** has a system for rating unit trusts, while Trustnet (**www.trustnet.com**) and Standard & Poor's (**www.funds-sp.com**) do the same for investment trusts. S&P provides two different forms of rating: stars based on a fund's performance over various timescales, and 'A' ratings, based on how a manager invests and their consistency of performance. Both help you to see how a fund is doing relative to its peer group. Of course, all this data is historic and therefore, as ever, no guarantee of future performance.

financial services industry are marketing masters (there's no bad product they can't make sound good) but very little of what they are selling offers us any value.

So, as an example, take the guaranteed equity bond, or Geb. The very name suggests it's the perfect investment: it's a bond, so it's safe; it's guaranteed, so it's extra safe; but it's also got equities (or shares) in it so it's a little bit racy too. All in all, it appears to offer upside with no downside. But strip the marketing veneer from most Gebs and they don't look quite so good. Last year I had a good look at one on offer from Birmingham Midshires. It offered a return of 19% over 3 years as long as the FTSE 100 index didn't fall over that period. If the FTSE did fall you would get no return at all on your money but you would get your original capital back in full. This sounded like a reasonable sort of a deal (so much so that I was only just in time to stop my mother investing in it) but it absolutely was not.

A 19% return over 3 years worked out at a measly 5.97% a year. But if you had put your money in an ordinary savings account at the time you could have earned interest of 5.1% a year, more in longer-notice accounts. So you'd be tying up your money for three years (meaning that if any better investments came your way you'd have to pass on them) and running the risk of losing money if the FTSE fell, all for an absolute maximum extra return of 0.87% a year. I say running the risk of losing money because that is exactly what might happen over the three years. The issuers of Gebs make a great song and dance out of how you will get your original capital back in full regardless of the state of the market, but thanks to inflation it won't be worth as much when you get it back as it is today. If inflation is running at 2.5% a year you can buy 2.5% less stuff at the end of each year than you can at the beginning despite having the same amount of money. This means that £100 invested today will be worth only £92.60 when it is returned to you in 3 years. And what if interest rates rise during the term of the Geb? That would make it look even worse value than it is now. Why? Because it would push up the returns from ordinary savings accounts (you would feel pretty silly if savings accounts were offering a risk-free 7% but your money was tied up with Birmingham Midshires at a maximum of less than 6%) and it would keep eating into the purchasing power of your capital. If inflation rose to 3.5% your £100 would be worth only £89.86 by the end of the bond's term.

I have two more gripes with the Birmingham Midshires Geb. First, it isn't even giving you real exposure to the racy stuff suggested by the word 'equity'. In the words of the brochure, your money is 'linked to the FTSE 100 rather than invested in it'. That means you wouldn't have ever got more than 5.97% a year from the bond: the Footsie may break out into the greatest bull market of all time (a bull market is when shares rise and a bear market refers to when they fall), but your 'equity' investment will still go virtually nowhere – the most you can make is the 19% we discussed earlier. Second, you won't get any of the dividends that people who invest in 'real' equities will.

I have rather picked on Birmingham Midshires here, but it's not the only one to offer this kind of utterly useless product. There are plenty more out there, using plenty more tricks to ensure that their providers make more money out of Gebs than you do. Not all Gebs are as completely awful as this one but they are all just as complicated once you start to look at them and I'm wary of complicated products; the more complicated something is the more money its provider is generally making. Financial service providers love complication mainly because they can hide their fees in the detail but as an investor your most basic principle should be to avoid it – for exactly the same reason.

How to buy shares and funds

Historically, trading shares was considered to be another perk of the rich: you had to buy and sell through certain stockbrokers and it was extremely expensive to do so. That's not the case any more. Today the stock market is open to everyone and if you go to the right broker you can trade cheaply and easily. You can't buy shares direct from the stock market yourself; you need to choose a broker to do it for you. Most brokers offer what they call an 'execution-only' service. This means that they don't bother you with their (often worthless) opinions on what you should buy and sell but simply do what you ask them to do. If you are, as I think you should be, investing mainly via ETFs and investment trusts this is all you need. Find a broker that charges under £15 for each trade you make (such as Barclays Stockbrokers or Hargreaves Lansdown) by visiting **www.fool.co.uk**. You can also buy and sell most unit trusts through the same brokers using the same account. And you should.

Why? Two reasons. The first is fees again. If you buy direct from the fund manager you will have to pay the upfront fees (up to 5.5%) in full but if you buy via a broker they will usually cut this fee right back for you (they get it as commission so can easily rebate 3% or so of it back to you). According to Bestinvest we waste upwards of £75 million a year paying fund fees we could easily avoid by using a discount broker.

The second is simplicity. If you buy a different fund from a different manager every year you will end up being completely defeated by paperwork and admin. Do it all via one broker and one account and you will only have to deal with one lot of paperwork and one institution. It makes life easier.

If you want to buy individual gilts (although there isn't really any need when, if you want bonds, you can buy bond ETFs) you can buy them through your broker or, if it is government bonds you are after, directly via the Post Office or the Debt Management Office (**www.dmo.gov.uk**).

Why women make the best investors

I am not a believer in the 'men are useless' brand of feminism, as propagated by bath-cleaning product manufacturers and a particular type of lady journalist, but I think we can all agree that the stereotypically accepted differences between men and women have more than a grain of truth in them. On my honeymoon three years ago my new husband drove down Italy's A26 in the wrong direction for two hours rather than stop and ask for directions, something I would have been irritated about – except for the fact we were driving the wrong way in the first place because I read the map upside down. If I'd been driving we would have stopped and asked after ten minutes and we would have had an extra hour and a half by Lake Garda (although, as he pointed out, if he'd been map-reading we wouldn't have been lost in the first place and we'd have had an extra two hours).

The fact is that there are intrinsic differences between men and women and their brains. Recent research from the University of New Mexico showed that women tend to use more of the 'white matter' in their brains (this is the bit that connects the brain's processing centres and is central to language, multi-tasking and emotional thinking). Men use more 'grey matter' (the tissue that deals with processing information, maths and map-reading). The results are well known. If you present a small baby with a face and a mechanical object to look at the girls will look longer at the face and the boys will look longer at the mechanical object. Girls learn to read first but boys are better at spatial tasks. Women are better at verbal reasoning and men are better at mechanical tests. Men like things and women like people. Men like to think they know everything already. Women ask questions. The differences are much debated but definitely there. And they make all the difference when it comes to investing.

Nicola Horlick, one of the UK's more prominent female investment managers, points to a few other things that might make women better at investing than men. We have an innate caution, she says, that stems from our traditional role as household managers and nurturers: we are hardwired to be more cautious, we have a good natural grasp of balancing budgets and we think more long term about money.

According to Sheila Gleason of Barclays Wealth Solutions it is the ability to ask questions and admit they don't understand that really gives women an edge when it comes to investing. We know what we don't know and aren't afraid to ask. Women tend to do 40% more research than men. They also collaborate in a way that men often find hard (using advisers, joining investment clubs, going to seminars to gather information) and they plan properly; they bother to find out the tax implications of what they are doing before they do it, for example. Finally, they have a tendency to act conservatively, diversifying and investing in industries they understand, such as leisure, retail and utilities as well as holding their investments for the long term. Men, on the other hand, are driven by the need to make money fast. They buy hot investments they don't really understand, such as biotech firms and small oil and gas companies, without bothering to research them, says Gleason. They refuse to cut their losses when their investments are failing because they don't like to admit to losing money. They ignore the tax consequences of their decisions, allocate too much to each investment they make and trade in and out of stocks much too often. Ask any broker and they'll tell you that when the technology bubble burst in 2000 they had very few women clients left in the market. It was the men with the get-rich-quick investing style that got hit the hardest.

It is tempting, I know, to dismiss this kind of thing – the idea that women are better investors than men – as nonsense, but the data

seems to back it up. A recent survey from Digital
Look showed that in 2005 the average
woman's portfolio grew by 17%, while that
of a man managed a mere 11%. And this,
says Gleason, is no isolated event: if you look at almost any
period you find that female stock pickers have outperformed
men. Yet 90% of the UK's fund managers are men! A study from
Terrance Odean of the University of California backs Gleason
up. Odean looked at 150,000 brokerage accounts between 1991
and 1997 and found that on average the women were making
1.4% a year more than the men. He isolated one simple reason
for this: men traded more often than women, 45% more, and the
costs of doing so reduced their returns. Why do they do it? For
the thrill, apparently. According to an ABN Amro survey 18% of
men said that their primary motivation for investing was the
'excitement and anticipation of investing'. Not making money
for their old age, but 'excitement'. Only 5% of women felt the
same.

In Chapter 1 on income we looked at how male confidence does
great things for them in the workplace – they ask and they get –
but when it comes to investing it doesn't work for them quite so
well. In 2005 63% of the women who had accounts at Hoodless
Brennan said in response to a survey that they considered
themselves to be either a 'novice' or a 'dabbler' and a full 98% said
they were beginners. Only 7% of them said they were risk-takers.
The men were much more confident: 16% of them said they were
risk-takers, for example. Yet despite their confidence we do better
than them: investing, it seems, is one area where we should
nurture our natural caution.

ISAs: much simpler than you think they are

There is a great deal of confusion about ISAs but they are so important that I am going to explain them from the very beginning. Most people think an ISA is an investment in itself, to be bought in its entirety from one fund management group – something those groups have a strong vested interest in us thinking. But it isn't. An ISA is not an investment. It is just a tax-efficient 'wrapper' for investments. Think of it like self-storage. When you use this you go to one of the companies in question, say Big Yellow, and you buy a cardboard box from them. You then fill up the box with all the stuff you want to store for a few years and they look after it – for a small fee – until you need it again. An ISA is pretty much the same. You buy the box – your ISA wrapper – from a financial provider of some kind and then you fill it up with investments that cost you up to £7,000 a year. There are currently two kinds of ISA available – the mini and the maxi. If you take out a mini ISA you can invest up to £4,000 in the markets and put up to £3,000 in a savings account. If you take out a maxi you can put £7,000 into investments. The chancellor has said this distinction is to be removed so that in future there will be no maxi and no mini ISA, just a £7,000 allowance up to £3,000 of which may be cash. At the time of writing no date has been set for this change but when it comes in to effect savers who have built up a cash ISA nest egg will – for the first time – also be able to switch their cash savings into a stocks and shares ISA without losing any of their annual entitlement.

The absolute key here when using your ISA allowance is to buy the wrapper from someone who allows you to put whatever you want in it rather than from one company that then lets you put only their funds in it. Every year the big fund management

companies run huge advertising campaigns in
which they refer to ISAs as investments in their
own right when what they are really trying to
get you to do is simultaneously to buy their
wrappers and one of their funds to put in it.
You shouldn't do this, partly because it is
expensive (you'll be buying unit trusts and
paying upfront fees of 5%) and partly because it is
so inflexible (there is no way you are going to want to stick
with the one company and their funds for ever so you'll end up
with the bother and expense of moving).

Instead you should buy what is referred to as a Self Select ISA.
This means buying the wrapper from a fund supermarket or a
stockbroker (again see **www.moneysupermarket.com** or
www.find.co.uk to find one) and then choosing what you want to
buy for it – funds run by any provider at all, ETFs, individual
shares, bonds or even just cash. Then you can add money into
your wrapper every year and invest it as you like, just as you
would with an ordinary share-dealing account. You aren't really
investing in an ISA. You are investing via an ISA. Indeed the only
real difference between an ordinary dealing account and an ISA
account should be their tax treatment.

Just as the Big Yellow box discussed above protects your dresses
from damp, your ISA wrapper protects any capital gains on the
investments you've popped into it from tax: if you invest outside
your ISA wrapper you will have to pay capital gains tax on
anything you make on your investments above the annual capital
gains allowance, but if you invest inside it you will not. You might
not think you need this – after all not many of us manage to make
capital gains of anywhere near the allowance let alone above it

every year – but it is a good safety net. If you invest sensibly and leave your money working for you for the long term you'll be amazed at how much money you do end up making. And if you then sell all your investments at once you will be extremely pleased you are doing so via an ISA. If you are a higher rate tax payer you also get a break on the taxation of any dividends you earn from the investments inside your ISA. You will be automatically charged 10% just as lower rate tax payers are but will be charged no more than that. Over the years that's a tax break that will add up nicely (you pay 32.5% outside an ISA).

"Those who have some means think the most important thing is love. The poor know that it is money."

Gerald Brenan (1984-1987)

Most of the banks and brokers offer Self Select ISA accounts so it is just a matter of choosing one. The main criterion? You guessed it, price. Some of the best execution-only deals come from the online brokers such as idealing.com and Self Trade so they are worth a look, but many of the high street banks such as Barclays are OK too. Before you settle on a broker check that you can buy everything you might want to through them: UK and international shares, gilts and corporate bonds, ETFs, unit trusts and investment trusts. When you start out you will just want to buy simple ETFs but you are going to have your ISA account for a long time and in a few years you may want to branch out. Also check what the deal is with having cash in your ISA account: you may want to put your cash into the protection of your ISA wrapper to be sure you are using up your annual allowance but you may not be sure what to invest it in right away. If this is the case you should be able to keep it in cash inside the ISA wrapper (the government is OK with this as long as you intend to invest it at some point) but you will probably find that the organization you are using will pay very little interest on it.

A final point to be aware of when opening an ISA account is simplicity. If you really want to keep on top of your finances you need to keep them simple. I have my ISA account, my ordinary investing account and my pension account all with the same provider. That way I can look at them all online at the same time and keep a picture of my investments in my head. I would suggest that you do the same: if you already have a variety of ISA accounts with providers transfer them to your Self Select ISA and make sure that any other trading accounts you have are with the same people. It might cost you a bit in fees and admin in the beginning but it will be worth it later. Simple is good.

Keeping an eye on things

In 2006 fund management group Isis surveyed investors about the state of their portfolios. The results were shocking. Thirteen per cent of the investors surveyed had no idea what they had invested in, while 25% were unable to say why they had invested in what they had beyond the fact that it had 'seemed like a good idea at the time'. This isn't the way to create long-term freedom. Instead, once you've sorted out your investments you need to keep on top of things with regular reviews. You have to reassess your position constantly. This means keeping an eye on the market in general: reading one business and personal finance section a week or subscribing to the magazine I edit (**www.moneyweek.com**) should do it and checking your own investments every few months. Are they going up or down? Why? Would you still buy them today at their current price? Do you have the cash to invest more? If so are you going to buy more of what you already have or diversify into something else?

It is important not to have too many different investments. Sure, you don't want to have all your eggs in one basket but you also don't want to have so many eggs that you won't notice if one breaks. That means having no more than 10 different funds, I think, and if you are investing in individual shares no more than 15 of these. If you have more just keeping an eye on them is going to take far too long for you to be bothered to do it. I know I keep saying this, but keep it simple.

Getting financial advice

Mostly when you buy things you are pretty wary of the salesmen; we all know that kitchen, car and double-glazing salesmen are on commission so we take care not to believe a word they say. But when it comes to our money that caution appears to go out of the window. We suddenly come over all trusting and do what we are told, nodding as though we understand what's going on as we do so. We ask many more questions of a travel agent booking us into a three-star hotel in Greece for a long weekend than we do of the people we consult to help us set ourselves up financially for the future. This is a major mistake.

Imagine you bought a new-build buy-to-let flat and the agent who sold it to you not only took the traditional 2% upfront commission on the sale, but also insisted on charging 1% of the rental income paid by your tenants every year for as long as you owned it. Furthermore, what if you then found out that the 2% upfront commission and the 1% annual levy had not been set by the agent, but by the developer of the flat? And that elsewhere in the area there were identical flats for sale from another developer that would have cost you only an upfront 1% but your agent hadn't shown them to you. You'd be horrified, wouldn't you? No way would you do the deal. But that's pretty much what happens every time someone in the UK buys an investment fund or a 'product' via a financial adviser.

Almost every adviser in Britain is paid on commission by the providers of financial products. Some is paid upfront and some is paid every year you continue to hold the investment they suggested you buy (this is called trail commission). The result? You end up paying your adviser for many years after you've used them. It's a bit like financing an annual holiday for your estate agent for every year you continue to live in the house he sold you, however long that may be. What this means is that most of us never meet a real financial adviser: we meet commission-hungry salesmen masquerading as advisers.

How then can you possibly expect to get reasonable financial advice? It certainly isn't easy. Advisers divide into three types in the UK. There are 'tied' advisers who sell the products of one provider only. There are Independent Financial Advisers (IFAs) who can suggest that you buy the products of any provider in the market. And there are multi-tied advisers, introduced only in 2005 by the Financial Services Authority (FSA) in an attempt to improve 'choice', who can recommend products from a panel of firms. The latter, said a spokesman from mortgage lender Bradford & Bingley when they were introduced, are a fine innovation as 'research shows that most people do not want to deal with all the products in the market. They are happy with a select choice from the most well-known or best performing companies.'

So people are happy not to get a good deal as long as they have heard of the company they get a bad deal from? What patronizing nonsense. I don't think I need to dwell on this at length: it should be clear that anyone wanting unbiased financial advice on how they should invest should avoid tied and multi-tied advisers like the plague.

That leaves IFAs. The worry with these is not that the advisers are formally linked to product providers but that thanks to the commission system they will be tempted to suggest investments based not on their suitability for you but on the levels of commission they will receive. They will also find themselves utterly unable to stop suggesting that you buy and sell things when you might be better off doing nothing at all. Note that if they look at your portfolio and say it looks just fine they get nothing. If they look at it and say you should sell everything and buy some new unit trusts they could make themselves 5% of the value of your investments. That doesn't make it easy to be honest.

A few years ago a friend of mine came to me asking about her pension investments. She had been to an IFA to check that she was on track with her savings plan. He suggested she change pension provider. Her email to me said: 'The annual fee on my new pension will be 1.5% and the commission will be £5,600 payable immediately. Does that sound reasonable?' It did not. The IFA was at pains to point out that the commission would be paid to him by the pension company, not by my friend directly: the pension company would then claw it back from her 1.5% annual fee over the life of the pension. But the end result would have been the same: she was to be charged five and a half grand for being advised to take out a savings plan that as far as I could see was no better than the one she already had. If her adviser was genuinely giving her his best advice why didn't he just tell her to do nothing? The answer is easy. An adviser who tells you you need nothing does not get paid. They end up working for free. If you were an adviser reliant on commission for your income and you could make thousands of pounds out of recommending someone buys an investment bond but nothing out of telling them all they really need is a good savings account, what would you be tempted to do?

The upshot of this nasty and corrupting system is that the only way you will get unbiased financial advice is to reject commission and insist on paying for advice as you get it. This is what we do when we consult other professionals. Do you pay your solicitor an upfront percentage of the value of your will when they write it for you? Of course not. You just pay them a flat fee for their time. So it should be with IFAs. The good news is that all IFAs are obliged to offer you a choice of payment methods. Either you pay a flat fee upfront and get any commissions on products you buy rebated to you, or you let the adviser take the commissions themselves. The obvious thing to do if you feel you need financial advice is to take the fee option and know that as a result the advice you are getting is good for you and not just for your adviser's bank balance. I doubt that your adviser will actively encourage you to take this option (commissions tend to run higher than fees) but they certainly should. You can find an IFA at **www.unbiased.com**. If you want a female IFA (of which there are now about 1,600 in the UK) you can specify this on the site. The other option of course is just to keep your financial affairs so simple that you don't need any advice.

WHAT DO I DO NOW?

✳ **Unless you are debt-free and have cash savings for emergencies, nothing. You aren't quite ready to invest. Just keep saving into your Freedom Account until you have six months' worth of cash in it.**

✳ **Choose a broker and open an account. If you are investing £7,000 or less a year make it a Self Select ISA account at an online broker. If you are investing more than £7,000 a year open an ordinary dealing account too – for simplicity's sake do so with the same broker with whom you have opened an ISA account. Make sure you are getting the cheapest deal on buying and selling funds and shares that you possibly can. The lower your transaction costs the higher your returns.**

✳ **When you are ready move money from your Future Account to your ISA and get started. If you do not intend to be a very active investor buy Exchange Traded Funds and investment trusts only.**

✳ Put aside an hour a month to check your investments, but unless you have a particular reason for doing so don't check them much more often than that.

✳ Start skimming the financial pages just so you know roughly what is going on.

✳ If you want to be an active investor do a little more reading – the business papers, at least one paper a day and a weekly magazine such as *Moneyweek* perhaps. Books you might look at include *How to Read the Financial Pages* by Michael Brett and *Investing for Dummies* by Eric Tyson.

✳ Think about your attitude to risk. How much are you prepared to lose if things go wrong?

✳ Think about your reasons for investing and how much you intend to invest on a regular basis: both of these will make a difference to the kind of thing you buy.

✳ Choose a broker to do your investing through and do it as cheaply as possible.

6
Pensions
Provide for Your Old Age

I have a friend who has the most wonderful black pearls. She always wears them, two as earrings and one as a pendant. For a long time I admired them enormously then eventually I asked her where they had come from. She told me that she had always wanted black pearls and one day she wanted them so badly that she used the money she'd been planning to start a pension scheme with to buy them. Now when I look at her pearls I don't see their beauty any more. I see the misery of her poverty-stricken old age instead.

It took me a long time to come around to the idea of paying into a pension. I hate the idea that I will ever be old. I hate the idea that I must give up pleasures now to pay for necessities in 35 years' time. I hate the loss of control that comes with having money tied up in a pension (you can't get a penny out until you turn 50, soon 55). And I hate the fact that the government and the financial services industry between them have conspired to make understanding pensions and taking them out so stupidly complicated.

On the other hand when I do think of being old I see myself living in some style. I won't be living in a tiny studio flat, counting my pennies at the Tesco's checkout and saving up for day trips to Blackpool. No, I'll be settled in a nice country house with a charming garden and a smart two-seater parked outside the front door. I'll be constantly entertaining friends and family and when they aren't around I'll be off on a series of exciting holidays. There'll be winter trips to the Caribbean and Canadian ski resorts. There'll be summertime cruises up the fjords of Scandinavia and adventure in the safari parks of Africa in the spring. I'm not alone in my retirement fantasies – we all think of retirement as the holiday of a lifetime – but sadly most of us don't arrange our lives in such a way that we will ever be able to live out those fantasies.

I now have a pension that I pay into (it's a SIPP – see below) but given that I only started it nearly two years ago when I was 34 I've got a bit of catching up to do if I ever want to go on that Norwegian cruise in my seventies.

Everyone knows that there is a pensions crisis in the UK today. According to IndependentAge, the average weekly income received by retired households is actually falling: it was £368 in 2003 and £356 in 2004. And one in three pensioners lives on a mere £150 a week, while the average pensioner is so strapped for cash that they spend less on food and drink in an entire week than the average non-pensioner spends eating out (about £20), according to Virgin Money. The result is that debt levels are now rising even faster among the old than the young. One in 20 of the over-fifties says they are always overdrawn – people are battling with debt even before they retire. And the CCCS says that the levels of extreme debt among pensioners are getting out of control: the average debt of over-sixties coming to them for help is now over £30,000. Why do you think you see so many elderly people behind the checkout at the supermarket these days? They aren't doing it because it's fun. They're doing it because they're living longer than they ever imagined they would and it's the only way they can pay their bills.

Part of the problem for today's pensioners is on the spending side. Prices are rising much faster for them than for the rest of us. The prices of the things they need to buy – water, gas, transport and so on – have been rising extraordinarily fast over the last decade while the prices of things they neither need nor much want (computers and Topshop dresses) have been falling fast. At the same time they have been aggressively targeted by the banks, loan firms and credit card companies who see them as easy pickings when profits need a boost. The other part of the problem, however, is simply that many of them haven't saved enough to finance their retirements: they made the mistake of thinking that the state would provide and it hasn't.

Given that all this is common knowledge, you'd think that those in the population who are not yet retired would be tripping over themselves to save, save, save, so they would find themselves in a more comfortable position come old age. But not a bit of it. No one in my family except for my very sensible husband and me has a pension and a quick straw poll of my friends shows that, apart from a few bits and bobs of company pension picked up from jobs along the way, none of them does either. The number of people making no provision at all for their retirement is actually rising and has been for a decade: two in five people are saving nothing. A recent survey from Accenture showed that while 71% of us think that we need £14,000 or more a year to retire in reasonable comfort over 40% of us are not saving nearly enough to meet those goals. Forty-one per cent of us don't even know how much we have in our pensions and a terrifying 21% of those surveyed had such dismal saving situations that they actually said they were pinning their hopes on having their savings topped up by lottery or pools wins.

Overall, says the Association of British Insurers, the nation is saving £27 billion less a year than it needs to survive in retirement. So little can we bring ourselves to think about the long holiday of retirement realistically that more of us are saving for our next week away than for our retirement: according to a 2005 study from Business Development Research Consultants of those under 30 with no children 1% are saving for old age and 23% saving for holidays for example. However, it isn't just the young. The study suggested that whatever stage of life you look at there are always more people putting money aside for short-term pleasure than long-term survival. Think about having just £20 a week to spend on food and drink. That might be OK for one week but could you manage it every week until you die? Keep ignoring your pension arrangements and you will be.

It's worse if you're a woman

But there is worse news. Horrible as the pension crisis is for men, it is a hundred times more dire for women: 98% of men qualify for the full state pension but less than a third of female pensioners do. And very few women have the kind of personal pensions that might fill the gap. The result? The typical man now retires with an income £100 a week higher than that of a typical woman: our income when we are old is less than half of theirs. And one in five female pensioners lives in poverty. How did this happen?

It's all about childcare. To get a full state pension a woman has to work for 39 years, but make childcare your main priority as an adult and you probably won't be able to do that – you can get credits if you have been caring for children or relatives but even then you have to have worked 20 years to get a full pension. Worse, while most of us will end up getting something, if you have been a full-time mother and worked for less than a quarter of the required years under the 25% rule you won't get a penny from the government in pension under the current rules. Nothing at all. The pension system was designed in the 1940s to deal with the existing status quo – a man working full-time and a stay-at-home wife with children. It didn't accommodate the needs of modern women then and it still doesn't. Some 2.2 million women coming up to retirement won't be getting a full state pension. The rules are set to change in 2010 – you'll only have to work for 30 years to get a full pension and you'll get credits towards those years during some of the time you are off work caring for children and relatives – but the playing field still won't be quite level: it isn't yet clear if the 25% rule will be abandoned for example and the government itself says it doesn't anticipate reaching equality in terms of state pensions until 2025. It doesn't seem fair that the way women live – stopping paid work to deal with family obligations – should leave us with such a financial burden, but it does.

"If you are given the choice between money and sex appeal take the money. As you get older the money will become your sex appeal."
Katharine Hepburn

The situation has been made worse by the lack of private pension provision made by women. Not only do we take long career breaks to have our children and stop contributing to our pensions when we do so but when we go back to work post-children we tend to take lower-paid jobs or part-time jobs – the boring ones in call centres and shops. Eighty-four per cent of women in work are part-timers against 10% of men and while the typical woman over 50 earns £60 a week less than a woman under 30, the typical man over 50 earns £140 more than a man under 30. Men of the same age earn £140 more than women. This means we have less cash to save and to put into private pensions. Only 35% of women have any private pension arrangements (two-thirds of us are saving nothing at all) and on average we save only £1 for our retirements for every £3 that men save: 75% of those of us who do have our own pensions have less than £10,000 in them. That's not going to get us far.

We also get our priorities wrong when it comes to our retirements. When we are young we have debts to deal with and discos to dance in so we delay saving. Then when we have children we can't quite bring ourselves to save money we feel would be better spent on the family now. When men have children they tend to up their savings – mainly into their own accounts. When women have children they tend to stop saving altogether, except for short-term family-related needs: we'd prefer to pay for new trainers for the kids now than tinned tuna for ourselves in 30 years. We think we are being unselfish, sacrificing, as we are, our futures on the altar of motherhood. And we'd probably say that the men saving for themselves are being shockingly selfish. But is this quite true?

Look at it the other way round. Your little girl might think her new pink and purple fairy dress is the best thing ever right now. But if the result is that when she's in her forties she's going to find herself subsidizing your income at the same time as she's trying to pay her own children's university fees, is she really going to be so pleased? We should perhaps think less about the impact of our actions on our children today and more about the impact our actions today will have on them in the future. A little bit of selfishness on your part now might make things a lot better for everyone in 30 years. Last year 56% of women told a government survey that their main concern about ageing was being a burden on their family. A good pension would take away that worry.

However, there is another reason why we don't get around to saving as much as we should for our retirement. We think –

whether we are prepared to say so or not – that someone else will do it for us. Yes, in my picture of myself cruising around the world as a well-dressed and properly elegant 70-year-old, there's a man in the deckchair next to me. And most of the time he's got his cheque book out. Survey after survey shows that even after 100 years of feminism young women still come over all dependent when it comes to old age: they expect to share their partner's pension or in some way to be provided for by a man in their retirement despite overwhelming evidence to the contrary. This is a big mistake. For starters there is every chance that you will be spending your old age alone: over the next decade or so four in ten women coming up to retirement will be unmarried. An increasing number of women will never marry and of those who do think they have met their Prince Charming, a large percentage will end up divorced. And divorcees rarely end up with perfect pensions. Divorcing women are now entitled to a share of their husband's pension on divorce but your ex-husband won't be contributing to your share post divorce and most pensions aren't designed to fund two separate retirements anyway: your share of your husband's pension is unlikely to be enough to keep you in any style.

And even if you stay married don't forget that when your husband dies (and the odds are that he will die before you) his pension will very often die with him. When you retire you use the money you have built up in your pension to buy a stream of income for the rest of your life (you give the pension company all your money and they then pay you an annual income for ever – this is called an annuity). You can do this in two ways: you can get an annuity that only pays out for the length of your own life; or you can get one that continues to pay out to your spouse even after you are dead (these tend to offer a slightly lower annual income as the providers expect to have to pay them for longer). And guess what? According to Age Concern, around three-quarters of the annuities arranged for married men provide no income at all for a widow after their deaths. This means that they leave their partners in the lurch when they go for the sake of a higher income when they are alive. Nice. The lesson? You have to look after yourself.

The other thing to remember when you are mulling all this over is that you can't rely on the state either. As we have seen, most women don't get a full pension, and even if they did it wouldn't be enough for them to live on in any comfort. That situation isn't going to get any better. You might think that the national insurance you pay out of your salary every month goes into some kind of special government savings account to pay for our pensions and our healthcare. You'd be wrong. There is no special account and the government is even worse at saving than the rest of us. The only way it can get its hands on enough money to pay pensions every year is to take it out of the pockets of tax payers (out of your pocket) every year. But this is getting harder and harder. Not so long ago there were ten people in work for every one person claiming a pension, now the ratio is more like four to one and soon it will be more like two to one. Back in the 1950s the average man retired at 67, having worked for five years for every year he claimed a pension. Now we live so much longer that he works for only two years for every year of pension he claims (he also retires a few years earlier at 63).

Worse, the government has massive financial commitments to meet on the pensions of public sector workers. They still retire at 60 on splendid pensions that are linked to their salaries and paying those pensions is going to cost £800 billion – that's around £30,000 in extra tax for every household in the country. See the problem? There isn't going to be enough money left for the rest of us to rely on; we are going to have to work into our seventies just to pay for the public sector to put its feet up early. Already the government has said that the retirement age for the rest of us is going to have to rise. It is already set to jump to 65 for women by 2010 but from 2020 is likely to move further upwards to 67 and then 69. The 40% of people who told a survey in 2006 that they think it is the government's responsibility to provide for their old age have a very nasty shock coming.

So what does all this tell us? The answer is pretty clear. The way things are going at the moment not only are many of us not going to be able to retire in style, we aren't going to be able to retire at all. We have to start saving into our own pensions in our own names and we have to do it now. If you don't immediately start thinking about how you will finance your retirement there is every chance that you are going to spend it eating tinned food and wearing all your clothes in bed – which won't be any fun at all, particularly given that if you are a woman in your twenties or thirties now you will probably live well into your nineties. If you retire in your sixties you'll have 30 years of life still to finance. Of course you can't delay gratification for ever. The present is as important as the future and of course you need to enjoy life as it comes. But you must also make sure that the future is at least as nice as the present: you need to strike the right balance between fun now and comfort later. Cashing in your pension in your thirties to buy pearls is not striking the right balance!

I have been bandying a lot of statistics around in this section but for those in any doubt that they have to sort out their pension arrangements I have just one more. A report out in 2006 showed that poor older people are much more likely to die prematurely than rich older people. Of those aged 50–59 at the start of the survey 2.5% of the poorest fifth had died by the end, but only 0.2% of the richest fifth had. Of the 60–79 age group the numbers were 5.9% and 1.3%. Get a proper pension sorted and not only will you live better, you'll probably live longer too.

The price of the dream

So now you know you have to do something what should it be? First of all think about how much you might need as a retiree. This is an inexact science, of course, but ask yourself a few questions. Where do you see yourself living? Will you move house? How old do you want to be when you retire? Do you think you'll do a lot of travelling? Have you the kind of career that means you might keep working part-time into your sixties and seventies? Will you get a state pension and if so how much (**www.worksmart.org.uk** to apply for an estimate)? What have you got in personal pensions already? Remember that however far off it seems you won't actually be old when you retire, assuming you do so in your sixties.

In her sixties my own mother is still bringing up a teenager, skiing, riding, and generally behaving in every way as though she were in her forties (if that). The same report I mention above (the one that told us poor people die before rich people) also asked a variety of questions about how older people felt about ageing. The results made it clear that they weren't convinced they were ageing and they certainly didn't see it as particularly negative. Three-quarters said they didn't see themselves as old – including most of the 75-year-olds surveyed – and most said they felt middle age went on well into their sixties, with the wealthiest saying they felt middle-aged until they hit 66. They also claimed to be travelling frequently and to have healthy sex lives. And 60% of women said they saw retirement as a time for challenge and risk. Basically the lives of the over-sixties are now much the same as those of the young: when you're thinking about your pension you are no longer thinking about financing a small bungalow and 14 cups of tea a day but about financing a lifestyle remarkably similar to the one you have now (or you want to have now).

"The real beauty of having material wealth is that you don't have to worry about paying the bills and you have more energy to be concerned about the things that matter. How do I accelerate my humanity?"

Oprah Winfrey

Once you've thought about your dreams for the future and how much they are going to cost you on an annual basis you can start to figure out how much you need to save to make them real. Then you can see if it is feasible or not. If not, you can set about finding ways to up the amount of money you can get your hands on (go back to Chapter 1 perhaps!) or on moderating your retirement requirements. In general, people find that they need 70–75% of their usual salary every year to live well in retirement. You need less because you have less in the way of expenses. No children to finance (hopefully they'll be independent by the time you hit your late sixties), the mortgage paid off and none of the costs of work (yes, work costs – think clothes, travel and lunch). So what does that work out at as a lump sum in today's money?

Again this is an imprecise science but for the sake of argument let's say you've decided you need £20,000 a year in today's money to live a reasonable life in retirement. You have no idea how many years you will live for so you really need to think in terms of a sum of money that will provide you with £20,000 a year indefinitely without running out; if interest rates are running at 5% when you retire (i.e. you can make roughly 5% return on your cash every year) that means you need a pot of £400,000 (in today's money) to be safe and that's before taking into inflation into account. Frightening, isn't it? Your retirement dream comes with quite a price tag.

It's easier than you think

However, there is good news too. Not all pensioners are poor. According to Brewin Dolphin Wealth Management there are 625,000 pensioners in Britain with assets of more than £500,000. And saving for your old age isn't as hard as you think. For starters you've got plenty of time and money does grow. When it comes to pension savings, the power of compounding (as discussed in the last chapter) means it really does pay to start young. Let's say that you invest £300 in a pension account every month and it earns an annual return of 8%. If you do this from the age of 24 to the age of 40 (a total of 15 years) you will have invested a total of £36,000. If you then stop adding money in but leave the account to grow, by the time 35 years have passed (i.e. you are 60) it will be worth around £315,000. By the time you are 70 if you have left it untouched it will be worth nearly £700,000 (and that's before adding back in the tax relief).

If, on the other hand, you leave saving until you are 40 as so many people do and then invest £300 a month until you are 70 (i.e. for 30 years) how much do you think you will have? The answer is not a good one. Because your contributions lasted for 30 years, you will have invested double the amount but thanks to your late start your money won't have had time to grow and you will have a total of only £300,000 on your retirement. The basic point is that in your twenties and thirties you have something older people would love to reclaim – time. And one of the best ways to take advantage of that wonderful asset is to start putting money into a pension scheme of some kind now.

Further good news comes in the fact that the government really wants you to do this (it'll cost it less later) so it provides some very nice incentives, in the form of free money. You get tax back on any money you put into a pension. If you are a lower rate tax payer the government makes every 78p you put in up to £1 and if you are a higher rate tax payer it makes every 60p you put in up to £1. You then don't have to pay income tax on any income that flows from your pension investments into the pension and you don't have to pay any capital gains on it either. You only pay tax once you start taking the money out as income after your retirement.

Exactly how much you put aside and what percentage of your savings go into a formal pension and what percentage into other investments is up to you: who knows how much of a return the investments you put in your pension are going to make or how fast they will grow and who knows what interest rates and investment returns will be when you retire? However, the basic rule is that the later you start the more you have to save: as a rule of thumb you should be saving as a percentage of your salary half the age you are when you start saving (this is known as Bouldings Law). That means that if you are 20 you need to be saving 10% of your income and if you are 30 you should be saving 15%. This may seem like a lot and you may think you can't do it. The young have it hard these days. We leave university with massive debts to carry around, house prices have moved far beyond our reach and day-to-day living seems to take up every spare penny we have. But none the less the sooner we start saving the better off we will be. Look at the sums above again.

And even when you don't have an income – when for instance you are home with children – you need to make sure that your contributions are kept up as much as possible. If you are married or have a long-term partner your pension payments should be just another part of the family budget. Your husband or partner's pension continues to be contributed to and yours should be too. Your future is just as important as his but if you rely on using his pension one day instead of maintaining your own you may find it isn't nearly as nice as his. You need more money than he does (because you are going to live longer) but, if you separate from him without a fully paid-up pension of your own, you'll end up with less.

Inertia is a huge problem when it comes to pension savings (and any kind of saving) so think about doing it automatically. Set up a direct debit from your Freedom Account into your pension every month and try to leave it alone. Then every time you get a pay rise make sure that you raise the amount debited so your pension gets a bit of it – this is quite painless as it means redirecting the money out of your account before you ever get accustomed to having it. It will be boring to make the phone calls to set all this up in the first place and boring to deprive yourself of a few luxuries now to be able to start pension savings but you will thank yourself for it later.

The pension possibilities

Pensions are a bit like ISAs. The pension providers all talk about buying a pension as though a pension were an investment in itself. But it isn't. It is – like an ISA – simply a box, a 'wrapper' into which you put investments. The box simply protects the investments you put into it from tax and has a lock on it to stop you from taking any money out of it until you are 50 (soon 55). The box and the investments are two different things. That means there are two vital points to bear in mind when you are looking at your pension arrangements. What kind of box have you got or are you going to get and what investments are going to be put in it?

Personal pensions and stakeholder pensions

There are three kinds of pension boxes around: the personal pension, the company pension and the Self Invested Personal Pension (SIPP). Having a good company pension is probably the best thing (mainly because your employer contributes to it for you – see below) but traditionally anyone who doesn't have one of these has been encouraged to take out a personal pension. This basically involves going to one of the big pension providers, buying one of their wrappers and then filling that wrapper with a selection of the investment funds they have on offer for that purpose. The problem with these is that they are expensive – you pay high commissions when you arrange them and massive annual fees. You also have to be prepared to put in around £250 a month in order to be allowed to get them. Personally I wouldn't touch an old-fashioned pension like this with a bargepole; I think that thanks to the general public's inertia and ignorance when it comes to pensions the providers use them as an opportunity to fleece investors at every turn. Buy one of these and you are pretty much guaranteed to get ripped off somewhere down the line. You can find yourself paying up to 2.25% a year in annual charges to say nothing of a whole host of other more opaque charges (total charges on one of these pensions can add up to 5% a year) and we've already seen the effect of charges on investment returns over the years.

As a reminder, note that if you invested £2,400 in a pension and managed to make 8% a year on your investments, after 20 years you would have £119,000. If you paid charges at 2% a year so made only 6% you'd have over £25,000 less – a mere £93,500. The difference between a pension provider that charges 1% and one that charges 2% a year might seem tiny now but the odd 1% saved in the early days could make the difference when you retire.

So if you do decide to take out an old-fashioned personal pension you need to keep an eagle eye on it to make sure the charges are low enough and returns high enough to make it worth while. If not move on. It isn't complicated to move your pension investments from one provider to another – it shouldn't be any more complicated than shifting a savings account.

All that said, there is one kind of personal pension that might suit a great many people – stakeholder pensions. These are offered by the same providers as most other personal pensions but they are simpler and cheaper. The charges are not allowed to be more than 1% a year and you can put in as little as £20 a month. The fact that they are both easy to access and easy to understand makes stakeholders well worth looking at: almost anyone working or non-working is allowed to get one and for people who are just starting to save or have only small funds stakeholder pensions are probably a good option. The problem with stakeholders, however, is that the firms that provide them only offer you a limited choice of funds to put in them. But if you don't want to stay with a provider and their choice of funds there is no charge for moving a stakeholder from one provider to another. For a list of firms that offer stakeholder pensions see **www.thepensionsregulator.gov.uk**. You can get one via an IFA but why pay his commissions when you can just as easily make the decisions yourself?

Company pensions

If your company offers any kind of pension scheme sign up now. There are three options here. The first is the final salary plan. These are a bit different from most pensions in that for you – the recipient of the pension in the end – the kind of wrapper used and what goes in it is irrelevant. You just get paid out on retirement an annual amount based on the length of time you worked at the firm that awarded you the pension and your salary when you left it or retired from it. It doesn't matter how much you have paid into the pension (you are usually asked by your firm to contribute 4–8% of your salary) or how the stock market has performed since. You get your money anyway. Final salary schemes cost employers a fortune but are fantastic for employees. If anyone ever offers you one grab it.

The next kind of company scheme is the money purchase or defined contribution scheme. With these your employer chooses the wrapper and the pension trustees usually choose the investments to put in it. You and your employer then both contribute money into the wrapper to be invested (in general you put 3–4% of your salary in and your firm will then put the equivalent of another 4–7% in for you). You do not always have to put in the investments chosen by the scheme's trustees. This is the default option and the one that 80% plus of people take but it isn't always suitable; if you are very young you may want to go for riskier investments than offered by the default, for example, or if you are very near retirement for less risky options. What you get paid out when the time comes will depend entirely on how the investments the trustees or you have chosen perform and how much the pension firm that provides the wrapper manages to cream off in fees and charges. The lump sum left at the end is used to buy you an annuity that pays you an income for the rest of your life.

Finally, your firm may offer something called a group personal pension (GPP). This is not an occupational pension in that your employer can but does not have to contribute to it on your behalf. If it doesn't (and usually it doesn't) it is no more than an ordinary personal pension organized for you by your firm. This is good in that the admin has been done for you and your employer may have been able to negotiate lower charges than usually available to individuals buying the same kind of pension wrapper, but, assuming you are the only one contributing to the pension on your behalf it might not always be the best way to go.

It's also worth noting that many employers now offer to arrange stakeholder pensions for you (they have to if they have more than five employees) but again when they do this they are only doing the admin for you and you might be better off just taking out your own stakeholder pension. That way you get to choose the provider and there is less admin involved when you change jobs or take a career break.

When you change jobs or leave a job you should get a statement from your old employer, which will tell you the transfer value of your pension investments (i.e. what they are worth now). This can be paid as a cash lump sum into another occupational pension, a SIPP, stakeholder or personal pension plan. You have to be careful doing this as the transfer value is often lower than it should be and you can lose out. However, if the transfer value is OK I'd be tempted to move the money just to keep life simple.

Take one example. A former colleague of mine has a pension with an old employer. Until recently the funds in it were managed by one firm, which charged a 1% annual management fee. Then last year she received a letter telling her that the trustees were going to move all the cash to a second firm, which is charging 0.65% a year.

This sounds fine – good, even. But it isn't. The move was compulsory, but she still got charged £744 for the 'advice' (payable to the financial adviser 'immediately'). That's 2.7% of the value of her fund. Worse, the deal comes with no guarantee that the second firm's rates won't rise as soon as the company gets the cash. It's all complicated and expensive and it seems to me she would have been much better off to simplify her life by moving the pension into a vehicle she could control when she left the company in the first place.

SIPPs

To my mind SIPPs are the best kind of pensions there are. I have one. A SIPP is simply a wrapper for your pension investments that you control. You go to a provider, you arrange to set up the wrapper and then you put into it whatever investments you like – from individual shares and bonds to investment funds and commercial property. You are entirely in control. SIPPs used to be expensive to set up and be used more by the rich than by ordinary people but the costs have now come right down: you can arrange a SIPP online and manage it online just as you would a Self Select ISA. You put in as much money as you like (up to the equivalent of your salary with a current top limit of £215,000 a year and increasing to £255,000 a year by 2010) as often as you like and then invest as you like using the SIPP provider as your broker for buying and selling investments. The government automatically tops up every 68p you put in by 22p whether you are a higher rate or a lower rate tax payer and if you are a higher rate payer you then claim another 18p back via your tax return. It's simple, it's reasonably cheap, it's flexible and best of all it means that you can save for a pension without having to leave your money hostage to the whims of the charging systems of the big pension providers. All in all, SIPPs seem to me to be a great way to save. I think that in 20 years everyone will probably have one.

Your house

A great many people think that their house will end up being part of their pension (30% of people told an Accenture poll in 2005 that they intended to use equity from their home as one of the main ways of financing their retirement). Women are particularly guilty of this, and divorced women even more so than most. Often they give up rights to their husband's pensions during their divorce in order to be able to keep the house and limit disruption for the children. Never mind, they think, when the time comes I'll just sell the house and live off the proceeds. This might seem like a good idea at the time but it doesn't always work out. Why? For starters there is no guarantee that your house will still be worth enough when you retire. The last decade has been kind to homeowners – the generation that has just retired has seen unrepeatable gains on the value of their houses – but there have been long periods in history when house prices have either stayed flat or even fallen. What if the decades to your retirement are like that?

And you are still going to need somewhere to live when you retire so even if your house is worth a lot you'll have to sell up and move on. This isn't cheap. You'll be paying 2% to your estate agent and up to 4% in stamp duty. Then there'll be moving expenses and so on. All this eats into nest eggs fast. You may also find that you don't want to trade down – you may need the space for grandchildren or find you don't want to leave a garden you have nurtured for 20 years to someone else. I've never really understood why people want a lovely big house when they are out

of it all day working but then when it comes time to retire – and stay at home all day – they think they can make do with a little and not quite so nice home. Surely it should be the other way around? Your house may be able to help you out but it is highly unlikely to end up funding your retirement completely. You just can't rely on it.

That said, there is a way of part financing your old age via your house without actually having to leave it – equity release schemes. Selling part of your house before you die and being able to live in the house on the proceeds is a great idea in principle and it is marketed as such by the providers; they suggest you use money from your house to 'take a trip' or to buy 'something for the family'. It is, we are told, all about 'life enhancement'. Sounds good but it isn't always. The problem is that it is often a shockingly expensive way to get your hands on money.

There are two types of equity release schemes: lifetime mortgages and home reversion schemes. A lifetime mortgage involves you taking out a loan against your house but continuing to own it. Unlike a normal mortgage you don't pay any interest during your lifetime – it all gets added to your loan and rolled up. Then when you die the house is sold and the loan repaid. This sounds fine but not only is the rate you will pay a few percentage points higher than that of an ordinary mortgage (for no better reason than that lenders can get away with it) but the interest will be compounded (every year you will be laying interest on the interest that has already piled up). This means that your final debt will be huge – in some cases it can be even more than the value of your house, something that would leave your heirs with nothing when repayment time arrives (most deals at least stipulate that the debt will never end up being greater than the sale value of your house). Borrow £20,000 at 7% on a lifetime mortgage and the amount you owe will double in 11 years and treble in 17. If you lived for 35 years (say from 65 to 100) your estate would owe £200,000 when you died, 10 times what you borrowed. Once you owe that kind of money your choices start disappearing: you couldn't at this point ever move house, for example, as you'd have no equity left over to buy a new one, however small.

With a home reversion scheme you actually sell a percentage of your house to a home reversion company. You get a cash sum immediately for the sale with which you can do as you like. Then when you die the company takes its share of the proceeds from the sale of your house. This is better than the lifetime mortgage to the extent that you at least continue to own a set amount of your house but again it costs you. The home reversion company won't pay you the market value for the percentage of your house that it buys. Why? Because it doesn't know how long it will have to wait until it gets to sell the house and take its cut and it also doesn't know what will have happened to the housing market when that day comes. However, even taking this into account, the sums they pay out are pretty measly – the effective interest rates are often well into double digits. You may not mind being ripped off by the equity release companies and you may be able to ignore the irony of having spent 25 years paying off your home loan only to take it out again at a higher rate; after all, if you get to stay in your house and get a cash lump sum that gives you more freedom than you would otherwise have had, what does it matter how much it costs and what happens after you die? However, if you do mind and you can't ignore the irony, you might be wiser to release equity by selling your house and moving to a smaller one instead. Note too that it is entirely possible to take out a standard interest-only mortgage even when you are retired. This does of course mean making payments out of your income but it at least stops the awful compounding of interest.

Another option that no one ever seems to consider is selling and renting during retirement. You get to cash in on a lifetime of house price growth and then just rent the place of your dreams whenever and wherever. Say you sell a £500,000 house. You pay no tax on the proceeds and if you pop it into a savings account at 5% you'll make £25,000 a year on it. You could then rent somewhere at, say, £1,500 a month and have nearly £600 a month left over for spending. If you really need your house to finance your retirement this seems to me to be a much better solution all round.

Your work

The whole concept of complete retirement is relatively new and you might ask yourself if you really want to be fully retired at the age of 60 or 65. You'll still be quite young and you'll have 30-odd years of life ahead of you. Do you want to spend them all doing nothing? You will need some kind of satisfaction – much of our happiness comes both from having and meeting challenges and from feeling needed (see Chapter 11) so giving up an environment where we get both of these things (and get paid for them) is not a decision to be taken lightly. Now might be a good time to think about whether the career path you are following is one that will allow you to work freelance or part-time when you are of official retirement age.

WHAT DO I DO NOW?

- Accept that no one else, the state included, is going to finance your old age (unless your Prince Charming really has come with both a permanent commitment and a cheque book at the ready).

- Review your pension arrangements. Are they sufficient? Work out how much you need to put away in order to live in your old age as you do now. One way of doing this is to take your age at the time you start your pension, halve it and save that percentage of your salary every month. You can also use the calculator at **www.pensioncalculator.org** to help you to work out how much to save.

- If not, or if you have no pension, look at a stakeholder pension (these offer set and cheap terms and conditions) or consider taking complete control of your future, as I have done, by investing via a **Self Invested Personal Pension**. Also ensure that you check what your employer offers and that you are making the most of it. If your firm has any schemes in place to put any money in a pension on your behalf get on them.

- If you decide to use a financial adviser to help you through the pensions maze make damn sure you aren't paying them any commissions, just fees for their time. And before you go to an IFA visit **www.askdavidson.com** where you may find you can get your questions answered for free.

- Do not rely on your house to finance your retirement. House prices can go down as well as up.

- If you are married and not working make sure that pension contributions for you fit into the family budget.

- If you have no pension of your own make sure that when your husband buys his annuity he gets one that will provide for you after his death (because odds are he'll die first). You have to make the annuity decision together – it will affect you every day for the rest of your life and there aren't many decisions you can really say that about.

7
Buying a House
Freedom or Slavery?

*I*magine if you'd bought a house in Notting Hill ten years ago. You could sell it today, buy a chateau in France and have enough left over never to work again. Think endless days pottering around the garden picking lavender and having coffee on the terrace. But what if you had decided buying was too much bother and rented instead? Then life wouldn't be so nice. There'd be no chateau. And no early retirement. In the UK houses can change lives.

137,000: the number of estate agents in the UK. We now have more estate agents than we have soldiers.

21%: the percentage of UK households made up of single women.

8,140: the number of houses repossessed in the first six months of 2006, up over 50% on the same period in 2005.

£7,500: the stamp duty payable on a £250,000 house.

£20,000: the stamp duty payable on a £500,000 house.

£106,000: the average amount borrowed by a first-time buyer in 2006.

£24,000: the average deposit required to buy a house in 2006.

34: the age of the average first-time buyer in the UK. A decade ago first-time buyers were in their mid-20s.

House prices have been rising in the UK for so long and so fast that the idea that they will rise for ever dominates our national consciousness. We all think that what we buy and where we buy it will have hugely profound effects on our financial futures. We believe that property makes the best possible investment and that many of our retirements will be financed by it. We're all terrified of missing out on the huge property profits everyone on TV seems to be making. The result? We are all mad to 'get on the ladder'. A survey by UCB Homes in 2006 showed that 89% of people between 16 and 21 expect to own their own homes and 92% would prefer to. And women are buying into property faster than men (the majority of first-time buyers in 2005 were women). Women love houses even more than men do. For us houses aren't just investments. We think owning a house will not only make us money but also bring us the independence we think we should have and the security and peace of mind our nesting instincts crave. It feels good to us. So we'll do anything to raise the deposit for a house and take on any debt burden just for the privilege of becoming an owner-occupier.

"I believe in love. But I don't sit around waiting for it. I buy houses."
Renee Zellweger

But are we right to do so? Is borrowing hundreds of thousands of pounds to buy a house really a good idea now or indeed at any time? Or sometimes might it actually be better to steer clear of the debt and responsibility of owning and rent instead?

Everywhere you find a property boom you will also find a nation that hates to rent – a nation that thinks renting is a waste of money, that rent money is 'dead money'. Look up the phrase 'dead money' on the Internet and you will find it in every discussion of a property purchase by a first-time buyer: 'Everywhere we wanted to buy was a bit too expensive ... we had to really stretch ourselves, the house isn't quite what we wanted ... but it is better than renting. Rent is just dead money.'

I hear it all around me, too, from one of my sisters who bought a house last year that we both know she can't really afford because she can't bring herself to 'waste' money renting, to my friends who are moving further and further outside London to buy houses they don't really want to live in because they won't rent nearer the capital, however much cheaper it may be to do so.

You see it all over the television, as well. I once watched property experts Kirsty and Phil on *Location, Location, Location* trying to persuade a young couple to move out of (very nice) rented accommodation into a (quite nasty) 'home of their own', the monthly mortgage payments on which would be higher than their original rent. The couple, we were told, had come to realize that renting was tantamount to 'paying someone else's mortgage', and that was 'madness'. There is a downside to buying, Kirsty told the pair. It comes with sacrifices. If you move from renting to buying you can find 'a real drop in your standard of living' as it can be 'impossible to replicate the space' for the money.

This seemed like a whopper of a downside to me, enough even to make the couple think buying wasn't such a top idea after all, but as far as Kirsty was concerned it was a sacrifice worth making: like most of the UK, she clearly believed that being on the property ladder was desirable in itself, regardless of the cost in either lifestyle or financial terms.

I think she is wrong. Sometimes rent is dead money, sometimes it isn't. It just depends on the market conditions – on the cost of buying and on the cost of renting. Basically, if house prices are rising and it costs less to pay the interest on a mortgage and to maintain your house (insurance, repairs, etc.) than it does to rent a similar property, then buying is a good idea. You are paying off your mortgage bit by bit and gradually gaining ownership of an appreciating asset but for less than it would cost you to rent it. If, on the other hand, house prices are flat or falling and it costs less to rent than to pay mortgage interest and maintain a property, renting is a good idea.

What you save by renting instead of buying can be saved or invested so you can buy when circumstances change if you want to.

Obviously a few other factors are relevant to your decision (when you buy you have to pay stamp duty, legal fees and so on, so you have to add these in when you do your sums) but the equation basically comes down to house prices, rental prices and interest rates.

I did the sums on flats in my building in Paddington, west London, in 2006. I added up the cost of taking out a new mortgage on a flat in the building (on a 90% interest-only basis), the service charges every year, any upkeep and maintenance costs and then also found out the cost of just renting a flat exactly the same. The result was clear. Overall it would have cost £5,000 less a year to rent a two-bedroom apartment than to buy one. So if I had been looking to buy in 2006 I could have rented instead and saved myself £5,000 in the process. That £5,000 could then have been invested with a view to buying when the situation changed and buying became cheaper than renting.

My building wasn't unique at the time: according to HSBC the average cost of servicing a mortgage on a London apartment worth £260,000 was around £13,000 a year in 2006, roughly the same as the cost of renting a similar one. Add on the cost of upkeep – which can come to half as much again as the mortgage – and anyone buying would have been well out of pocket. The same was also clearly true in the area where the couple being advised by Kirsty and Phil were buying: if they bought they were going to have to live somewhere less nice than if they rented. This was the case in most big cities around the world in 2006: rising house prices meant that monthly mortgage payments, maintenance and taxes all added up to a great deal more than it would cost to rent a property. In Madrid, says HSBC, it cost 24% less a year to rent an apartment than to buy one and even in Paris, where prices appear relatively low, renting works out cheaper in the end. It isn't rent that is the dead money for buyers in this kind of market, it is mortgage payments.

You will say – as everyone does – that it doesn't matter that it costs more, at least if you buy you end up with something at the end of the day. Well, maybe yes, maybe no.

That argument works well when house prices are rising: what you lose in monthly costs you win in capital gain. But what about when house prices are not rising? You pay more every month but you make no capital gains to compensate. And what if house prices are falling (as they often do, by the way)? Then you get to pay more every month just for the right to lose money. And when house prices fall you do lose a great deal of money. Say you put down a £7,500 deposit on a £150,000 house (5% of the cost). House prices then only have to fall 5% for your equity in your house to be wiped out. The house will be worth £142,500 and your deposit will be gone.

You think you are an owner-occupier but you don't own the house. The bank does – every single brick of it. Worse, if prices fall any more than that you'll be in negative equity: you'll owe money you can't pay back even if you sell your house. And that's before you take into account the money you spent on stamp duty and legal and estate agent's fees. Contrary to popular belief and to the misinformation peddled by property reality TV, it really isn't hard to lose money on property in the UK.

So how can you tell if house prices are more likely to rise than to fall? This is a tricky one. The direction of house prices is notoriously hard to forecast. But the key thing to look at is interest rates. When interest rates are low people can afford to borrow more money so house prices are likely to be pushed up by rising demand. When interest rates are high people can borrow less so demand at each price level is likely to fall, pushing prices down overall. This makes sense in terms of the renting/buying equation too. When interest rates are falling, buying will probably be cheaper than renting and when they are rising renting may well look cheap relative to buying. It is also worth looking at what the property industry refers to as affordability ratios. Over the long term in the UK the average house price has been equal to 3.6 times the average salary. So if prices are lower than that you might think they are a good deal and if they are much higher you might think they are not. In 2006 the average house price was 5.6 times the average salary – probably not a good time to use all your savings to buy a house.

Can you afford it?

Before you buy you need to ask yourself a few questions. First, is it a good time to buy in general? Is it cheaper to rent than to buy and in which direction might interest rates go? Next you might want to ask if, regardless of the state of the market, you can actually afford to buy at all. You need to think about how much you need for a deposit, how much you will need for all the various fees involved in buying (estate agents, legal fees, surveys, removal vans, stamp duty and so on), how much the repayments will be on a monthly basis and also how much it will cost you to maintain your property. It all adds up.

But even if you can come up with the upfront cash and you can afford the mortgage repayments on your loan, can you afford the ongoing costs that come with owning a house too? A study from the ONS in 2005 revealed that the proportion of our incomes we use to cover our housing costs has jumped from a mere 10% in 1947 to 22% now. Just owning a house costs double what it did 60 years ago. People say – endlessly – that your home is your biggest asset but if owning it makes you a slave to its bills surely it is instead your biggest liability?

When you are pondering all this bear in mind that this passion to own is relatively new. Before the Second World War and indeed in the decades after it, it was entirely normal for lower-income households and for a large part of the middle class to rent not own: today around 70% of houses are owner-occupied but in 1947 less than a third were.

Buying when the numbers don't add up may get you on the ladder but it doesn't bring freedom or independence. Instead it brings slavery in the form of huge debt repayment, payable every month for 25 years. It doesn't bring security either – if you can't make those repayments you won't be allowed to keep the house (this isn't unusual: 8,140 homes were repossessed in the UK in the first six months of 2006). Where's the security in that? And never forget about the risk of negative equity. Ask anyone who found themselves owing thousands more than their house was worth (and paying out double in mortgage what it would have cost them to rent) in 1992 and they will tell you that for them the burden of unrepayable debt was a life destroyer. If you can't sell for a price that pays back your loan you can't sell at all. And you can't move house. You've no get-out clause. You're stuck.

I know I sound as if I am completely anti buying houses. I'm not. I'm just against buying them automatically because 'you know where you are with bricks and mortar. 'You see, you don't know where you are with bricks and mortar: buy at the right time and a house can bring you freedom, buy at the wrong time and it might only bring you slavery.

Getting started

So what if you have decided it is the right time and that you want to buy? First you need to find the start-up cash, the deposit. It is entirely possible to get a 100% mortgage these days, no deposit required. This might be something to consider if you are utterly convinced that house prices will be moving up by a large percentage in the very near future. If that is not the case a 100% mortgage is simply foolish. You are immediately at risk of owing more than you have in equity (house prices only have to fall minutely for you to be in trouble) and that means you won't be able to move house if you want to. Anyway, if you haven't even managed to save a tiny deposit, what makes you think you'll be able to get together a couple of hundred quid every year for your

Beware land banks

If you can't afford a house at the moment you'll be looking around for all sorts of other ways somehow to get on the property ladder. And there are hundreds of scamsters out there who would like to 'help' you do so. One scheme to keep well clear of is land bank sales. They work like this. Companies buy up large plots of agricultural land (which costs around £3,000–£4,000 an acre) and then sell it on in tiny plots to investors (for more like £20,000 a quarter acre). The sales pitch for the plots says that the UK needs thousands of new homes every year and that planning rules are bound to be relaxed so that this land can be built on – pay £20,000 for a plot now and it will be worth triple that in a few years. You can use your profits to put down a deposit on a home of your own. This is usually nonsense. There may be a need for more houses in Britain (or may not be – it depends who you ask) but that doesn't mean it will be open season on green belt land. Most of this land will never get planning permission and will never be worth what people pay for it.

building insurance or find the money to cope when the boiler blows? Are you really ready for the responsibility? So try to have a deposit: 20% of the cost is best; 10% is good; 5% is just about OK; any less and you should probably delay buying.

The fact that houses are so expensive these days and that the deposits needed are therefore pretty hefty (the average deposit was £5,500 ten years ago according to Halifax numbers, today it is £24,000 and takes five years to save) has meant that the nation's 'experts' have been working overtime to find ways for the young to get their hands on the cash. Their favourite suggestion? Your parents. Between 40% and 50% of new buyers under 30 get help from their parents and are given around £34,000 each – roughly one and a half times their salaries, says the Council of Mortgage Lenders. In 1995 that number was just 5–10% and they got only £13,000, around one year's worth of salary. According to Scottish Widows, between 2000 and 2005 500,000 graduates borrowed more than £2 billion from parents to buy.

This may all seem a bit mad but it does make some sense: the child gets a house, and by giving money away early the parent gets to move money out of their estate and cut their eventual inheritance tax bill (although given that they'll be dead when that bill comes in they may not be much bothered). That said, if you are going to get the deposit from a parent you need to be sure you are both agreeing to the same thing. Is it a gift? Is it a loan? If it's a loan is there interest payable on it and if so how much and when will it be paid? Does the parent have any call over any capital gain or any say in the kind of property bought? What if you marry and divorce? Is the money ring-fenced or will it end up with a stranger?

But if your parents don't have the cash or don't want to give it to you what next? The property magazines and television programmes

have been full of ideas for this, all absolutely terrible. You do not want to take out a personal loan for a deposit (why have two debts?). You absolutely do not want to use a credit card (why have two debts, one of which has a criminal rate of interest attached to it, when you clearly can't afford to have any?). You do not want to invest in the stock market to make the money (it might not go up). You probably don't want to buy with friends (too much potential for falling out). You definitely don't want to buy with a stranger despite the fact that several websites have been set up to help you to do so: it might just work if prices are rising fast and you get out with some equity in a hurry but it probably won't be much fun if prices fall and you and the stranger are stuck living together for years.

And most of all you do not want, as one television programme I watched suggested, to buy a cheap house in Bulgaria, wait until its price goes up, sell it and use the proceeds to put down a deposit on a house in the UK. Why? It's hard to know where to start with listing the problems with this kind of thing, but see below for the pitfalls of buying abroad and then think for one minute about the absurdity of owning a small breeze-block house in a tiny village in the back end of Bulgaria when you live in Bristol. It just won't work.

Once you have the deposit you need to make sure you have the money to complete the deal. Stamp duty is a killer. It is charged at 1% on houses costing between £60,000 and £250,000, 3% between £250,000 and £500,000 and a huge 4% above £500,000. It also isn't incremental as most taxes are: so if you buy a house for £254,000 you pay 3% on not just the £4,000 over the £250,000 threshold but on the entire lot (this is a classic stealth tax). Then you will need up to £1,000 for your searches (to make sure the house legally belongs to the seller and so on) and your legal fees plus another £400 for a survey. (If you're selling a property, you'll also need to budget for your estate agent taking a commission of up to 2.5% of the value of your house or flat.) Then there is the mortgage. I'm going to look at all the different types of mortgages below but when you are calculating your upfront costs you need to be aware that you will often have to pay an 'arrangement fee' of up to £500 just to get your loan sorted out. All in, your fees are going to come to a good few thousand pounds. Add them up before you start house-hunting or you'll have a nasty shock when the bills come in.

Next, you need to know how much you can borrow. It used to be that the standard mortgage involved borrowing no more than three times your salary and doing so for no more than 25 years. Even in the mid-1990s the average female first-time buyer was borrowing only 2.5 times her salary to buy a house. Not any more. Today she's borrowing four times her salary (an average of £106,000) and could borrow even more. It's a far cry from the 1950s when it was practically impossible for a woman to get a mortgage of any kind at all. Mortgage lenders have long been easing their terms: you can now borrow four or even five times your salary if you fancy it (particularly if you can get your parents to act as a guarantor for you) and you can extend the term of your mortgage well beyond 25 years – to 35 or even in some cases to 50 years.

There is nothing wrong with this in principle but it doesn't really make any sense for the borrower: not only is it wildly expensive to take out long loans (see the box on how mortgages work) but why would anyone want to be burdened with one debt for 50 years? Do you really want to be paying off a mortgage when you are supposed to be retired? Taking out loans of much more than three times your salary is also pretty reckless. You may think you can stretch to afford the payments and that as your salary is bound to rise they will soon become easier to cope with anyway. But what if your salary doesn't rise? What if interest rates rise instead, pushing up your payments? It all smacks of danger to me. Just because you can borrow five times your income doesn't mean you should.

Then you need to think about where you want to buy. As far as estate agents are concerned there is no such thing as an area that isn't up and coming. And most Brits appear to agree – we are relentlessly optimistic when it comes to property. A survey by **www.propertyfinder.com** in 2006 found that an overwhelming majority of Britain's homeowners firmly believe that prices in their area will outperform the national average. Six times as many people believe their district is up and coming compared to those who think that it is doing less well than other areas. The reasons for their optimism? The main one is that their area is somehow special: not only do they believe their area is up and coming relative to other areas but they also think that it is a honey pot for property investors and will see its prices propelled upwards by investment money. As a result more and more people will want to move to their area, thus pushing up demand and, naturally, house prices.

But it isn't very likely that all areas are up and coming, is it? Everywhere can't beat the market. Some prices will go up more than average and some less than average.

There is a theory – put about by estate agents – that you don't have to like your first house. All that matters is getting into the market, getting on the ladder, so buying in an 'up-and-coming' but horrible place isn't a problem. But this only makes sense in a very fast-moving market – when prices are rising quickly the costs of moving seem irrelevant. Most of the time, however, prices aren't going up fast and the costs of moving are crippling, as discussed above. The result? You really have to like your first house because you are probably going to be in it for a while. Say you buy a house for £200,000. Your upfront costs (excluding the deposit but including legal fees, stamp duty, the survey and estate agency fees) will come to at least £5,000 and probably more. This means that for you just to break even when you sell the house prices have to rise by 2.5% – and there is no guarantee that they will.

Getting a mortgage

Mortgages are simple things that mortgage lenders manage to make very complicated. You borrow a large amount of money from a bank or building society and you then pay it back in monthly instalments over an agreed term – usually 25 years but sometimes more and sometimes less. The longer the term the less you pay every month but the more you end up paying in total. Say you borrow £150,000 (this original lump sum is called the principal) at 5% and pay it off over 20 years. The monthly payments will be £1,003 making the total (principal plus interest) repayable over the term £240,720. Now imagine you borrow the £150,000 over 25 years. Your monthly repayments will fall to £886.90, the total repayable will rise to £266,070. That's the magic of compounding working firmly in the lender's favour: they let you pay £116 less each month but get to charge you an extra £25,350 for the privilege of doing so.

But interest isn't the only cost you are going to come across when you borrow money to buy a house: mortgage lenders are as tricky as everyone else in the financial services business. They have, for example, recently cottoned on to the fact that they can cut interest rates to get themselves in the best buy tables but then claw back their profits by charging you 'arrangement fees' of hundreds and sometimes thousands of pounds. The average is now £500, double what it was five years ago. Another great new scam comes in the form of exit fees – a charge for 'administration' made when you have finished paying off your loan. These rose, on average, 30% between 2005 and 2006 as lenders realized they are a grand way to squeeze a few hundred extra pounds out of everyone before they escape back into the land of the debt-free. Other shockers include offering you cash back when you take out a mortgage. This might seem like a good deal at the time but it never is. The banks aren't actually giving you the money (this isn't something they do), just adding it on to your long-term loan. You're just borrowing more to pay back over 25 years, and that will, as we know, compound up to make it very expensive cash back.

Watch out, too, for how often the interest on your loan is calculated. Doing it just once a year instead of every month or every day is a great money-spinner for the banks. Why? Because it is calculated on the amount of principal you owe at the beginning of the year despite the fact that with a repayment mortgage you are paying the principal down during the year. The result? At the end of the year you are still paying interest on money you paid off months ago. It's a complete outrage. Make sure your interest is calculated daily so that you are only ever paying interest on money you actually owe.

Two other things to avoid are extended tie-ins and Higher Lending Charges (HLC, also known as Mortgage Indemnity Insurance or MIG). Extended tie-ins lock you into keeping a mortgage with one firm for years after your original deal with them has expired. So you may pay a cheap rate for a few years but then find yourself having to pay a high one for another five years. HLCs are fees charged if you borrow a very high percentage of the cash needed for your house. The fee is used by the lender to purchase insurance to cover the amount should you default on the loan, but why should you have to pay for this? It gives you no protection and they are already protected by the fact that your mortgage is secured on your house. You default, they get the house. Why do they need more? Finally, remember not to automatically take buildings insurance out from your mortgage lender – they'll suggest strongly that you get your buildings insurance, contents insurance and so on via them and it might seem like an easy option at the time (you'll be exhausted by all the house admin by the time you actually complete your purchase). But you'll find that it will end up being much more expensive than buying similar insurance from a discount broker.

The upshot of all this is that you can't look at any of the costs of a mortgage in isolation. The fees mean that the lowest interest rate deal might not be the cheapest deal overall. So don't get hung up on the monthly costs of a deal alone. Instead look at the big number: what is each loan on offer going to cost you in total over the full term of the deal?

How interest rates work

The base interest rate is set by the Bank of England (its Monetary Policy Committee meets every month to decide whether to change it or not depending on what is going on in the economy) and mortgage rates tend to follow it very carefully: when the base rate goes up so do mortgage rates. When they come down so will mortgage rates. So what makes the base rate go up? And what makes it come down? The answer is the rate of inflation. The Bank of England has one responsibility: to keep inflation around 2%. If it goes much higher the governor has to explain why to the chancellor, and if it goes much lower he has to do the same. Raising interest rates tends to reduce inflation. Why? Because when borrowing money gets more expensive people tend to borrow less. And as they borrow less they spend less. So demand falls and so should prices. The opposite happens when interest rates fall. So if you want to know where interest rates might go the best thing to do is to think about where inflation might be going.

Repayment: the ordinary mortgage

Most ordinary mortgages are repayment mortgages. This means you pay back both some capital and some interest every month. However you don't pay back the same amount of each every month. Instead lenders tend to 'front load' the interest: they assume that you won't keep your mortgage for the full term (you'll move house and so on), so they like to get as much of the interest off you upfront as possible (remember the interest is their profit).

In the first few years you will find that your repayments are largely interest despite the fact that the payments will be much higher than they would be with an interest-only loan, but by the end of the loan they are mostly capital. If you are keeping your loan for a long time this doesn't really matter but if you are borrowing for the short term (say under four years) you might be better off to take out an interest-only loan and save the difference. Again, you need to get all the numbers from the lenders you are considering and add them up yourself.

When it comes to choosing your interest rate the key number to look at is a lender's Standard Variable Rate. This is their benchmark rate, the one they price all their other rates off and the one that moves as base rates move. One in five borrowers ends up paying this rate on their loans. But you shouldn't. It is usually a good 1–2% higher than the best deals on offer, so taking it can boost the final cost of a mortgage by 25% or so. Take the case of a £100,000 mortgage. The annual difference in interest between paying 4.5% and 6.5% is £2,000 a year. That's £2,000 out of after-tax income, remember, so £2,650 out of the earnings of a basic rate tax payer and £3,330 of the earnings of a higher rate tax payer. Why would you want to waste that kind of cash?

Instead you might look at any discounts from the SVR offered by lenders and take those instead – you could go for a straightforward discount or for a rate that is fixed at a set level for a few years. Note, however, that most deals only last a few years so you have to be vigilant: when your deal ends you have to look for another one. This takes planning – if you leave it to the last minute you'll end up paying the SVR for a few months while you organize a new loan. It might be better to look to the few banks that offer good rates that stick for the full term – so-called lifetime mortgages, the rates on which are designed always to be just above the base rate (0.2% for example). I'd be tempted by these. They might cost a tiny bit more in the end than constantly changing deals but life is surely too short to spend too much time filling in mortgage application forms.

Living on the edge: interest-only mortgages

Interest-only deals sound great. Instead of paying back bits of the capital on your loan every month you just pay the interest owed on the capital. That's it. Take a loan of £100,000 on an interest rate of 5%. If you took a repayment mortgage it would cost you £591 a month. Make that interest only and it is going to be a mere £416 – over £2,000 a year less. But what happens at the end of the term of the loan? If you haven't paid back any capital you'll still owe £100,000 in 25 years. It used to be that you weren't allowed to take out an interest-only mortgage without being obliged to arrange some way of saving up the money to pay back the loan: you'd set up an investment plan (known as an endowment) into which you would pay monthly with a view to growing the capital enough over time to meet your debt. However, this is no longer the case.

These days you just take out the loan and how you pay it back is your problem. Is this necessarily a bad thing? Very often the answer to this question is yes. It takes enormous discipline to save up that much money – say £100,000 – if no one is actually making you do it. So a great many of the people who have taken out interest-only mortgages over the last five years or so simply aren't bothering. The result? They won't own their houses at the end of their mortgage term: they'll co-own it with the bank. Paying off mortgages, like building up a pension, takes discipline and that's why most of us find that we need to do it automatically – with direct debits into our SIPPs and repayment mortgages. Otherwise we won't save, we'll spend.

Balancing act: the offset mortgage

I love the sound of the offset mortgage. The idea is that your savings are offset against your borrowings: instead of earning interest on your savings you reduce the interest you pay on your debt. It works like this. Say you had a mortgage of £100,000 and savings of £20,000. If you offset you would end up paying interest on only £80,000 of the loan. However, your monthly payments would be unchanged, as they would still be based on you owing £100,000. The result? You'd effectively be overpaying every month and end up paying off your mortgage significantly earlier. This could save you a fortune (remember the faster you pay off a debt the lower your total interest bill) but it also has tax advantages (if you aren't earning interest on your savings – which technically you aren't in this situation – you don't have to pay tax on them).

The problem with this is that while the concept is great the actuality is not great. The banks that offer offsets tend to charge much higher interest rates on them than they do on ordinary mortgages so anything you gain from the offset you lose on the interest rate. Don't forget that for every 1% more you pay on a £100,000 mortgage you pay an extra £1,000 a year. Instead you might as well have an ordinary mortgage and just pay it down as fast as you can anyway: most lenders allow you to overpay as and when you like.

Peace of mind: paying it off early

More than anything you want to get rid of your mortgage as early as you can. Not having it hanging over you as a huge debt burden is enormously liberating. It is also an extremely tax-efficient way to use your savings. A higher rate tax payer would have to have their money in an account paying 7.6% to get the equivalent benefit of overpaying on a mortgage charged at 4.5%, for example. A basic rate payer would need to get 5.6%. Overpaying can also save you thousands. A £100,000 repayment mortgage at 4.5% over 25 years will cost a total of £166,700. Cut that to 15 years and it is only £137,700 in total. So overpay as much as you can and pay off lump sums if and when you can too. It's the best way there is to save money.

Buy to let: hype, spin and debt

The housing boom of the last decade has meant that thousands of people have made vast profits from the property business. Buying houses and letting them out is now thought to be the best possible way to make money, the best way to finance retirement and the best way for those who don't want to or can't work full-time – i.e. women – to produce an income. Buy to let, it is often said, is a woman's business. Their nesting instinct makes them better at creating homes people want to rent. And at the same time they find it less threatening than the stock market or other more esoteric investments. 'They know where they are with bricks and mortar.' This is nonsense. You don't need nesting flair to fill a two-bed buy-to-let flat with Ikea furniture, and as we already know women should be in no way threatened or confused by the stock market. Buy to let isn't a woman's business. It's just a business.

Houses for students

Going to university is expensive. And one of the biggest costs of all is housing: most student halls cost between £50 and £70 a week. Many parents look at these numbers and wonder if they might not be better off buying a house for their children to live in while they study – a sort of buy-to-let investment but with students (one of whom belongs to you) as tenants. When house prices are rising this is a great idea: you get rent from your child's housemates to cover your costs and then when your offspring graduates you get to sell on for a profit. Between 2000 and 2005 prices in the UK's top 20 university towns rose by 77% (Halifax) so anyone buying over that time period would have done very nicely out of the whole thing. But if house prices are falling things aren't so good: you still get the rent but when your child moves on you are stuck with either a capital loss or a default buy-to-let investment in a town you don't really know. And even if prices are flat, after buying and selling expenses you may find you've lost a packet. Once again you need to do the sums very carefully before committing.

If you do decide to buy you will probably want to do so as joint owners of the property with your child – that way there will be no capital gains tax to pay, at least on the child's part should you have capital gains when you come to sell. You will also be able to have your child receive the rent and avoid income tax on that too (your child will have to pay but they will be able to use up their income tax allowance and the £4,250 rent-a-room relief before they start to do so).

And the only question we need to ask about it is: Is it a good business? In theory it is. You buy a house and rent it out. The rental income covers all the costs and hopefully produces a surplus too and at the same time the house rises in value. Then one day in the distant future you sell it for several times what you paid for it and pocket the profit. Free money!

However, this only works as long as the rental income really does cover all the costs (not just the mortgage when the flat is rented out but any voids when it is not, as well as the maintenance and upkeep) and when house prices are rising. If this is not the case you may find that you are effectively subsidizing the housing costs of your tenants. That's not so good. I know one woman who has three buy-to-let flats. After she's paid the mortgage and upkeep every month she loses around £80 on each flat. That's £240 a month. She's a single mother with three children and thinks that she should hang on to the flats anyway – 'for their futures'. But what if house prices don't rise like she thinks they will? She'll have wasted £240 a month when she could have saved it instead. The latter might have done a bit more to safeguard her children's futures.

You've got to watch out for a lot of spin when it comes to buy to let: there are now a great many people with a vested interest in us continuing to think it is a marvellous investment when it might not be. I got a press release in 2006 from the Association of Residential Landlords (Arla) telling us that the return on buy-to-lets in the UK was 22%. At first glance the numbers looked pretty sensible. They assumed that each UK landlord was buying a property for £285,315 with a 25% deposit to earn a gross annual yield of 4.99%. So far, so good. But, Arla admitted, after allowing for mortgage repayments, voids and repairs, that means that in cash-flow terms the landlord is actually making a loss of £212 a month. So where did the 22% come from? This is where things became a lot less sensible. Arla assumed that, every year for the next five years, property prices in the UK would rise by 8.8% (the average rise from 1984 to 2003), meaning that at the end of the period the value of the investor's deposit would have doubled – giving a 22% return a year. The problem with all those sums was that there was no way of knowing that prices would rise by 8.8% a year for the next five years. Instead, according to Arla's own members at the time, the average value of new build rented flats 'throughout the country' had fallen by 9% in three months. Buy-to-let investors weren't making 22% a year. Instead, they were losing 8.9% a year (the £212 a month as an annualized percentage of the average purchase price of £285,315). Over the last five years developers have built thousands of two-bedroom flats across the nation with buy-to-let investors in mind: now there is something of a glut in the market and that means some people are beginning to lose money.

Like all property deals buy to let works in some kinds of market and not in others. Do your sums very carefully before you fall for the hype.

Flying and buying

The British obsession with property doesn't end at Dover. In fact it doesn't end anywhere – it doesn't matter how far-flung the place, if a property looks cheap enough a Brit will buy it. A Nationwide survey in 2006 suggested that 32% of the UK's young (16–21) would prefer to live abroad, and according to the Office of the Deputy Prime Minister 254,000 of us now own homes abroad, 70,000 of us in Spain but the others everywhere from Estonia to Australia. Why? Because house prices in the UK are so high that much of the rest of the world looks practically free to us. Buying abroad isn't necessarily a bad idea – property yields in many parts of the world are still much higher than they are at home – but I do wonder if people who are buying in more out-of-the-way places are really taking account of the risks. Much of 'abroad' is cheap for a reason.

I can't understand why anyone would want to own a house in Montenegro, for example. It may be hyped as the next big thing and parts of its coastline are certainly very beautiful but that doesn't necessarily make it a nice place to be. I visited several years ago, intending to stay for a few days. But after trouble at the border, a huge everything-in-your-wallet fine (from some very heavily armed policemen) for speeding when we were practically stationary, various run-ins with aggressive war-hung-over youths and one of the most disgusting lunches I've ever had, we called it a day and drove back to neighbouring Croatia. It may be true that you can buy a beachfront villa in Montenegro for the cost of a garage in Clapham and I know not everyone has the experiences we had (I have friends who adore Montenegro), but, given the choice, I'd rather holiday in Clapham. So it makes complete sense to me that Montenegrin houses should be cheap.

Bulgaria is another example of a place packed with cheap-for-a-reason property. For years now we have been told that the deals there are extraordinary, that we should rush in to take advantage of win-win opportunities on the Black Sea coast or in the nation's developing ski resorts. We could buy them for nothing, rent them out for more than enough to cover the mortgage and live high on the surplus. The problem is that it hasn't quite worked out like that. Instead rental returns are hopeless – if you can rent your property out at all – and oversupply means that huge numbers of properties not only aren't making capital gains but can't be sold at any price. Bulgaria is just one big building site. And not a very efficient one either. Anyone who has bought there with a mortgage intending to service the debt by renting out the property is going to end up in trouble.

What my day trip to Montenegro and the tribulations of buyers in Bulgaria should remind us of is that in eastern Europe the rules still aren't the same as they are in the West. The level of legal protection available to the consumer is nothing like it is at home; corruption is common; wars have muddled ownership issues, so buyers often find themselves caught up in endless battles over title; building standards can be poor; and differing tax and inheritance laws can make things very confusing to say nothing of expensive. Finally, it is worth noting that buying a property abroad, wherever it is, comes with all the same difficulties as it does at home – voids, repairs and the like – only in a foreign language.

I'm not saying you shouldn't buy abroad. There is probably money to be made in some places and some people love owning holiday homes (me, I'd rather save the money and hassle and stay in hotels but that's a personal preference). I'm just saying that buying at home is hard and buying abroad is harder: you need to know what you are doing, you need to go into it with cash in your pocket rather than expecting it to make you rich, you need to have a good lawyer and to read all the small print in the contract, and you need to be prepared for all sorts of difficulties you have never thought of to turn up.

My mother is a property investor and currently owns several small houses in France, which she rents out. Here are her tips on how to buy abroad successfully.

1 Never touch a time-share. They are usually overpriced. You can't borrow against them and they are hard to sell on.

2 Always buy somewhere easy to get to. If you don't no one will rent it and when you are staying there no one will come and stay with you. People are lazy.

3 Buy through a local agent not a UK one if you can – you'll get a better price. But if you don't speak the language always take a translator.

4 Try not to think of a holiday home as an investment – it may go up in price but there is no guarantee and in the meantime you will have to pay all the usual expenses of owning a home: running and repair costs and taxes. Note that in most places property taxes are higher than they are in the UK.

5 Never believe a new-build salesman: just because they are selling the flats for high prices doesn't mean they are worth those prices and just because they tell you prices will rise further doesn't mean they will. They can also rarely be believed on rental yields. Remember, too, that if they are offering rental guarantees they have usually inflated the price of the property to cover anything they might have to pay out.

Mortgage Brokers

You don't need a mortgage broker these days – you can just do your own research online at all the usual websites (**www.moneyextra.com** or **www.moneysupermarket.com** for example) or just type mortgage comparison into your search engine. If you do want a broker, however, you can find a list of authorized ones at **www.fsa.gov.uk/register**. Be aware that as is the case with other financial advisers there are three kinds of mortgage adviser: tied (selling mortgages from only one lender), multi-tied (from several lenders) and independent (who have access to the whole market).

WHAT Do I Do Now?

✳ **Do your sums. Is it cheaper for you to buy or to rent? Include stamp duty, fees and the upkeep of a house in the figures.**

✳ **If you decide to buy make sure you are doing it inside your comfort zone: your mortgage must be completely affordable.**

✳ **Pay as little as possible for a house: you don't have to pay the asking price if there aren't any other bidders.**

✳ **Never forget the agent works for the seller not for you. They are working on commission so the more you pay for a house the better they do.**

✳ **Don't just assume property is a good investment because it has been for the last decade. It may not be.**

Section 3:
Sharing the Money

"The sum which two married people owe to one another defies calculation. It is an infinite debt."

Johann Wolfgang von Goethe

8
Marriage
Working the Money Together

When I was in New York a couple of years ago I saw a beautiful black dress by a well-known US designer in Barney's going for $900. I was looking for a wedding dress at the time and the style seemed just the thing so I tried it on. It looked fantastic but they didn't have it in white or cream so I left it. However when I returned to London I found it in white, at a bridal shop in Central London – same dress, same size, same material, just a different colour. I tried it on again and again it looked pretty good so I thought I might get it. Then I looked at the price. It was £3,500. 'That's crazy,' I said to the saleswoman. 'You can get these for $900 in black.'

'Yes, madam,' she said, 'but this is the bridal collection. It costs more.'

£300: the average cost to a guest of attending a wedding (World Vision).

£3,000: the average cost of a honeymoon. One in three people told an NSI survey they intended to pay for it with a credit card.

£17,400: the value of the unpaid housework the average woman does every year.

$100,000: the annual value of a happy marriage.

£150: the amount couples say they spend on Christmas presents for each other (Skipton Building Society).

£450: the amount couples say they spend on birthday presents for each other (Skipton Building Society).

£17,000: the average cost of a wedding in the UK.

£4,356: the average cost to a couple of getting married abroad (the most popular destinations are South Africa, St Lucia, Mauritius, Las Vegas and Antigua).

Marriage is an amazing institution. It provides a basic insurance against all the nasty things that can happen in life: if your marriage works, every burden is a burden shared. Indeed, if you add up all the emotional benefits a happy marriage brings, say US economists David Blanchflower and Andrew Oswald, you will find that it is worth the equivalent of $100,000 a year in income to a couple. Even the most grouchy of people are happier after they have married than before. A study from the University of Zurich a few years back showed that the single are pretty much always more miserable than the married: only by the time they reach 60 do their happiness levels begin to hit the same levels as those of their married friends. The married also live longer and are healthier than the single. They have more antibodies in their blood and get flu less often as a result, for example.

And the married are not just richer in emotional and physical terms: they have more real money too. According to Ohio State University they have almost double the wealth (defined as equity in houses, shares and cash) as single and divorced people: on average the married increase their wealth by 16% every year whereas the single increase theirs by a mere 8%. These days most couples earn two salaries at least some of the time but have living expenses not much greater or even lower than those of someone living alone. Marriage is cheap: you get to economize both by staying in together and when you go out together (you share hotel rooms, only bring one bottle of wine and one birthday present to parties and only take one taxi home). Over a couple of decades that makes a real difference.

Not many people get married any more: 60% fewer tied the knot in 2003 than in 1970 and the ONS predicts that the proportion of people between 45 and 54 who are married will fall from 71% in 2003 to a mere 48% in 2031 for men and from 72% to 50% for women. Why? Largely, it seems, because the young perceive it as pointless (a BBC survey in 2005 found that 27% of 7–12-year-olds thought marriage was a surefire path to unhappiness and boredom). But the statistics above show that that's not true.

Solo living: the modern spinster

In the nineteenth century being a spinster was considered to be a hideous fate. Carol Clewlow in her book *Not Married Not Bothered* points out that they were referred to in Parliament as 'the problem of surplus and excess women' and in the newspaper columns of the time as a 'mischief' and a 'disturbance'. Even for the generation before mine spinster was something of a dirty word. But my generation has, I think, reclaimed it as something of a badge of pride. According to the ONS a third of women now in their twenties will be alone in their mid-forties. Half of those will be divorced or separated but the other half will never have married. And a large number of those will not have married out of choice: they can finance themselves (so marriage isn't necessary any more) and prefer the freedom of living alone to the compromises of marriage. As Clewlow herself puts it: 'I don't want to have to take another person into account. I'm only going to be on this planet once and while I am here I don't want to waste one minute doing what someone else wants to do.' Some people just don't want other people.

Still, when you consider the attributes men look for in a woman you can understand why many women may prefer to live alone. It has often been noted that men like to marry women they consider an intellectual inferior – their secretary being the classic. A study from the University of Michigan a few years back confirmed this: most men looking for long-term relationships said they would prefer to have one with a woman in a subordinate job of some kind. No wonder so many clever women prefer not to marry: UK research shows that the higher a woman's IQ the less likely she is to get married – every 16-point rise in a woman's IQ reduces her chances of getting married by 40%.

Need another reason to be wary of the motives of men? Here it is. McMaster University (Ontario, Canada) did some research into lonely heart ads and found a remarkable difference in understanding between the sexes. When men said they were looking for GSOH (good sense of humour) they meant someone who laughs at their jokes. When women said they were looking for GSOH they meant someone who made them laugh. There's more. When asked by Mintel what the biggest disadvantage to being single was the most common answers from men were having to do their own housework and not having enough sex. Knowing what men really want … it's enough to make spinsterhood look really good.

The financial implications of living alone for ever are obvious: you won't accumulate wealth as fast as married couples and you won't have anyone else to support you through a career break if you have children or to share a pension with you. This means you need to have your finances seriously under control. Your savings need to be automatic and your pension started as far in advance as possible. On the plus side at least you won't have to have the joint account conversation with a husband and, for good or bad, you will never relinquish your independence.

Marriage is not a religious institution, and it isn't a pointless one. It's a legal one that creates a secure and hopefully permanent core – something you just don't get when you cohabit – around which lives can be lived. The average marriage lasts 11.5 years, the average cohabit a mere 3. You may think that loving, honouring and obeying is a tad outdated and maybe it is (the last bit certainly is) but creating a legal structure for the care of your children and your joint finances is not. Indeed if you intend to stay with your partner for ever and if you have children I can't see any reason not to marry, particularly given the non-legal benefits (the long life, the money and the happiness levels that appear to come with it). The only time you may not want to marry someone who you think is a long-term partner is when you have both come out of previous marriages, have children already and see no need to entangle your financial affairs and complicate your relationships. However, this aside, long-term relationships need contracts and this is the best one we have. I'm all for it.

Anyway, back to money. The studies I've quoted above tell us that on average marriage can bring financial benefits. But when a marriage is unhappy the pain can frequently be traced straight back to money problems – sometimes a shortage of money but more often a difference in expectations about money, different spending habits and attitudes to debt between spouses and most of all a lack of financial intimacy. Very few couples are completely honest, frank and upfront about their financial affairs with their partners from the beginning. They should be. Arguments about money are the most common in every household (ask your mother if you don't believe me) and many arguments that don't appear to be about money really are about money:

would the time your husband spends on his hobby, be it photography or drinking, be as irritating if it didn't use up so much of your household's surplus cash?

The decisions you make about money and the problems you have with your finances are with you and your partner every moment of every day for ever. They affect everything from how you cook (are you buying expensive ready meals or cheap basic ingredients and how does that fit into your household budget?), how you get to work (new car or old car?), where you live (risky big mortgage or conservative small one?) and what you wear (Prada or Primark?). So if you don't feel the same way about money as your partner or you don't know if you feel the same way because you haven't ever discussed it you will end up with ongoing tension in your marriage, absolutely no doubt about it. It follows, then, that in marriage too love is not enough; you need to sort out the money stuff as well if you want to be happy.

The Big Day

You can't wait to start talking about your marital finances. Most conversations of this sort should come well before the wedding, and the wedding itself is a fine place to start. The average wedding cost well over £17,000 in 2006, up 13% on 2005. The typical couple spends £1,289 on the engagement ring, £665 on the wedding rings, £1,500 on the bride's dress, £317 on the groom's outfit and a massive £6,076 on the reception itself, according to figures from Alliance & Leicester. This is ridiculous. For most people that's a whole year's worth of post-tax income, an amount that would take a good four years or so to save up, and that you are sorely going to need if you want a house deposit or a couple of children. So why would you want to blow it on just one

day? Or borrow money to do it (the average amount saved up to pay for each wedding is only £6,650 so one in ten couples ends up paying for the rest on their credit cards)?

Yes, it's a special day but can't it be special without sugared almonds, over-the-top flowers, fiddled-with food and big name dresses? As the story at the beginning of this chapter shows, designers see brides coming. So do hoteliers, florists and travel agencies. And they aren't just going to overcharge you, they're going to overcharge you for the same muck all your friends had at their weddings. There are loads of ways to cut the cost of a wedding (don't tell anyone it's a wedding when you are asking for quotes, for starters) but it's also worth asking how much of the so-called traditional wedding stuff you really want.

Wedding magazines and planners are no different from other businesses: their job is to make you think you need things you really don't need. Like a vintage Rolls to take you from church to reception, tacky waistcoats, bridesmaids' bespoke dresses (why? You can get them for £80 in Monsoon), flowers in little baskets, presents for the guests (this is a new 'traditional' invention and just silly) and so on. Buy into all this and you'll end up spending thousands of pounds on things you wouldn't allow anywhere near you or your family on a normal day and that everyone there knows you couldn't afford on a normal day.

The final irony, of course, is that your guests don't care. They've been to tons of weddings and they've all been the same. It's not new and it's not interesting: they'd probably rather be celebrating your wedding with a picnic in the park anyway. Most of this stuff also isn't traditional at all – it's been invented by the wedding industry in the last 20 years. Ask your mother if she had a sit-down dinner for 150 at her wedding. I bet she didn't. The same goes for everything from the weird master of ceremonies hotels suggest you hire (£200 for someone to tell you when to stand up and sit down at your wedding) to the swords they lend you to cut your cake with.

This is an industry that just can't leave anything alone. With the legislation that allowed same-sex couples to formalize their relationships a huge gay wedding industry has sprung up too, as though a party for them was somehow different to a party to celebrate a heterosexual union. It is very complicated, one 'wedding coordinator' was quoted as saying. If two women are getting married you need to organize two photographers so 'the two brides shared the limelight' to say nothing of two aisles so that both their fathers can walk them down the aisle. Doesn't sound that complicated to me.

There's also a new craze in the US for having a special pre-wedding wedding 'action' photographer to photograph brides in the run-up to the wedding (getting their legs waxed and hair done) and then getting dressed on the day. That way, the sales pitch goes, they will end up with a nice pile of sexy photos that will remind their husbands when they are in their fifties of why they married them. I rather like the idea of this. I was in pretty good shape when I actually got married but having got pregnant within 24 hours of saying my vows, I find that the figure that slipped into my wedding dress is now nothing but a distant dream. That said, were I to have my time again I certainly wouldn't be paying £6,000 (the going rate in New York, I gather). This is a job for a sister.

Bling Bling: The story of Carly O'Brien

Influenced by the likes of Posh and Becks and glamour model Jordan, silly couples all over the country are splashing out on too much bling on their big day. Meringue dresses and underwires have been dragged out of retirement and white doves have been working overtime (six flew out from the folds of Jordan's dress when she married singer Peter Andre in 2006).

But of all the silly stories of excess the story of Carly O'Brien, an ordinary girl from Gloucester, is the silliest. It took Carly more than eight hours to be dressed in her wedding gown. It had 30 layers of material including 120 metres of silk, 1,600 metres of tulle and thousands of metres of net as well as dozens of steel hoops – several of which had to be removed to get her through the church door. It was decorated with 30,000 Swarovski crystals, weighed 25 stone, came with a white gold tiara to top it off and was said by the tabloid papers to have cost £15,000. The train was so long (60 feet) and so heavy that ten or so of her guests had to help her up the aisle. The result? Her father couldn't walk beside her up the aisle: the wretched dress and its assistants took up so much room that he had to walk in front of her. Carly's self-confessed heroine? Jordan.

So when you are arranging your wedding never agree to anything before you've asked yourself if you really need it to make your day feel special or if someone else wants you to think you do. Also never accept a price for anything until you know what the non-wedding price for the same thing would be. And while you're at it ask yourself why you are having the same wedding as all your friends – the kind invented by bridal magazines and wedding venues not by tradition nor indeed by you. Why let the wedding industry persuade you to start married life in debt? I read recently of a couple who had spent an absurd £25,000 on their wedding. They had borrowed £10,000 of that on a credit card on which they were paying interest alone of £125 a month. That's not a nice thing to welcome you back from honeymoon. Talk about the wedding early, agree a budget, agree that you don't want to waste money on something no one will really remember and you will find that you won't have to.

One final word on weddings. Wedding presents were invented in the days when people married young and lived at home until the wedding. They started out with nothing, setting up house from scratch when they left the church. So people gave them toasters, cheese graters, corkscrews and knives and forks to get them started. It isn't like that any more. Most of us get married later on in life when we already have at least two toasters and several different kinds of corkscrew. We just don't need anything else. So perhaps all we should ask from our guests except that they turn up to celebrate our union and wish us well. It already costs the average guest around £300 to attend a wedding, once travel, accommodation and clothes are taken into account. Surely they don't need to give us presents too.

The prenup

Next is prenups. Prenuptial contracts have become increasingly popular as people have left it longer and longer to get married – everyone in Hollywood has one. By the age of 35 or so you will (hopefully) have built up something in the way of assets. You may have some equity in your house, a reasonable sum in an ISA and some pension savings, for example. And if your marriage fails after a year or two you won't want to share those hard-won assets with your ex-husband. So you need to think about ring-fencing them.

Prenuptial agreements are not legally binding in the UK (as they are in Australia and the US) and they are also not of much interest if neither of you brings any assets into the marriage (or if you bring equal assets into the relationship) but that doesn't mean they aren't worth considering anyway. If you do end up in court they will give a judge an idea of what your pre-marital intentions were but also because in discussing one you will both end up with a clear idea of each other's financial assets and aims. It's a good way to get the conversation going – to force communication. Prenups are particularly advisable, by the way, if you are marrying late or for a second time and already have children: you don't want to get divorced and see your assets end up in the hands of the children of your ex rather than those of your own children.

If you do go ahead with a prenup you might want to keep it under regular review: after you've had a man's baby and given up your job to care for it you may feel differently about how much money you are entitled to in a divorce. Note that to give it as much validity as possible you will both want to take independent advice on the document, it has to be reasonably fair (if you sign something saying you don't want a penny, it will be ignored), both parties have to have made full disclosure of all their money in advance of the deal being signed and it has to be clear to the judge that both parties signed it entirely voluntarily.

The cost of dating

Life may be cheaper once you've found a husband but it's pretty pricey in the run-up. According to NSI figures 25% of women raid their savings to buy new clothes before a first date, while American Express research in 2006 found that the average date in the UK costs £120. Given that most people tend to go on at least three dates before they decide if there is mileage in the relationship that adds up fast. Finding love isn't cheap. Then again neither is staying single. The only financial benefit to it is the 25% you get off your council tax. Everywhere else you pay a singles supplement: holidays are more expensive, travel insurance is more expensive (families get discounts) and so is car insurance (insurers see single people as higher risk than married). And of course you'll probably go out more, much more. Add it all up and it's probably worth persisting with the dating.

After the honeymoon

You need to make clear decisions about how you want your finances to work inside your marriage. Marriage is probably the most important contract any of us will ever enter into but too many of us mess it up before we even walk up the aisle by going into it with no discussion of how its practicalities will work and no knowledge of the financial personality of our husband-to-be. This may have made some sense 100 years ago when men automatically took charge of almost everything anyway, but it makes no sense now. The odds are that when you marry you'll both be working and earning so you'll need to lay down ground

265

rules about how things are paid for and how your finances are joined and separated. You don't want complete financial separation – there's something very odd about watching married couples paying for their dinner separately as I have seen some friends do. But you don't want to sacrifice your independence either. So what's the solution?

Communication and a system. Talking about money is tough – you may think it impinges somehow on the romance of your perfect love, but if you talk about it properly now, I think you will find your love will last longer than if you do not. You may have found out all you need to know about your husband's attitude to money during the wedding and possibly the prenup conversations but if not now's the time to start. If you can sleep in the same bed together, have sex and share food, you can talk about money. So, is he a spender or a saver? How much money does he have saved up? How much debt does he have (remember, post-marriage his debt is your debt)? How much money does he earn? Is he a risk-taker or a risk-shirker? You have to talk about it to find out where you both stand and be able to manage your money together. You also want to share your dreams so you can make sure you are both working towards the same goals with your work and your savings: what if you are saving to retire early to the south of France when his dream is to climb the promotion tree at work until he can afford a swanky pad in Notting Hill? Note that 64% of people surveyed told NSI last year that they felt financial security was important to the success of their relationships. But if they don't talk about it properly how will they know if they have financial security?

You may find that you don't feel quite the same about money, but recognize that a shared approach to it is important. This is bound to mean making compromises and this is another reason to make sure all the money conversations come early in a relationship, when you are both in the mood for compromise and before the red bills start arriving.

"It's like a comedy everyone's so flash. It's like who's got the best watch on, who's got the best bag, which wife is dressed best, which wife's got the best hair? I'm like, I've got my own career...... If I'm going shopping I'll pay with the money I've worked hard for...... I was in Girls Aloud before I met Ashley and have my own successful career. I'm not going to quit the band and sit around in the sun all day or go shopping with Ashley's plastic."

Cheryl Tweedy, pop singer and wife of footballer Ashley Cole, on footballers' wives

So what's the system? There is no one way of doing it, everyone has different ideas about what makes sense, but my husband and I thought about it very carefully before our wedding. Our solution leaves us both with our independence and our own money but it gives us a way to pay all our joint bills fairly. But best of all it removes the difficulties surrounding who might make more and who make less. It doesn't have us contributing to our household equally in absolute terms but it has us contributing fairly. Fair is

Doing the numbers on the system

Partner A nets £1,000 a month and Partner B nets £1,500 a month. The couple's monthly income is £2,500. They decide that their joint account needs £1,750 a month to cover all their expenses. This is 70% of their joint income. The result? They must both contribute 70% of their individual income to the joint pot. A puts in £700 and B puts in £1,050. A then has £300 left for personal spending and B has £450. In an ideal world I would then like B to give A £75 to equalize their personal spending money (they'd have £375 each) but I know that might not be an easy sell.

the key and I don't think that when one person earns more than the other (as is usually the case) paying the bills 50/50 is fair at all. Our system also has the advantage of being fair to the extent that should one of us stop working, short or long term, that person won't feel financially dependent on the other.

It works like this: our salaries continue to be paid into our personal accounts and we continue to use those accounts for our personal expenses (fishing gear in his case, Starbucks coffee and shoes in mine) but we also pay a percentage of our salaries into our joint account, which pays for our mortgage, household bills, joint expenses (holidays, dinners out, etc.) and also our joint savings. We added up our total joint income. Then figured out how much we needed in our joint account every month, worked that out as a percentage of the total and then both agreed to contribute that percentage of our net incomes to the account (see the box for calculations). The key here is that it is a percentage not an absolute amount so that whoever earns more pays in proportionally more but once in the account the money is considered to belong to both of us. One-off income is dealt with in the same sort of way: if one of us gets a bonus for example the appropriate percentage of it is deposited in our joint savings account.

This doesn't make that much difference right now. But if I decide to stay at home with children for a few years and perhaps work at home one day a week or so it means that my contributions to the account will plummet but that my right to consider it as much my money as my husband's money will not. The only problem with the system is that it can still leave partners with wildly different surpluses in their own accounts (in the example above one partner has 50% more personal spending money than the other, for instance). I think this needs addressing too: in an ideal world the higher earning partner should hand over some of their surplus to the other so that their spending power is equalized. This is particularly the case if one partner suddenly sees their income fall dramatically: it makes sense to agree that if you stop working half your husband's surplus over and above the needs of the joint account will be diverted to you so that you never find yourself in the situation I have seen so many women in of having to ask their husbands for money to buy their mothers a birthday present.

Instead your spending power will remain equal and you will both continue to feel independent. Not all men are going to agree to this one in a hurry; the idea that work in the home is as valuable as work outside it may have been one of the most basic tenets of the feminist revolution but that doesn't mean many men ever actually agreed with it. But it is worth persevering to get a deal done in the early days (i.e. before the need to split his surplus actually arises) when you are in a reasonably strong position; leave it until you need it and it'll be a lot harder.

I have noticed, by the way, in conversations researching this book that in cases where the woman earns the most my system is very often used – making all the household income a joint income makes sense to men then. But when the man earns the most it is rarely used – instead the woman gets an allowance; her disposable income is in his gift. That isn't quite right! As far as I can see our system should work well in all households, whether both or only one partner is working. It isn't the only system out there but I think it is the best one.

Having just one joint account into which all the family income goes seems like a nice idea but it doesn't quite work, as it doesn't give each party any independence. If you want to buy your husband a birthday present do you really want to do it out of a

joint account? And do you really want any treats you buy for yourself to come out of a joint account? It's also asking for rows. What if one partner does almost no personal spending from the account and the other spends every Saturday morning having an aromatherapy massage at £70 a go? It's just not fair. And as I keep saying, fair is the key to success with a money marriage system.

> "I'm sick of everyone saying I married my husband for his money. It just happens that I get turned on by liver spots."
> Anna Nicole Smith

I can't overstate the importance of making some kind of financial arrangement such as ours. And the sooner the better. The longer you leave it the harder it will be: financial resentments build up fast and stay for ever. It's also the case that while a lot of modern marriages these days start off equal in financial terms we all know they don't stay equal. The *Guardian* can run as many articles as it likes about house husbands but the truth is that they are rarer than a non-sexist boss in the City. The fact is that women have a habit of having children. So they work outside the house less, their income falls and if they haven't sorted things out at home they suddenly find themselves financially dependent. This isn't a nice feeling, particularly for the 23% of married women in the UK who have no joint accounts with their spouses, but it is a very common one. And there is only one way to prevent it happening: you need to make sure that your joint accounts really are considered to belong to you both.

It's also important to think about joint savings. Anything left over from our joint account at the end of the month goes into our joint

savings account and we then discuss together its
destination from there. This again is of the
utmost importance. Too many women leave
what should be joint investment decisions
in the hands of their husbands and have
no idea how it all works. My grandmother
was like this (she didn't even have her own
cheque guarantee card until my grandfather died and
when we got her one she didn't have a clue what to do
with it), after a few bad experiences my mother is not,
but to my horror some of my friends still are. I asked one
recently how she intended to invest her new baby's Child Trust
Fund. Her answer? 'I don't know, Stuart deals with that sort of
thing.' London's networking queen Carol Stone told me that while
she's 'extremely organized and efficient' at running her own
business it wasn't until her husband was suddenly rushed to
hospital with stomach pains last year that she realized she had no
idea if they had any health insurance or not. Too many women
still think that marriage gives them a fine opportunity to pass on
the bother of making long-term financial decisions to their
husbands.

A survey last year from market research company Synovate
announced with great satisfaction that 80% of UK women now
say that they are given an equal say in decisions about whether to
buy big-ticket items such as cars and properties. How great, said
the papers that reported it, that feminism has come so far. Hmm.
I think it is a horrible sign it hasn't come nearly far enough.
Twenty per cent of British women still get no say in what kind of
car their household has? Worse, however, is the fact that had the
survey asked about pensions and ISAs the number of women who
said they played an active part in the decision-making would have

been an awful lot lower. It's amazing how many young women think they don't have to deal with family finances and how very wrong they are.

We already know that overall men aren't as good at investing as women and we also know that we are likely to live longer than our husbands so why would we let them deal with our family savings and investments alone? If they make mistakes we'll be the ones dealing with the consequences of those mistakes in our old age. We may still make mistakes if we deal with our finances together but at least we won't be able to blame the other party. We also won't ever find ourselves in what we might call a Tessa Tragedy.

In 2006 Tessa Jowell proved herself to be precisely the kind of woman I talked about in the Introduction: one who couldn't have been much more successful career-wise (she was Secretary of State for Culture, Media and Sport at the time) but who simply hasn't got to grips with money. When her husband David Mills appeared to get caught up in a variety of financial shenanigans in Italy, some of which centred around the remortgaging of their house, the presenter on *Woman's Hour* asked her: 'As the feminist you are, are we to believe that you signed a mortgage form on your home for your husband without knowing exactly how it was going to be paid back?' Jowell had no answer. She muttered about how she signed a form that allowed the bank to 'take a charge on our house in order that my husband could buy some investments that he wanted to do'. She didn't, she says, ask him what the money was really for or when it would be paid back because 'I was perfectly happy, in the division of our finances, to sign the charge.' Should she have been? Of course not. The division of finances in her household was clearly wrong: household financial decisions should not be divided, they should be shared. Jowell and Mills separated soon after.

The final reason to stay on top of family finances – should you need any more – is divorce. Around 40% of marriages now end badly: many women find that when they get divorced and are already an emotional wreck they suddenly have to think about money for the first time. They have to find out from scratch how much they are worth as a couple and hence how much they might be worth alone. Then they have to organize their own money for the first time. That doesn't make divorce any easier.

Keeping your career

Terry Martin Hekker is a woman who should act as a living lesson to all of us. For years she was a rabid cheerleader for the stay-at-home housewife and mother: her book *Since Adam and Eve*, published in 1980, was a bestseller and she toured the world explaining the benefits of housewifery and the emotional support of husbands. Then something happened to change her mind. After 40 years of marriage her husband presented her with divorce papers. She couldn't believe it. She had, she said, thought being married was a 'tenured position', that she had a deal with her husband: she kept house nicely and he stuck around. Not so. Instead he had found a younger 'sleeker model' and she was 'cancelled'.

She got some alimony but it was less than her housekeeping allowance had once been. Having not been near a formal workplace for decades and having very little in the way of work-related skills she wound up in low-paid work and relative hardship. Divorce settlements are fairer than they used to be but you can still be pretty sure that if your marriage ends you are going to need to support yourself: one of the reasons modern marriage demands self-sufficiency is because so many people leave it. As Hekker says, marriage used to be a long-term contract but today married women need to look out for themselves: to be ready 'for being abandoned so that if you end up alone you will have the skills to look after yourself'.

That means that you always need to have one eye on your career: don't ever just give it up to live on your husband's income and if you have children and take a career break do it thoughtfully. The longer you take off for children or for housewifery the harder it will be to get back in. Out too long and you'll come back to a rubbish title and low pay. So always be aware that you might have to go back. Keep your contacts, consult if you can and network at any opportunity. Also consider charity or part-time work to keep your hand in. Never forget that you don't know how life will turn out – you might get divorced, your husband may lose his job. And if you ever find yourself thinking that none of these things will happen to you, think of Terry Hekker selling her engagement ring to pay for her basic living expenses while her husband of 40 years partied in Mexico with his new lover.

Note too that it doesn't have to be financial hardship that pushes you back into the workplace. It could be babies. For every friend I have who revelled in nappies and milky smiles I have another who couldn't get back to work fast enough. 'The door shutting behind me as I leave the house on a Monday morning is the sweetest sound there is,' says one.

Your bank account and your career are your routes to freedom should you need them. You worked hard for them: don't let marriage mean you lose them.

Taxes and togetherness

It used to be that getting married wasn't just about love but about money too – you got great tax breaks for tying the knot. These days the taxman doesn't reward your love quite so well but he does none the less offer a couple of small bonuses. You can, for example, shift assets between yourselves to use up allowances and cut capital gains and income taxes. Say that one of you is working and the other not. Any income-producing assets (shares paying dividends or savings accounts paying interest) should move into the name of the non-earner to use up their income tax allowance. And if one of you is selling an asset that might push your capital gains over the annual allowance you can transfer the asset to the other before sale to take advantage of their allowance too. You can also avoid some inheritance tax, as there is none to pay on assets left to spouses. But that, I am afraid, is about it.

Making a will

You may think that all your money will automatically go to your husband when you die, leaving no need for a will. But you'd be wrong. Instead, if you have no children, he will get the first £200,000 worth and half of the rest (the remainder goes to your parents if they are alive and your siblings or other relatives if they are not). If you have children he will get £125,000 of your assets and a life interest in half of the remainder (the rest goes to the children when they are 18). If that's not what you want you will definitely need a will. This can be simple – you can get a kit from

WH Smith for a few pounds, write it up and have two witnesses sign it and you're all done.

Living in sin: the bad news about not being married

In 1965 5% of couples dared to live together before they got married. Now 70% do. There are over 2 million couples living together, a rise of 50% in the last decade, and it is estimated that there will be 4 million within the next 25 years. The problem with this is that most of the 2 million women who live with someone they aren't married to think that their union gives them some rights. They believe in common-law marriage: the idea that if you've been living with someone for a long time as though you were married to them you have roughly the same legal and financial rights as if you were actually married to them. Bad news: you don't. In fact you don't have any rights at all. If you live in a house with a man and the house is in his name, he can just ask you to leave. With nothing. It doesn't matter how long you've lived there and it doesn't matter how much you have contributed to the costs of the house, to the general household bills or even to the mortgage over the years: if the house or part of the house isn't actually in your name, you have no *set* legal rights to any share of it and that's that. You are on your own. When you split, he'll get the house and you'll get a leftover can of baked beans and your DVD collection back – if you're lucky. If you want legal rights you have to get married: marriage is a union in law, cohabitation is not.

And if you don't want to get married you will have to make other arrangements to protect yourself. You might find it hard to imagine that you will split up with your partner but on average you will do so after three years. And you might find it hard to believe that your partner will be unfair when the time comes, but all the evidence suggests that he will be. This means that if you are pooling your money in any way at all you will need to write a lot of contracts as you go.

Start with the house. When you buy together you can do so in two ways, as joint tenants or as tenants in common. With the latter you own the property in shares in accordance with your contributions to the purchase. When you die that share is passed on according to your will. With the former you own the house in equal shares and when one of you dies it automatically passes in full to the other (although the recipient might then be liable for inheritance tax on it). Make sure that you buy your property in one of these ways if you buy together. Either way, get your name on the title deed and if you paid more of the deposit or pay more of the mortgage get that in writing too. Otherwise, if you move into a house already owned by your partner and you contribute towards its upkeep and mortgage you can get a solicitor to make up a trust deed for you specifying that you are entitled to a share of it and what that share is. If you rent you will want to look at your tenancy arrangement too. If it is in his name you have no right to stay if your partner asks you to leave or if he dies.

Next you will want to make a will. If you do not your partner will get absolutely nothing when you die – it will all go to your blood relations. This may be what you want but if it is not make a will fast, defining your partner as your next of kin. You might want to draw up a list of your possessions and how you think they should be divided if you split up. This isn't legally enforceable but it might keep the rows to a minimum when the time comes. If your partner isn't nuts about doing all this perhaps you shouldn't be cohabiting with him. And perhaps you shouldn't be having children with him.

For more on how to put a legal structure around your relationship without getting married see **www.advicenow.org.gov/livingtogether**.

WHAT Do I Do Now?

- Get married.

- Don't ask for money as a wedding present: if you don't need any household goods don't ask for anything at all. It's just tacky.

- Consider a prenup: they aren't legally binding in the UK but they do set out each partner's intentions and as such may be useful to both of you.

- Don't lose your own identity: have your own accounts and your own cards.

- Don't sever your ties with your career, ever.

- Save for your own retirement.

- Be frank about money: you must be able to discuss things openly and make decisions together. If you don't know how much he earns, or how much debt he is running up you're in trouble (it's your debt too now).

- Take advantage of any tax breaks you can.

- Don't do everything yourself: it doesn't matter how much men say they understand that housework in a dual-income house should be shared, it never happens. These constraints will hold you back, hold back your income and hold your family back as a result. Make a deal with your husband early. On the plus side all this free time is ill used by men – they get bored. A study by Victoria University in Australia found that while they have more leisure time than us they don't spend it in 'meaningful activity'. Instead they watch TV, play computer games or just do nothing. Boredom meant they smoked more, drank more and sat around more – obesity, diabetes and early death, anyone?

- Make a will.

9
Children
Nuturing with Your Money

In the first five years of your child's life it will cost you an average of £46,695 to provide for their needs. You will then spend another £31,000 on looking after them between the ages of 6 and 11 and another £33,747 on the same during their teens. And it doesn't stop there. The rising cost of university means that parents get hit for another £30,000 in their child's nineteenth, twentieth and twenty-first years. In all, it costs parents £140,398 to nurture their child into adulthood. That, according to the Halifax, is more than the cost of an average house. It's lucky we love our children more than we love our houses.

The cost of a baby

£2,350: the average spend on essentials such as nappies, clothes and toys in year one (Abbey).

£795 million: the amount spent annually on children's hobbies such as ballet and riding (Halifax).

£9,500: the amount parents spend on 'extras' such as field trips during the time their child is being educated in the state system (Birmingham Midshires).

£8.13 billion: the total amount parents spend on their children's education every year – including uniforms, school trips and fees (Capital One).

£13,000: the average final-year debt of a medical student (Children's Mutual).

£200,000: the average total cost of sending a child to a private day school.

£330,000: the average total cost of sending a child to a private boarding school.

£140,398: the cost of raising one child to adulthood (Liverpool Victoria Friendly Society).

£405: the average spent by mothers on designer-label clothes for their under-threes, every year (MINT).

£124: the amount they spend on designer labels for themselves.

£24,000: the value of the work of a mother in the house every year (Legal and General). This number was calculated using average wage figures for cleaners, cooks, childcare workers and drivers. The average mother serves her family for 66 hours a week, making her total annual value higher than the national average wage.

£172 million: the cost of the damage done to property by toddlers in 2005 (Direct Line).

£8.37: the average pocket money per child paid weekly across the UK in 2004 (Halifax).

£1.4 billion: the amount spent on Christmas presents for children in 2005 (Abbey).

£4,800: the cost of a pre-university gap year (Mintel).

£50: what the average parent spends per child on entertainment every week during the summer holidays (Daycare Trust).

£3,212: the family spend on 'outings' every year. The average family ticket to a theme park costs £80 (*Mother and Baby* magazine).

£64: the weekly cost of a 16-year-old.

£40,000: what it will cost to give a child a university education in 18 years' time (Abbey). It currently costs around £25,000.

Babies. What a shock they are. First they take over your body, then they take everything else – all your free time, all your space, most of your brain and, in the end, all your money. When you don't have a baby you look at people who do and wonder why they need so much stuff. Then when you have a baby you understand. They just need stuff. As soon as children enter your life, your costs go up (they need a lot for such tiny beings) and your income usually goes down (as you take maternity leave and then try to slash your hours in the office). And things carry on that way for a long, long time: the older your child gets the more they are going to cost you. It used to be you could say goodbye to your child financially at age 18. Not any more: university fees and the UK's insane housing costs mean that you are going to be paying out for another three years at least. Parenting is always more expensive than anyone thinks it is going to be.

So what do you do? The point of this chapter is to try to answer that question. I'm going to look at spending on your child and saving for your child as well as the thorny issue of whether you should or shouldn't be going back to work when your maternity leave ends and your rights in the workplace if you do go back.

Maternity leave: from commuting to cuddling

The sooner you tell your office you are pregnant the better. You don't actually have to do it until 15 weeks before the baby is due but if you want everyone to get used to the idea and there to be ample time to arrange cover for you and so on you might be wise

Shopping for your baby

Nothing is more exciting than pregnancy. Not only are you getting a new baby but that new baby is going to need stuff, lots of stuff. Everyone you meet will tell you about a special something you won't be able to do without. Special breast-feeding chairs, baby baths and playmats, special chairs, prams, cushions, cots and bras. It's a licence to shop!

But before you launch yourself into Mothercare at speed remember this. The baby/child stuff industry finds it even easier to tap into our emotions and to make us shop than any other industry (even the wedding industry). When it comes to our children we'll do anything and buy anything to make sure they are safe, to make sure they are warm and sleeping well and of course to make sure they develop faster than the baby born in the next-door bed. When we are pregnant and when we are the mothers of small children we are sitting ducks for the marketing men. The result? We spend thousands more on our children than we need to, buying new when we should buy second-hand (that's what eBay is for), or borrow (that's what sisters-in-law and friends are for) or not buy at all.

Let's face it. Clever as your baby is, they can't tell the difference between a new Fisher-Price musical clock and a second-hand one and if they could they wouldn't care anyway. The same goes for prams (a new Bugaboo is generally in no way superior to a hand-me-down from your cousin), clothes, playmates, car seats and cots. And when it comes to baby safety you generally need more in the way of common sense than products – something to bear in mind as the retailers do all they can to play on your baby paranoia. I once saw advertised for sale a special shopping trolley seat cover you could use in supermarkets to make sure that your child doesn't touch anything that isn't spotless. 'I didn't want my son to hold the germy metal handle of the carts,' Missy Cohen-Fiffe, the designer of the 'Clean Shopper' told the *New York Times*. Hmm.

Before our baby was born we bought a pram, a small cardboard cot (only £27 and biodegradable too!), a starter kit of Babygros, two swaddling blankets and some breast milk-expressing equipment. Everything else we thought we might need immediately (a car seat, baby sleeping bags, ear plugs) we borrowed and then we just waited to see what we would really need. It turned out that we needed quite a lot, but nowhere near the amount of things the industry propaganda and baby-shopping services told us we would need. There is one basic fact to remember with babies: they change so fast that anything you think they need on a Monday will probably no longer be needed or wanted on a Friday.

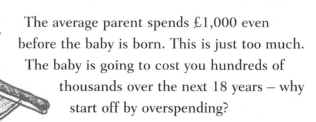

The average parent spends £1,000 even before the baby is born. This is just too much. The baby is going to cost you hundreds of thousands over the next 18 years – why start off by overspending?

to do it at nearer 12 weeks. Then you need to find out what's on offer in terms of maternity leave at your firm. Some companies offer fabulous benefits so you may find that you have little in the way of financial worry. Others offer just the statutory minimum, which means you need to get saving to cover some of the costs you are going to be hit with when you aren't working but your baby is growing – fast. Everyone gets statutory maternity leave (i.e. the right not to be at work but to have your job kept for you) for 26 weeks and provided you've been with your employer for at least 26 weeks by the beginning of the fifteenth week that your baby is due (i.e. you worked for a couple of months before you conceived) you will be entitled to be paid during those 26 weeks. If you qualify to be paid you will then qualify for another 26 weeks off (so 52 weeks in total).

So how much do you get paid? Usually not very much. Basic maternity pay is 90% of your salary for the first 6 weeks and £106 a week for the remaining 20 weeks of the first 26 weeks of maternity leave. Most people will find that this is all they get. However, some will do better. It is rare to be paid anything for more than six months (employers really don't want you to be away for longer than that) but those in professional white-collar jobs will often find that they get 90% of their salary for four or five months and some will even get 100% for up to six months: the more valuable you are to your employer the more likely they are to pay you proper money while you are off. A word of warning, however. A lot of these good payouts come with a sting in the tail: if you don't return to work by the end of the 52-week period you have to pay the money back. This seems entirely reasonable but it does mean that if you aren't sure whether you are going back to work or not you had better not spend your maternity pay. Keep it in a separate account until you know what your plans are.

The key for most people when it comes to financial survival during maternity leave is to spend as little as possible in the run-up to the birth: the more you save pre-birth the more you'll have to spend post-birth. The good news is that saving money isn't that hard when you are pregnant. Once you've bought a few bits of stretchy black jersey clothing you won't need anything else except for a few ugly bras for the next nine months and you won't be going out much either – no late nights, no cocktails and not much in the way of expensive dinners out. I barely spent a penny when I was pregnant (except on vast amounts of cake). Saving is also pretty easy in the few months after the birth: in the first six months of being a mother I found out exactly how much babies hate shopping.

Next you have to make the really big decision. Are you going back to work? There are many non-financial things to think about here. But before you start thinking about it in emotional terms you need to do your sums too. How much will it cost you to go back? First look at the cost of childcare. Then add up all the other expenses of working. A survey from Benjys in 2005 showed that it then cost the average woman £4,000 a year to work. We spend £1,300 on commuting, £1,060 on office clothes and accessories and the rest on incidental expenses such as dry-cleaning, after-work drinks, colleagues' birthday presents and food and drink during the day (£352 on breakfast at our desks, £422 on coffee and snacks). Over a lifetime this adds up to a total of £170,000. Can you cover all this and clear enough cash at the end of each month to make working worthwhile? If your costs are greater than your salary you probably aren't going back to work for now. You'd effectively be paying for the privilege of doing so and who wants to do that? There is a case to be made for working even if it makes you very little – see below – but it isn't an easy decision.

But what if working does make you money. It may be that you don't in fact have a choice between working and not working. With the cost of living as high as it is and housing costs being the burden they are, many women have to work: they need two incomes to stay afloat. It may not be your passion for work but your mortgage that forces you back to the office after six months. If you have to work you have to work and that is that. I saw a survey in *New Woman* once that had 7 out of 10 women saying they didn't want to work as hard as their parents' generation and 1 in 4 saying they would be chucking in work if they had babies. All very well, except that these same women admitted to being up to their eyeballs in debt with 7 out of 10 saying they spent more than they earned. They may want to stay at home but odds are they just won't be able to afford it. Wanting, as ever, isn't getting.

But what if you can afford it? What if your partner can support you as a stay-at-home mother if that's what you want? What then?

This is where it gets tricky. The basic choice is this: you can maintain your financial independence and leave your child in someone else's hands or you can give it up and look after your own baby. And you know what? It doesn't matter which one you choose, someone's going to make you feel bad about it. My plan? To make you feel bad about wanting to be a full-time mother for more than a few years. I've banged on endlessly in this book about the absolute necessity of maintaining financial independence: you have to be capable of self-sufficiency even within marriage because one day you might find that you have to be self-sufficient. And if you stay at home for 15 years making beds and changing nappies you won't have a hope alone. Remember the case of Terry Hekker? And remember the statistics on divorcees living in poverty for want of a pension of their own? Divorce judges are getting much better at compensating women in some way for careers lost to childcare but mostly when ordinary couples divorce there isn't enough cash to set up two new homes and two new lifestyles in any comfort at all: if you can't bring home at least some of your own bacon you will have a miserable time. You have to be able to take care of yourself and that means that you have to – in however small a way – stay connected to the workplace.

Feminism has been hugely successful. It isn't complete – recent research shows that bank managers still routinely assume that women are worse risks than men and lend them less as a result, for example – but it isn't far off. Until the 1970s it was practically impossible for a women to take out a mortgage without a man acting as her guarantor; until 1990 women were not treated as separate entities from their husband for tax purposes (even Mrs Thatcher); and until a few decades ago it was perfectly legal to discriminate against women in the workplace simply because they were women. All this sounds ridiculous now but changing it – to allow women to have the financial tools to create their own independence – was a long hard battle. That's why my heart sinks when I read surveys like a recent one from *New Woman* in which more than 50% of women said they would be happy to live entirely

The best time for baby

When's the best time to have a baby? It's the question that most vexes modern women. Do you have your children in your early twenties when you know you are most likely to be able to conceive, or do you have your fun and get your career under way and then have them in your thirties and even forties? As far as the medical profession is concerned, there are huge advantages to it being your twenties. Wait until your thirties, they say, and your chances of conception are vastly reduced. There are constant scares, avidly reported by the *Daily Mail*, about the baby hunger of the selfish women who put work before babies and are now being punished for it with sterility. It may be true. I don't know. All I know is that I can't imagine where the *Mail* finds all these case studies of women who can't get pregnant in their thirties. So far I know of only one person in their thirties who has wanted a baby and found that they have not managed to have one. I also know that I was pregnant within 24 hours of walking down the aisle (at 35). That it has taken my sister two weeks from thinking she might have a baby to being pregnant on two occasions (aged 36 and 37), that my mother conceived her last child naturally at 46 and that my grandmother had her last child at 41.

Does it happen? Of course it does, but there are women of every age who can't conceive and I'm yet to be convinced that women who wait have only themselves to blame. How do we know how many career women would have trouble conceiving in their twenties given so few try? And how do we know that the women having trouble at 35 wouldn't have had trouble at 25? The statistical evidence seems pretty muddled to me and whatever the doctors say the fact is that 23% of first babies are born to women over 30 and 1 in 7 women in England now conceives after 35.

So that's the fertility scaremongers dealt with. Don't let them get to you! But what of your career and your babies? There are two camps here: the have them early, get it out of the way and then have a career camp; and the get your career going and then have them camp. I fall very firmly into the latter, a stance strongly backed up by the numbers.

According to research by Amalia Miller of the University of Virginia there are very rational reasons for putting off becoming a mother. On average, the younger a university-educated woman has a baby, the less she will earn over a lifetime. A 24-year-old who has a child will earn 10% less than a 25-year-old until retirement; a 25-year-old 10% less than a 26-year-old and so on. The optimum time financially to have a baby is 30 or later, when your career is firmly on track and you have something to come back to. Women further down the career tree when they give birth very often just stop climbing it. Why? Their salaries aren't high enough to pay for childcare and their jobs aren't yet senior and interesting enough to drag them away from their babies. And even if they do go back to work they are unable to put in the long hours the workplace requires of juniors trying to get ahead these days so they are fast overtaken by ambitious co-workers without dependants. If they wait until they are more senior in an organization they will have the clout to demand flexible hours and the confidence to go home when they need to.

> Miller's research is backed up by research done in the UK by the Institute of Public Policy Research. This suggests that women face a 'fertility penalty' if they have their first baby early. A mid-skilled woman on a salary of £22,000 who has a baby at 24 will earn £564,000 less over her lifetime than a childless woman. If she waits until 28 that figure drops to £165,000 and so on. So there you go. Enough with the guilt about delaying motherhood. Doing so makes perfect financial sense. The longer you wait the less it will hurt (career-wise that is).

off a rich man and that they'd not mind posing topless in men's magazines for money.

It sinks too when I read the rantings of the members of the so-called 'cupcake revolution': the women working to convince us that being a housewife is fulfilling in itself, that it isn't a backward step but a forward one – they even have a name for it: 'choice feminism'. There is a lot of muck talked about the romance and joy of being at home. And it may be true that full-time housewifery and mothering works for some people but it clearly isn't enough for the majority or the feminist revolution would never have happened: if dusting and washing were so much fun why would anyone have bothered fighting so hard for the right to vote, to be educated and then to become a middle manager?

The truth is that much of being at home is repetitive and boring. It isn't fun and it isn't particularly sexy either. There may have been a time when being a full-time stay-at-homer was all most women were capable of doing (pre-contraception anyone remotely fertile was usually either pregnant or breastfeeding) but these days most mothers only have a couple of children each and after they've left home we live for another 30–40 years. How can motherhood be enough to fill all that time? And as for most of the women who turn up on chat shows, in the *Daily Mail*, as authors of odd books such as Darla Shine's *Happy Housewives* and writers for a scary new American magazine called *Total 180* ('The magazine for the professional woman turned stay at home mom'), I've noticed one common thread between them: they have plenty of cash. Not working probably looks pretty good when you can have childcare, a cleaner and two skinny lattes a day regardless. In the US the percentage of women with small children not working is rising fast (up 15% in a decade) and the highest drop-out rate is among the best educated and the best paid.

We mustn't let ourselves be guilted by these people into thinking that our children will only develop properly if we dedicate ourselves to their well-being. It just isn't true. The stay-at-home lobby has somehow managed to convince us that traditionally mothers have been full-time mothers but they haven't. They've been non-working mothers but until very recently that simply wasn't the same thing. Rich women have never looked after their own children. Until relatively recently they even hired other people to breastfeed them, for heaven's sake. Even middle-class women used nannies to do most of the work until the turn of the last century. And poor women certainly never looked after their children in the way we think we should now: as Carol Sarler pointed out in a recent *Times* column they worked in fields and in factories 'with babies strapped to them until they had given birth to enough of them that the older cared for the younger in a haphazard daisy chain of comfort'. And until not so long ago most women were full-time housekeepers however, many children they had. Think no freezer, says Sarler, no fridge, no pre-trimmed beans, no washing machines, no tumble dryers and so on. Pure drudgery.

'Traditional' mothers didn't have time for endless reading of *The Hungry Caterpillar* and several hours of educational play a day: instead they barely sat down. The full-time mother is an entirely new concept, made possible only by the large number of labour-saving devices we all have at home. Still not convinced? Then consider this: a study done by Suzanne Bianchi at Maryland University found that mothers spent the same amount of time on average caring for their children in 2003 as they did in 1965: the time they spent working outside the home in 2003 was offset by the fact that, while they did get less sleep than before, thanks to the rise and rise of the household labour-saving device, they did less housework when they were at home.

It's also worth noting while we are at it that being at home full-time isn't always much good for your relationship. The *Journal of Family Issues* recently printed a paper pointing out that working women are less likely to have marital problems than those who stay at home. Why? I imagine that the family has less financial stresses than those with only one worker but it's a matter of conversation too: if you are out and about you have more in common with your partner than if you are not. How often do you read about men who leave one stay-at-home mum to run away with another? Not very often. By the time they've got around to leaving one stay-at-home wife they never want to have another conversation about how hard it is to get the kiddie parking spaces outside the supermarket ever again.

The new father

For years now the papers have been full of stories about house husbands and new-age dads: the men who give up their own careers to stay at home and look after babies. But the truth is there aren't very many of them about. Indeed far from embracing the new man within and taking on half the work that comes with a new baby most fathers are back working the same hours they were pre-baby within weeks of the birth. Research by Esther Dermott of the University of Bristol shows that men have changed – they certainly want to have more time with their children than their fathers did and they want to have a more emotional relationship than in the past – but not to the extent that they have any intention of adopting a 'female model' of parenthood. They aren't going to give up their work to look after children and they aren't going to go part-time and do both either. They like being involved but they aren't going to share childcare duties equally. They, unlike us, often get to have it all – enough time to bond with their babies but a career and a clean house too.

Finally, it is worth repeating one more time that two in five marriages end in divorce. You think it won't be yours but so does everyone, and two in five of them are wrong. So what happens when one of those is you? When it all goes wrong after 30 years and you are dumped a job might look pretty good, but if you haven't worked for 30 years your choices will be limited: hospital cleaning or supermarket checkout, anyone? You need to keep the ground for earning your own living constantly prepared. I'm not against full-time mothering for a second in theory, I just worry that in glorifying it we are falling back into a trap we have only recently escaped from: giving up our money and our independence to become domestic slaves subject to the whims of our breadwinners. That we might do so willingly doesn't make it any less frightening.

I'm not suggesting that all women with small babies work full-time. Absolutely not. If you can take a full year off and still go back to work, do it. If you can work three or four days a week, do it. If you can arrange to leave the office at three every day and then do your emails from home at night, do it. If you can work from home, do it. The generation that paved the way for women in the workplace – those who are currently 40–55 – are the ones who have really suffered for our freedom. They are the ones who have needed to work as much as or more than men to prove that it is possible. They've worked silly hours, delayed having families until their forties, pretended their children don't exist when they are at work and generally been overworked, overtired and overstressed. And mostly they've done it with no help from their partners – UK women still do 90% of the housework whether they work or not.

Thanks to them I don't think the next generation needs to work like that. We can have the confidence to reject the superwoman obsession. The principle that women are capable of giving birth and working too is now well established so our generation needs to move the workplace on one more step. We need to establish that it is entirely possible for a woman (and indeed a man) to be capable of doing a good job without actually working in an office from 8 a.m. to 6 p.m. every day. My generation was educated to think that they could have it all – children and a career just like a man's – but the generation above mine has proved that not only does that not quite work but we probably don't want the kind of 'all' we thought we did. We can't actually have children, work in the same way that men do and be happy. So let's demand not to have to. Instead we need to be able to find quality, well-paid work that comes with flexibility.

This is the next stage: we no longer just need the right to work but the right to work in a way that suits our sex. And it should be entirely possible. Women are going on 50% of the UK workforce – 70% of mothers now hold down a job of some kind. They need us as much as we need them so we have to keep on asking for what we need until we get it. I couldn't not work – 1980s feminism is burned into my soul – but I don't want to mould myself to fit work, I want work to mould to fit me.

The good news is that your employer is legally obliged to consider your requests for flexible hours. The Flexible Working Regulations which were introduced in 2003 give parents with children under the age of six the right to ask for flexible working arrangements including the right to work from home. So when you are ready to go back to work figure out what would work for you and ask for it – remember your office benefits too if you work from home: you'll cost less as you won't be using up office space, you'll be happier and more likely to stay in your job as well as being more committed and less likely to need sick days for yourself or your children. I'm not saying your employer will agree straight away. Bad attitudes are everywhere (I've been told that I didn't need as much money as the men I worked with because I didn't have a family to support – that was ten years ago and the man who said it was only in his forties and he's still a boss; do you think he has changed his attitude?). But if they refuse they have to explain why in writing and tell you how you can appeal against the decision.

So keep asking. The worst that can happen is that someone will say no. A survey from software company Inter-Tel recently showed that nearly 60% of office workers think requesting more flexible working practices would damage their career prospects. It shouldn't. And if it does don't forget you can get redress in industrial tribunals.

How to make working life easier

1 Don't be a martyr. There was a lad on *Big Brother* a few years ago who when asked what he learned in the house said, 'I learned how to wash up.' What a rod for her own back his mother made! What was she thinking? He was well into his twenties. Lastminute did a survey last year which found that the average British man has 41.5 hours a week – nearly 6 a day – me time. That's time entirely to himself to do as he pleases. Women have half that. They also get 10 hours' sleep a week less than men. The average woman also does 14 hours of housework a week. The average man? 2.5 hours. That'll be how he manages to meet up with friends for 18 hours a week compared to 6 hours for women. Note too that a Zurich University study found that while women are happier when only one of a couple works men are just as happy whether their wives worked or not. Why? Because it doesn't make any difference to them: 'Women still do most of the housework independent of whether they participate in the labour market or not.' The answer? You need help. You need it from a cleaner if both you and your husband work hard and you can afford it, but you also need it from your husband or partner: if you

both work he needs to do half the housework. Younger men are better at this than older men. My husband and I seem to have a pretty even split worked out and it seems to be standard among the under-35s for men to be as together in the kitchen as their wives.

2 Remember that, whatever the cupcake brigade may say, deciding to go back to work even if you don't absolutely have to is no comment on how much you love your children and shouldn't be thought of as such. I adore my daughter. But that doesn't mean I want to be with her and only her all the time. If it were an absolute choice – work or daughter – there would of course be no question. But it isn't an absolute choice. I can work four days a week and spend the early morning, the early evening and three days a week with my baby, so I choose both. And I think it works.

3 Remember that everyone knows your children come first so there is no need to apologize for it. Your conversations with your child carer don't need to be furtive. If they are necessary just have them.

4 Keep aiming high. The more senior you are the more likely you are to be able to force flexible working on your employers: 28% of new mothers return to work in a lower-paid job than they had pre-babies; among the lower-skilled that number rises to 50%.

5 Visit **www.workingmums.co.uk**, **www.womenlikeus.org.uk** and **www.mumsandworking.co.uk**. These sites specialize in finding work for qualified mothers who don't want to or can't spend five days a week in a traditional workplace. A huge number of mothers return to the workplace in jobs for which they are grossly

overqualified: they sell themselves cheap to get regular or flexible hours. It is a shocking waste of talent. This shouldn't be necessary and these websites are a good step in the right direction.

6 Don't let the myth of the superwoman make you feel inadequate. She did exist and we should all feel enormously grateful to her for the way she paved for us to the workplace. But we don't have to be like her. We can demand to work at different paces depending on our needs.

7 Remember we all want the same thing: a balance where we can make our children our priority but still fulfil ourselves in the workplace. And if we all keep asking for it we will get there in the end.

8 Remember that we are all muddling through.

Replacing you: the cost of childcare

Sixty per cent of mothers with children under five are now in full- or part-time work. And they are all going through exactly the same kind of anguish over childcare. Do you use family? Childminders? Nurseries or nannies? What's best and, more to the point, what can you afford? As I've already said, unless you love work for work's sake or have expectations of a large leap in salary, there is little point in going back to work immediately if you net only a few pounds a month for yourself after costs. And childcare certainly isn't cheap (not that there is any reason why it should be). The overall costs have risen by 25% in the last five years and parents now pay an average of £7,300 a year per child for care, according to childcare charity Daycare Trust. That's £142 a week, a sum that can soar to £500 a week in the summer. This means you need all the help you can get.

On the plus side there is help out there. You can get tax credits if your child is under one year old even if you have a family income of up to £66,000. If your income is low you can also get Working Tax Credit. The two are assessed together and can be applied for on a single form available from your local HM Revenue and Customs Office (**www.hmrc.gov.uk** or for information on all government assistance **www.direct.gov.uk/moneyandtaxbenefits**). This is worth doing. If your family income is, say, £30,000 and you have two children in childcare you could end up better off by nearly £10,000 a year. Even if your combined income is £50,000 you will still be better off by over £2,000. I'm not terribly in favour of the benefits system being extended so far up the income tree but as it is you might as well take advantage of it.

The next place to look is the childcare voucher system. Not all employers offer a voucher scheme but if yours does you should use it. It works like this. Instead of taking £238 of your salary in your pay cheque each month you take it as a voucher exchangeable for childcare with registered nurseries, nannies and childminders. This might sound pointless but here's the good bit: the voucher is given to you pretax so you end up paying no tax at all on that £238. This means basic rate tax payers can save a total of £858 a year in tax and higher rate tax payers can save £1,066 a year. Note that both parents can claim the relief, so if you are both working you can save a total of over £2,000 a year. That's effectively free money, something you don't get very often, so, if you can, make sure you take advantage of it. The other money you might want to put aside for childcare is your child benefit: £17.45 a week for your first child and £11.70 a week for each additional child may not seem like a fortune but it does make a difference.

Remember that while it is easy to assume that a nursery is the cheapest way to go when it comes to childcare, that isn't necessarily so: if you have more than one child or can perhaps share with a friend, a nanny may actually work out more cheaply, good news given that it is usually the case that a nanny is the best option for very young children: they need more personal care than they ever get in nurseries. If you do take the nanny option (and many do – there are 100,000-plus nannies working in the UK) remember that you will have to pay her taxes (she is your employee). This can be complicated, particularly if you are sharing, so it is probably worth taking advice or using an agency to sort it out for you. These will charge £180–£250 a year to do the taxes for you (see **www.nannytax.co.uk** or **www.nannypayroll.co.uk**). To find a nanny share in your area see **www.sharingcare.co.uk**. To find a registered childminder see **www.childcarelink.gov.uk**.

Finally, think about flexible working. Can you spend mornings in the office and then work from home after the baby is in bed? Can you shift down to four or even three days a week? With a bit of creative thought you might be able to rearrange your work so that less paid-for childcare is needed. You might also get away with taking your baby with you when it is very little. Mine went everywhere with me for her first five months when I was breastfeeding her. I changed her nappy on boardroom tables and breastfed her while having discussions about everything from American house prices to Chinese inflation. I've interviewed people for jobs while she chewed on their

How babies make you clever

For generations we've been told that having babies makes us stupid. But it just isn't true. Instead, as it turns out, it actually makes us cleverer. According to researchers from Richmond University, pregnancy improves our learning and memory skills and gives us enhanced sensory abilities. After childbirth our senses of smell and hearing are better. We also live longer than if we don't have children. Interestingly, this is particularly true of women who have babies in their forties – birth enhances their brain power just as middle age kicks in and starts cutting everyone else's.

Having a child is effectively 'a revolution for the brain', says Dr Michael Merzenich of the University of California. Brain cells thrive the more they are used and when you have a child you have to start using your brain in a whole new way. The bad news is that at the beginning our extra cleverness is hard to spot because we are so physically exhausted by giving birth and then getting up three times a night for two months (who isn't going to be a bit forgetful if their sleeping time is halved at the same time as their workload is doubled?). However, once the sleep deprivation bit is over we are left with a brain that has risen to a challenge and has an enhanced ability to multi-task. I haven't come across any formal studies that tell us whether that makes us better in the office or not but most employers I have spoken to tell me that mothers are their best employees. They are focused and efficient, balanced and hard-working, and best of all they practically never have hangovers.

CVs and had her sitting in her pram at the table in City restaurants. Was it a problem? Not when she was tiny – people are much more open to this kind of thing than you think – but I wouldn't do it any more. Once she was off the breast and old enough to want to play non-stop she got left behind.

Saving for the baby: your money, their gain

There is a very popular book for new parents called *What to Expect the First Year*. In the chapter on what to expect during the fourth month there is a list of things your baby should be able to do. One of these is 'pay attention to a raisin or other very small object'. This seems like an innocuous sort of idea but it is exactly the sort of thing that induces panic in a first-time parent. The result? Scores of sleep-deprived parents, keen to make sure their little ones are developing as they should, routinely spend hours trying to persuade reluctant babies to concentrate on raisins when they would much rather be sucking their fingers or staring at ceiling lights. Thinking about babies and saving, or investing, induces much the same kind of panic. But it really shouldn't. Yes, your children are going to want endless amounts of money but that doesn't necessarily mean you should be saving for them in a special way.

If you really want to secure your children's future you must first secure your own. Most people of new parenting age are in debt (the average under-30 has over £7,000 of non-mortgage debt) and have done little or nothing about saving for a pension. To start saving for your children before these things are sorted out is to get your priorities wrong: they won't thank you if you save a few thousand for them but they have to use that and more to pay your nursing home fees. According to research from Scottish Widows,

50% of women stop saving when they have children and most of those who do keep saving do so not for themselves (pensions, etc.) but for their families. They think that their children's needs today take precedence over their needs in the future, that it is selfish to put away money for the long term that might be needed in the short term. This is often an attitude they regret later. In fact your own financial security is one of the best gifts you can give your children: they may not know it now but in 30 years they'll be grateful.

"Saving is a fine thing, especially when your parents do it for you."
                                                    Winston Churchill

Once you are in the clear yourself you can start saving. But even then I can't see why it is necessary to save specially for babies: there is little tax advantage in it, so why not just save and invest the best you can and leave the choice of what to spend the money on until later? When your child is 18 you may want to finance them through university but you may also, after all those years of selflessness, prefer to spend it learning to kite-surf in Vietnam, and let them work in Tesco at the weekend. Who knows?

That said, there is one thing you must do for your child: decide what to do with their Child Trust Fund. Some time in the few months after your baby is born a voucher for £250 (or £500 if you are in a low-income family) will drop through the door. You are supposed to invest it in a fund and then encouraged to top it up by £1,200 a year so that when your child hits 18 they have a nice pot of cash built up to get them started in life. But once you've got it how on earth should you invest it? The answer is not a

simple one, but luckily, while pacing the corridor with a grizzly
baby on my shoulder every night, I had plenty of time to think
about it.

My first conclusion was that topping up your baby's CTF by the
allowed £1,200 a year might not be the best use of your money.
Why? Because when your child is 16 they will get the right to
manage the money themselves. You may have spent 16 years
carefully selecting the right shares and funds to give them the
best possible start in life, but if they fancy shifting the money into
start-up diamond explorers that will be their business. Then at 18
they get the cash. Just like that. So far no restrictions appear to
have been placed on how it is spent so they may take the money
and spend it on clothes. How will you feel about that if you want
it spent on university? If you topped up the fund it will be your
money – its existence in the fund will represent spending you
sacrificed years ago – yet instead of spending it on university they
might spend it on drink. I'm just not into the idea, particularly
given how contrary my little one looks like she is going to be. The
tax breaks on Child Trust Funds are great (you pay no income tax
on the income and no capital gains tax either) but I'm not sure
that's enough to make me want to place my money at the mercy
of the whims of a teenager.

None the less, I am, of course, going to invest the £250 we have
just received and the £250 she gets when she is seven years old.
But I am not going to do it prudently. There are three
ways of investing your CTF money. You can put it
into an approved savings account (and just
keep it in cash for the duration), into what's
called a stakeholder account (where it is
initially invested in equities and then shifted into

less risky investments as the child gets older), or you can opt for a shares account where the money is invested in the equity markets for the full 18 years (see **www.childtrustfund.gov.uk** for the full list of providers and eligible funds). The problem with the first two is that £500 invested in them is unlikely ever to amount to enough to help with the big things in life so I'm going for the third, and picking the riskiest fund I can in the hope that it works out and my little girl wakes up on her eighteenth birthday with enough money to keep the retailers of Oxford Street happy for many months at no expense to me.

However, there is one way it makes sense to top up a CTF: if grandparents, godparents and so on want to give cash to your child the CTF is probably a good place for it to go given how tax efficient it is. If it gets filled up, really is worth a meaningful amount in 18 years and your child then spends it sensibly that's great.

CTFs aside, I really wouldn't get drawn too far into specialist savings or investment products for your children. It is absolutely true that having a lump sum at some point in the future will make a vast difference to your child given today's housing and university costs but if you are in a position to offer one why can't it just come from your regular savings pot? That way it stays your money and you keep controlling it (as you should, you earned it after all). Most children's products are pretty useless anyway: children's investment funds have historically performed rather worse than ordinary adult schemes and designated children's savings accounts and bonds offer no better returns than ordinary ones.

The only thing you might consider is taking advantage of your child's personal income tax and capital gains allowances by designating an investment in their names but you need to be investing a reasonable amount to make this worth while and you run into the control issue again: anything you designate to them they get when they are 18. It is also often suggested that you start a pension for your baby – or encourage your parents to start a pension for your baby. As mentioned in Chapter 6 anyone can have a stakeholder pension (newborn babies included) and put in £2,808 a year (which will be £3,600 once tax relief is taken into account). If you do this for five years and then just leave it they'll have £370,000 by the time they are 65, assuming a growth rate of 5%. This sounds nice and may well work out just like the optimists think but I'd be wary of putting too much money into a pension that won't be accessible for more than half a century: pension legislation is endlessly fiddled with and there is no guarantee the money will be safe from the intrusive fingers of the taxman for so long.

Money education: the best thing you can do

The government's aim in introducing CTFs is to try and promote financial equality between young adults. This is an admirable idea but I'm not sure that this is the right way to do it. The thing is that inequality is rarely a matter of a couple of hundred quid here or there; instead it's a matter of education. Some people understand how bank accounts, mortgages, credit cards and compound interest really work and others do not. Those who do not are at serious risk of spending their entire lives struggling under the burden of unsuitable financial products sold to them by the financial services industry. Ignorance is far more likely to ruin a life than £250 is to improve it much: a study from the Institute for Public Policy Research in the US recently showed that children who are taught about personal finance at school are on average £32,000 richer by the time they hit their forties than those who are not. Twenty-eight US states have compulsory financial education. Given this evidence I would have much preferred the government to use the money going into CTFs in a different way – on making sure that every child gets the kind of financial education that could really make a difference to their futures.

Sadly, the education system doesn't look like it is going to be giving your children much of a financial education so you are going to have to do it yourself. If you don't they will have only the financial services industry to rely on for information. That's not good: the CTF tells them that money can be free; student loans tell them that there is nothing wrong with debt; the mortgage business tells them that borrowing five times their income for 30 years isn't a problem; and the credit card industry tells them that all glamorous people have debt. If you don't intervene your children really will grow up thinking that money grows on trees. So how do you educate your children?

The main answer here is by communicating with them. Many women, brought up in households where women didn't talk about money, still find it hard: they see money conversations as somehow rude or wrong. 'I just wasn't brought up ever to mention money,' says one 60-year-old. This got her into a great deal of trouble in her first marriage (the first time she knew about her husband's financial difficulties was when the bailiffs arrived) but it also meant that she never discussed money with her own children – why, she thought, should her innocent babies have to deal with learning about nasty realities. Big mistake. Her daughter, as a young adult, knows no more about money than she did when she opened the door to the bailiffs 35 years ago.

Money, the lack of it and how what there is should be used, is a huge part of every relationship. We've talked about how it affects your relationship with your partner but it is just as important with your children. They need to understand why they can't have everything they want. They need to know where money comes from, how it is worked for and how decisions are made about how it is spent. How else can they develop the skills they need to survive once they leave your house (which one assumes they will one day)? You won't help them run their futures by trying not to sully their present with money talk.

I'm not suggesting you should traumatize your toddlers with endless tales of your money woes, just that, like you, they should learn to think of spending in terms of earning (shouldn't they know that the trainers they want cost you 14 hours of work?), they should understand the balance between earning and enjoying and they should get from you the right messages about how to get that balance right.

Practical ways to do this include giving older children a set monthly allowance and not topping it up when it runs out, and linking money to responsibility by paying an extra amount for out-of-the-ordinary chores (not bed-making but car washing, for example). Lessons in saving and compounding are also of use: let smaller children see how their pocket money piles up if they don't spend it for a few weeks and how much more they can buy with it as a result. But the main way to be sure that your child learns to treat money with the respect it needs is to treat money with respect around them: show them that shopping isn't a recreational hobby, that not everything always needs to be bought new and that fun doesn't have to be expensive. Your child will learn most of their adult behaviours from you: if you treat a trip to the shops as though it were more fun than playing pretend at home so will they. Finally, never let a child hit their late teens without understanding compound interest: once they understand how it can bury them in debt if they use it wrong or make them rich if they use it right they should be OK.

School and university: spending and learning

Many parents given the choice would educate their children privately. Unfortunately most parents can't afford it. School fees have been rising much faster than inflation for years now. A reasonable secondary school now costs a good £12,000 a year and if you want to board your child that can easily double to £24,000–£25,000 a year. The average total cost of a private education? Just over £200,000 per child at a day school and £330,000 at a boarding school (including inflation and extras, see **www.education-fees.co.uk**). Why are fees so high? The schools will tell you that it's all about teachers demanding higher salaries and about having to keep up with other schools by buying expensive equipment. But there may well be less to it than that: they make the fees so high because people are prepared to pay them.

Still there is good news too: nearly a third of pupils at private schools get some help with the fees in the form of bursaries and scholarships and if your child is gifted in any way they can too. See **www.isc.co.uk** for more details on ways to get help with fees.

That said, most of us are still going to have to come up with the cash ourselves if we want our children to be privately educated. This means saving, a lot of saving. There are – as usual – a variety of products specially designed for school fees saving but again as usual most of them aren't worth the fees you'll pay for them. Instead, saving for education is just the same as saving for everything else: put aside as much as you can via all the usual methods and start as early as possible. Use your entire ISA allowance if you can so the returns are tax free and then outside that just invest in the funds or shares you like best for the medium term.

Then when your child reaches school age, if you haven't got enough cash put by but you still really want to go private think about borrowing. This probably means remortgaging, this being the cheapest way to borrow. If you take this route you don't want to have to borrow all the money at once and pay interest on it when you are likely only to need it in chunks of a few thousand at a time. This is therefore one of the rare occasions when an offset mortgage might be a good idea: these allow you to agree an amount you can borrow against your house but then take it as you want it so you don't have to pay unnecessary interest on it. You might also see if you can't get the school you are using to give you a discount for paying upfront: depending on how many terms in advance you pay you can get discounts of up to 30% (something that would make it easily worth borrowing money on your mortgage at, say, 7%).

It used to be that the financial burden of your child's education stopped being your problem when they hit 18. Not any more. Student grants no longer exist and tuition costs up to £3,000 a year so if you don't help out your student child is going to enter adulthood seriously in debt: 90% of students are in debt at the moment (in 1992 only a third were) and the average undergraduate lives on a mere £30 a week after paying rent. Seventy-five per cent of students work in term time and 30% of those do so for more than 20 hours a week. This is despite the fact that their parents spend over £4,000 a year trying to help them to stay solvent. It's all slightly depressing, particularly given that there is no guarantee that the income of a graduate will be any higher than that of a non-graduate (see p.18), and there really isn't much you can do to cut the cost. You can encourage your child to study nearby and live at home, you can make them work in the holidays, and you can visit **www.studentswaps.com** to see if you can save on accommodation by having your child housed by a family near where they are studying and taking another studying near you in exchange. Otherwise all you can do is save into your general pot and hope for the best. I'm tempted not to worry about it too much myself given that things change so fast. In 18 years when my baby reaches university age will the education system be the same and will the method of financing it be the same? I rather doubt it.

Wills: you can't take it with you, so who gets it?

Not talking about money causes problems not just at every single stage of life but after death as well. To prevent that happening you need to think about what you want to happen to your assets on your death well in advance of your death. I'm rather of the view that you shouldn't aim to leave too much behind. Money can only be spent once and if you're the one who earned it and saved it why shouldn't you be the one to spend it rather than your children? A big inheritance might be nice for your children but is it necessarily a good thing anyway? Expectations of wealth weaken ambition (why work when you can wait?) and your children's drive to control their own finances. This isn't particularly desirable given that even if you intend to leave money behind you can't ever be sure you will: with life spans getting longer and nursing care more and more expensive you may end up getting through the lot. You should be sure your children aren't living in the expectation of living better after your death.

Still, even if there isn't much money as such left when you go there'll still be an awful lot to divvy up – furniture, jewellery and pictures, for example. And you do need to think about that as well as making it formal with a will. You may think that you don't need to make a particularly specific will but if you have children you really do. Stipulating how your financial assets are to be divided up is simple stuff. You designate percentages and your executors sell the lot and divide up the cash according to your wishes. But what about your other possessions? Think jewellery, your wedding album, favourite paintings. Money can be split in two or three or four but engagement rings cannot.

This means that you have to specify in your will who gets the things that are important to you and to your children: you may find they all want the same Christmas decoration that reminds them of their childhoods or the same picture that hung in the kitchen for 30 years. This is particularly important if you have children from more than one marriage: you don't want a situation where something that originally belonged to the father of the children from your first marriage is left not to them but to the children of your second marriage. This might sound like trivial stuff but family feuds can last for decades on less than an argument about a much loved necklace. So make your division of the spoils fair and put it all in writing; verbal promises carry the seeds of conflict too.

Another reason to be sure that you have a will once you have children is to appoint a preferred guardian for them should you die before they reach adulthood. Your nominees won't automatically get custody of your children but your wishes will be taken into account.

If your estate is likely to breach the inheritance tax limit you might want to consider giving some of your possessions away before you die. You can hand over anything tax free as long as you live for another seven years, so if you want to pass items on and can afford it the sooner the better really. However, you cannot hand things on and still use them, so be very sure that you are happy to lose control over them completely before you make the gift: if you give your house to your child you can only continue to live in it if you also pay a commercial rent to your child to do so. Finally, note that you can give away £3,000 a year to anyone and £5,000 as a wedding gift to each child and still pay no inheritance tax on it even if you do die within seven years. You may also hand over as much money as you like if it comes out of your income and doesn't affect your own standard of living – so the more money you have the more likely you are to be able to avoid paying inheritance tax.

Insurance: now you need it

Once you have a child you might actually need some life insurance if you don't have sufficient assets to guarantee that your partner or the child's guardian will be able to look after them properly if you die. I'm not suggesting you go crazy here, just that you get some term insurance that lasts as long as your child will be dependent (see p.82).

WHAT Do I Do Now?

✳ **Find out about your maternity leave rights and start saving extra if you can.**

✳ **Don't overspend on your baby.**

✳ **Do your sums to see if you are going back to work.**

✳ **If you are not, make absolutely sure that your financial arrangements with your partner are worked out in such a way that you do not become a dependant (reread the last chapter).**

✳ **Exercise your right to ask for flexible or part-time working hours if you need them or just want them.**

✳ Claim and invest your Child Trust Fund. It's the only free money you'll ever get.

✳ Keep paying into your pension even if you stop working. Your children won't want to support you in your old age.

✳ Make a proper and specific will.

✳ Try not to worry too much about your child's university costs. Who knows how it will all work in 18 years.

✳ If you really want to get ahead even as a mother, says Linda R. Hirshman, author of *Get to Work: A Manifesto for Women of the World*, have just one child. A second child doubles all your childcare duties from lunch-making to getting up in the night. Most women who give up their jobs to look after their children do so on the birth of their second child.

10
Divorce
An End and a Beginning

D ivorce is a nasty end to relationships that are
supposed to last for ever, that we all want to last for
ever. But it doesn't have to be a disaster. Many women
find that their standard of living falls dramatically in the
immediate aftermath of a separation. But longer-term
things often come good. The independence divorce forces
means that divorced women work longer, earn more and
have higher overall household incomes than single or
married women. How's that for a silver lining?

£165,000: the value of the average divorcing couple's assets (Moneyexpert.com).

£15 billion: the annual direct costs of divorce (Grant Thorton). This includes welfare support, legal aid, court funding, counselling and lost productivity at work.

£25,000: the cost to a couple of the average divorce including the cost of the legal process and of setting up two new lives (*Independent*).

In Chapter 8 we looked at how marriage makes you happy. What I didn't mention then was that, while as a married woman you are pretty much always happier than a non-married woman, the margin of contentment you have over her declines every year. The happiest year of most marriages is the first one and for many people it is all downhill from there. This makes sense. In the first year love and romance are everywhere, babies probably haven't yet wormed their sweet but tiring way into your household and if there are going to be money worries they won't yet have surfaced. All this very often changes after a couple of years: two in five marriages now end in divorce. I haven't been through a divorce myself as an adult, but I'm one of the few over-21s in my family who can say so. And every divorce I have watched the others go through has been incredibly traumatic.

In marriage every burden is shared. In divorce every burden is doubled. And not just emotionally, but financially too. One house becomes two houses, one phone bill two phone bills and one set of insurances two sets of insurances. Suddenly there are two lifestyles to deal with. A total income that is sufficient to run one household rarely allows two households to survive in a similar style: when a marriage breaks down everyone usually has to suffer.

The good news is that poverty is no longer the natural state of the single divorcee, as it was even 20 years ago. When divorce was first enshrined in English law in 1670, only men could apply and to get the deed done actually required an Act of Parliament. Not many people got divorced back then. From 1857, under the Matrimonial Causes Act, women were finally able to apply for divorces themselves but only if they could prove some thoroughly nasty things about their husbands: they needed not just to have committed adultery but also to have subjected their wives to rape, sodomy or cruelty or to have committed incest. And if a divorcing woman could prove all this, her only right was to leave: she got no property, not even what she had brought into the marriage. Worse, she had no guarantee that she would ever see her children again.

In 1870 the Married Women's Property Act arrived, entitling women to keep £200 of their own money, which while mean was at least progress. Then in 1873 a breakthrough: women were finally guaranteed access to their children post-divorce, something that made it possible for more women to contemplate finding a way out of their marriages. From then on things improved rapidly. In 1932 women were allowed to ask for divorces simply on the grounds of adultery (men had already been able to do this for some time). By 1937 a few more legal justifications had been introduced: you could divorce on grounds of cruelty, habitual drunkenness or desertion for more than three years.

Then in 1969 came the Divorce Reform Act which made things much more straightforward: if you had been separated for two

The women who did well

£5 million: what City fund manager Alan Miller was forced to pay his wife in settlement after a mere four years of marriage, the equivalent of £5,000 a day. It would, said Miller, have been cheaper to have run her over in his car and pay her compensation for that instead.

£1 billion: the estimated amount Rupert Murdoch handed over to his first wife Anna when they separated in 2000.

£100 million: the amount paid by computer entrepreneur Peter Harrison to his wife Joy on an amicable parting.

£48 million: the final settlement received by Beverly Charman from her insurance underwriter husband in 2006. They had been married for nearly 30 years and had two children. The settlement represented 33% of his fortune.

£100 million: the estimated settlement between construction tycoon Steve Bell and his wife Pamela. The deal catapulted her straight on to the rich list.

£50 million: the estimated amount handed over by French Connection founder Stephen Marks to his ex-wife Alisa.

£20 million: what former model Sally Croker-Poole was said to have received on her divorce from the Aga Khan in 1995.

£17 million: the amount awarded to Diana, Princess of Wales on her divorce from Prince Charles in 1996.

£10.5 million : the amount awarded to Caroline Conran on her divorce from Sir Terence in 1995.

£28 million : what Mark Dixon, chief of office space rental firm Regus paid his wife of 17 years. He was left with £360 million.

years and both agreed, you could divorce right away (although if one party did not want it it was five years) and you could do so on the very flexible grounds of unreasonable behaviour and irretrievable breakdown. For the first time no one had to be to blame. You could simply say it had broken down. This concession came just in time – as life expectancies really started to rise. A hundred years ago if you didn't get along with your husband too well you could console yourself with the knowledge that he'd be bound to be dead by 50. These days it's possible he'll see 85, so if he is irritating you at 40 you'll probably need to find a way out sooner rather than later. In 1965 there were 40,000 divorces a year. By 1975 there were 120,000.

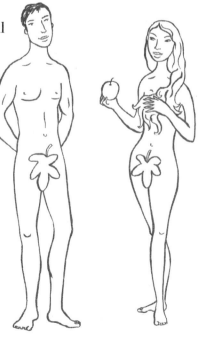

Since then any changes have been all about the money. The Matrimonial Property Act in 1973 finally took women's work in the home into account when dividing property, for example. However, even then and for some decades afterwards women came out of divorces pretty badly. When our mothers divorced they were entitled to little more than the bare minimum to live on and had no rights to things such as pensions. When their children turned 18 and their child support stopped they often found themselves not far off destitute. Worse, many of them had little way to help themselves: if you've never had a proper job, as was the case with much of the last generation, entering the workforce at 45 as a single mother is no joke. There's a reason why 40% of divorced women over 65 are poor enough to qualify for income support.

"I'm not taking a penny from him. I think that's disgusting."

Billie Piper on her divorce settlement with Chris Evans

However, in 1996 things changed dramatically – thanks to Pamela White. She had been married for 33 years and had run, with her husband, a farming business worth £4.6 million. When they divorced a judge awarded her £800,000 – enough, he said, for her to have a house and a reasonable standard of living. It may have been that but it wasn't, said Pamela, fair. She went to the Court of Appeal and after a long battle eventually won £1.5 million in the House of Lords.

The result of this precedent has been much fairer divorce courts. Settlements used to be made on the basis of making sure the 'reasonable requirements' of the poorer partner (usually the wife) were taken into account, but now when there are more assets than needed for just this (when there is a 'surplus') the ideas of 'fairness' and equality have taken over. Even if your husband has been the main breadwinner and has been responsible for bringing in the cash used to build up the family's assets you are now entitled to maintain your wealth and your living standards post-divorce as much as possible (as is he – this works both ways): domestic contributions are considered to be as valuable to a family as the role of a breadwinner. Property is now usually divided fifty-fifty, for example. There is also now scope for women who have given up careers to be stay-at-home mothers to be compensated for this in the settlement. The other difference between our generation and that of our mothers, of course, is that we should be rather more financially aware than they were and either in work or more than capable of returning to work. The modern woman has many more post-divorce options than her mother.

Getting started

If you think you want a divorce you must first get advice. January is the busiest time for anyone in the business of divorce: Christmas is the last straw for many a warring couple and it makes many willing to do anything to get out of their relationship fast. But just as you shouldn't rush into marriage you shouldn't rush into divorce: one of the main reasons to go to a solicitor and get proper professional advice is to slow things down a bit. Most good solicitors will start off not by looking at a list of your assets to figure out who might get what but by asking if you can be reconciled. A great many couples are apparently shocked into sense just by visiting a solicitor's office. It is possible to file for divorce online – you input your details and you're off – but to my mind you really shouldn't be able to file for divorce on the spur of the moment: computers don't stop to ask if you are sure, good solicitors do.

So how do you find a good solicitor? You don't just need someone who is good at their job, you need someone you feel you can trust: if your divorce drags out you could be seeing them regularly for a couple of years. The best way, as ever, is personal recommendations. If friends suggest someone good meet them – but don't think you have to use them if you don't think they're quite right. Solicitors don't take offence. Otherwise you can ask at your local Citizens Advice Bureau or contact Resolution – an association of matrimonial lawyers who work with a code of practice designed to help you make a settlement with your husband in a positive and conciliatory, rather then overly litigious, way.

If you are sure you want a divorce and you think you can be even the smallest bit amicable about it you might want to consider something new – collaborative law. This is a system under which lawyers and their clients agree not to go to court to work out a settlement but to work it out themselves. In court differences and arguments can become exaggerated, making the whole process even worse than it has to be. This system avoids the acrimony as much as possible by having the two sides meet at a round table with their lawyers and talk it out until they have a sensible settlement. Think Mick Jagger and Jerry Hall rather than *War of the Roses*. See **www.collabfamilylaw.org.uk** for more on this common-sense route.

You could also consider mediation – using trained help to sort out all your divorce-related problems without recourse to lawyers for anything but checking over the final settlement. See **www.divorce.co.uk** for a list of mediators. You can also get information on them from your local Citizens Advice Bureau.

The cost of divorce

Divorce comes with endless problems but one of the biggest and least understood is that, if you don't manage to arrange matters via a mediator or collaborator, getting divorced is in itself very expensive. When you are caught up in a legal battle instructing your solicitor to fire off letter after letter to your ex-husband and to his solicitor it's easy to forget that the cost of every letter will come out of the final pot of cash that you both have to live off. As Imogen Clout points out in her book, *Divorce*, people in nasty divorces often talk about 'fighting for their rights, or justice or the principle of the thing', forgetting that the law is pretty clear on how assets should be divided and 'that divorce law is not designed to deliver abstract redress or compensation'.

Don't forget that solicitors charge for their time – every minute of their time. You will pay for every letter, every phone call and every meeting. You will even be charged for their travel time when they come to court. And their rate can be anything from £120 an hour plus VAT to a great deal more. That's a cost to you of about £2.30 a minute. Big-money divorce can cost from £20,000 in fees. When it comes to lawyers' time it is a lot of money, and to make sure they get it they may well ask you for an advance payment, and then let you pay the rest on a monthly basis. They may also agree to wait for their fee until after your settlement with your husband is made (if, of course, they think you'll be getting enough to be able to pay their bill). Either way, you will want to be careful only to consult them when you really need to. Never forget they are a lawyer not a therapist: don't call them when you are angry or upset, just when you need legal advice. If you need to let off steam call a real friend instead – they won't charge you by the hour to listen. Your lawyer probably doesn't much care about how you perceive the rights and wrongs of your case; they just want to sort it out and get paid. This means that the second you decide you want a divorce is the second you need to slash your spending to the bone and start saving every penny you can: if you are going to end up in litigation you will need them all.

If you are a non-working wife you may qualify for legal aid to fund your divorce case even if as a couple you and your husband have significant assets; the courts know that if you have no income of your own you may not have ready access to cash until your divorce is final. Your solicitor should be able to help you to get any aid you are entitled to.

What you deserve and what you get

Divorce asks the courts to decide about something you probably never expected to have to put a price on: what has your contribution to your marriage really been worth? Once we thought we were worth no more than what we brought into a marriage, if that. Then we were worth a bit more to compensate us for loss of earnings and the fact that we reared children. Now we see we should be worth the value we bring to a marriage and the opportunity cost of giving up careers.

There were howls of protest from men all over the country in 2006 when Julia Macfarlane was awarded £250,000 a year out of her husband's earnings of £750,000. But was that really too much? Macfarlane had given up her career to look after her husband and her children (she was out-earning him when she stopped work) but after a decade-long break can hardly be expected to pick up where she left off. By becoming a wife and mother she gave up a huge earning potential. So why should she, because she stopped work to look after children, have a lower standard of living than her ex-husband? It's a vexed question. Some say she was entitled to everything she got: if you are dumped after such a long time you are 'due a lot of back pay' as one ex-wife put it in *Style* magazine. But some say that giving up work was her choice (clearly the Macfarlane family could afford childcare) and that having less money now is simply the price she has to pay for making that choice. Fairness, as law lord Lord Nicholls of Birkenhead said in his judgement on the case, is 'an elusive concept'.

However, for most of us what we think about the Macfarlane case or indeed any of the high-profile divorce cases that hit the papers is by the by: the assets of most married households, when divided, simply aren't enough to keep two households well, let alone to allow arguments about the surplus: settlements are less about who gets the house in the Bahamas and more about how assets can be divided so that both parties can survive. The average divorcing couple in 2006 had only £165,000 in assets to divide between them – hardly enough for both to be even satisfactorily housed post-divorce. Anyway, the courts have a fairly standard way of sorting out financial settlements. They will take into account the needs of each part of the family, the length of the marriage, your ages and the contributions each of you have made (making no differentiation between financial contributions and household contributions) and divide all your assets accordingly, sorting out everyone's basic needs first and then divvying up the surplus if there is one. This is all traumatic but it isn't that complicated: there tend to be set answers depending on how long you have been married, whether you have children and what each party brought to the marriage and contributed during it.

You don't want the house

That said, women tend to make one big mistake when it comes to divorce settlements, and it's worth knowing to be sure you don't make the same one: they insist on keeping the house at any cost. This is well meant – it's usually about not causing any more trauma to the children than absolutely necessary – but it is often a financial disaster. Why? Because mostly you don't get a whole house – you get a little bit of house and a whole lot of mortgage. And your lender will want to reassess that mortgage pretty quickly if it was given on the basis of your husband's income or your joint income. If the sums don't add up they'll force a sale anyway. Note that most mortgage lenders won't take maintenance into account when assessing how big a mortgage you can have. This is partly down to the fact that they don't know that those payments will keep coming in but also that maintenance tends to end when children are 18 while mortgages go on for 25 years. When you are thinking about the house you'll also need to remember that if you keep it you'll have to deal with the costs of the marital home on a divorcee's income. That's rarely easy.

"I'm a marvelous housekeeper. Every time I leave a man I keep his house."

Zsa Zsa Gabor

Add it all up and usually the best you can hope for is to sell the old house and get enough equity for two new mortgages (estate agents do better out of divorce than anyone else). Selling up and moving house is no fun when you are already bruised but usually the sooner you do it the better. And whatever you do, don't be tempted to forgo any share you might be entitled to of your husband's pension in return for a bigger share of the house or a lump sum that might allow you to

stay in the house unless you already have pension arrangements of your own. The lack of any pension provision is the one factor that has made so many older divorcees so utterly miserable. You are now entitled to share pension benefits so make sure you do. In 2004 of 167,000 divorces fewer than 4,000 involved pension-sharing orders. That's probably not enough.

Looking to the future

In Chapter 8 I told you about Terry Hekker, disappointed divorcee. Well, here's the end of her story. She's back on form. She's written another book called *Disregard First Book* and is a huge success all over again on the chat show circuit. 'With divorce,' she told the *Guardian*, 'when one door closes another one always opens. But until then it is hell.' Note that the average divorcee is only 40, that remarriages now account for two in every five weddings and that 60% of divorcees remarry within five years. Better still, modern divorced women now work longer, earn more and have higher household incomes than their married or never married peers, according to economists in the *Journal of Human Resources*. There are two reasons for this. First, they get a bigger slice of their ex-husband's earnings and even future earnings than ever before. And second, because they find themselves with both the freedom and the determination really to get ahead in the workplace, after the initial trauma it often turns out to be a life-changing experience in a good way.

WHAT Do I Do Now?

- **Get advice.**

- **Be amicable.**

- **Change your expectations of your lifestyle.**

- **Make a detailed report of all your finances. The sooner this is done the sooner you can move ahead.**

- **Know your rights and understand the divorce process before you start. The more you know the less you will have to ask a lawyer.** *Divorce* **by Imogen Clout (published by** *Which?***) contains all you will need to know.**

- **Don't try to keep the house if you can't really afford it: you might regret it.**

- **Don't sign anything just to get it all over with as fast as possible: you will regret it.**

- **Remember divorce isn't all bad: it forces responsibility and that can bring great satisfaction.**

- Manage any money you do get in settlement very carefully: it may have to last a long time.

- Rewrite your will. Divorce negates any will made during marriage. And if you remarry rewrite it again. Remarriage invalidates your old will and your new spouse will automatically inherit, leaving your children from other marriages out in the cold. That might not be what you want.

Section 4:
Beyond the Money

"You can be too rich. I like to have enough money to go on holiday or buy a dress but I don't want a yacht or a jet. Peace of mind is what you really need to be happy."

Lulu Guinness

11
Money
A Facilitator of Happiness, Not a Source of It

How much money makes you happy? The answer is much less than you think. Studies by Ruut Veenhoven, a professor of Happiness Studies at Erasmus University in Holland, show that those who have an income of less than around $10,000 a year are generally unhappy. Yet in countries where the average annual income is more than $10,000 money and happiness stop having much of a relationship: those with $100,000 are only marginally happier than those with $11,000. Could it be that once our basic needs are covered the best things in life really are free?

If you were to graph a line of living standards in the West over the last 50 years you would see that it moved in only one direction – up. We are all reasonably housed and fed. Almost all of us have electricity, running water and central heating. At the same time many of us can afford to take a proper holiday or even two every year, to drive cars that rarely break down, to have more changes of clothes than we could conceivably ever need and to eat out when we can't be bothered to cook. These days we want for nothing. Except, that is, contentment.

If you were to try to graph our levels of happiness over the same 50 years you would find that, instead of rising in tandem with our good fortune, the line meanders along in more or less a flat line. Polls taken in the US since the 1950s regularly have only one-third of Americans saying they are 'very happy'. In Germany things are better but still not improving: around 60% of people said they were 'content' in the 1970s and 60% do now too. And the situation is the same in the UK. Our incomes have risen by 80% in real terms in the last 30 years but our levels of happiness have barely budged: a study by Professor Ruut Veenhoven, an expert on well-being, and editor of *Journal of Happiness Studies*, shows that on his 'life satisfaction index' the population of the UK is now only 1.36% happier than it was in the mid-1970s (which, I should point out, was not a particularly happy time for most people). Happiness levels in the UK are now ranked below those of 20 other countries in the world, including Ghana, Colombia, Uruguay and Mexico. Getting richer, it seems, really doesn't bring us much joy.

This rather suggests that once your financial position is sorted out so that you know you will have enough to cover your basic needs for the remainder of your life (i.e. you are saving properly and your pension arrangements are satisfactory), continuing to fight for more is not the best way to improve your life. Having enough to get by is important. A flat in Mayfair is not. I am far from sure that the $10,000 suggested by Professor Veenhoven counts as enough to get by – in modern Britain I think £30,000 would be more like it – but the basic point stands and there's a perfectly good reason why. It all comes down to the difference between needs and desires. Once your basic needs are covered everything else tangible that you might have is not a need but a want. And we know that wants can never be satisfied: as soon as we get what we want, instead of wallowing in our good fortune we find that we just want more and more.

"Money never made a man happy yet, nor will it. There is nothing in its nature to produce happiness. The more a man has, the more he wants. Instead of its filling a vacuum, it makes one." Benjamin Franklin

When I was young I thought being able to buy a new piece of clothing in Topshop every few weeks would bring me joy. Now I yearn for pieces by a few favourite designers stocked only by Selfridges and silly boutiques in Notting Hill. And if I can ever afford those you can bet your bottom dollar I won't be satisfied. No, I'll be wanting couture. It's the same with houses. When we buy our first flats we think all our dreams have come true but it isn't long before we think we deserve a three-bedroomed house, then a larger garden, a pool, a holiday home abroad and so on. We are very quick to adjust to thinking of our current position as not a luxury but the norm, so to be happy we constantly crave a new luxury. 'You get used to eating caviar,' Boris Becker once said, 'and at some point it begins to taste as ordinary as everything else.' The growing gang of happiness experts calls the fleeting nature of the joy we get from material possessions 'hedonic adjustment' and points out that everything we buy that we don't genuinely need is subject to it. Think of it in terms of cars, says behavioural finance expert James Montier. 'We might get a new fast car and at first be out washing it every weekend, but six months later we have become accustomed to it, the kids have scuffed up the seats in the back and the boot is full of dog hairs.' The pleasure is gone.

What is true of individual possessions is true of money as a whole. We all think that if we won the lottery we'd be happier but we are wrong: study after study shows that while lottery winners are absolutely ecstatic in the immediate aftermath of a big win, within a year they say they are no more happy than they were before the win. Money just doesn't buy them happiness.

This is not to say that lack of money doesn't make you unhappy. It does. Until you have the base amount of money you require to cover all your needs, life will be hard and you may well be miserable. And if, once you have the money to cover your needs, you misuse it, you may well still be miserable: being in debt is horrible (note the regular tabloid stories of debtor suicides) and having money trouble is a famous relationship destroyer. And the rich are happier than the poor, albeit marginally.

There is nothing wrong with having money or with taking pleasure in material things: the problem is just that many of us seem to think that happiness comes *exclusively* from making money and buying stuff with it when it does not. Making, controlling and spending our money properly gives us a base of security and peace from which we can work towards long-term happiness. The rest we have to work out another way.

But how? Finding an answer to this question is vital for the modern woman. Right now most of us aren't particularly happy: surveys in the US suggest that today's women, despite their many freedoms, are actually less happy than their grandmothers. This is partly because – as this book discusses – we haven't used the money we are now allowed to earn to create long-term security for ourselves. But there is more to it than this. Despite all the wonderful opportunities and choices we have life is oddly hard for women today. If we stay at home we fret. If we go out to work we fret. We want too much. We want good relationships, lots of sex, happy children and husbands, designer clothes, bikini bodies, high-status careers and regular manicures. We want to be good businesswomen, good wives and good mothers and we want to be them while looking good in high heels and pencil skirts – just like the women in women's magazine land.

The pressure we put on ourselves is huge and the result is a degree of self-obsession: we look in not out. In an article on women and happiness last year *OM* magazine pointed to research by historian Joan Jacobs Brumberg showing how the way young women look at themselves has changed. A typical girl's diary entry from 1892 read: 'Resolved not to talk about myself or my feelings. To think before speaking. To work seriously. To be self-restrained in conversation and action. Not to let my thoughts wander. To be dignified. Interest myself in others.' By 1982 the typical entry went more like this: 'I will try to make myself better in any way I possibly can with the help of my budget and my babysitting money. I will lose weight, get new lenses, already got new haircut, good make-up, clothes and accessories.' The modern girl looks for self-worth through creating what she thinks is a better version of herself whereas her grandmother looked to improve herself via her attitude to others. The former, as we shall see below, is not conducive to long-term happiness: studies show that the more we connect outside ourselves the happier we are.

"If you want to know what God thinks of money just look at the people he gave it to." Dorothy Parker

So, back to what can make us happy. There are a great many 'experts' on this and they have done much useful work on the subject but if you take all their results and boil them down it seems fair to say that once you've moved out of poverty the things that will make you happiest are those that have no price – love, family, friendship, respect and a sense of purpose of some kind. We yearn for intimacy and love, but we also need to feel connected to a community and to have something to work towards. Below I look at ten ways you can find real long-term happiness. You will see that money facilitates a lot of these – in that it can buy you the time to pursue them – but can't possibly replace them. What good is being rich if you have no friends and your children don't love you? And how much better is it to go for a walk in the park with your partner than watch TV alone while he earns enough money to buy you a new bracelet? The fact is that however much you love your money it isn't ever going to love you back. Your friends and family, on the other hand, might.

1 ONLY CONNECT

The most important element in human happiness is connection to others – community, friendship and marriage. We are genetically designed to prefer to be in groups than to be alone (in primitive society survival outside a group was no easy affair) and to love and need to be loved. When we have none of these things we are destined to be miserable but when we have them, or some of them, we do have a good stab at happiness. Tom Rath in his book *Vital Friends: The People You Can't Afford to Live Without* claims that almost all the failures in our lives are down to lack of friendship. He points out that patients with heart disease are twice as likely to die if they do not have four or five close social connections, and that friendship within a marriage is five times more important a factor in determining its longevity than sex.

His views are backed up by research from economist Ed Diener who notes that no one who does not have good social relationships ever calls themselves happy and by the fact that countries that have managed to maintain warm family and community networks (Malta and some of the Latin American countries) come so far up the happiness index. Note too that a survey by London freesheet *Metro* suggested that to 59% of Londoners friends are the most 'meaningful things' in life. Aristotle agreed with them. 'Without friends no one would choose to live though he had all other goods,' he wrote. The fact is that those who belong to community groups are happier than those who do not. The married are happier than the unmarried and the generally social are happier than the generally solitary.

This all makes complete sense. Something embarrassing happened to you at work? Go home and tell your husband. Suddenly it's not embarrassing, it's hysterically funny. Failed dismally to get your baby to eat carrots? Call a friend to discuss it and suddenly you aren't a failure, you're just one of many mothers with a contrary child. Can't get below a size 14 and fit your bottom into the bikini you wanted to take on holiday? Tell your sister all about it and you may find that it isn't you that's chubby, it's the sizing that's all wrong. Good relationships deliver a constant buffer against anxiety: nothing is as bad after it's been talked through over a drink. They also give you security and a wonderful long-term sense of belonging and of self-worth – the liked and loved are much more comfortable in themselves than the solitary.

The simplest way to make yourself happier, therefore, is to have long-term friendships and to make yourself part of a community. This isn't as easy as it sounds. Having a large group of good friends (the scientists tell us we need to be close to at least four people and that they should be as diverse as possible) and being close to our families can be hard work (you have to give as much as you get). However, given that everyone agrees relationships are absolutely fundamental to happiness, it is clear that other things – work, laundry, shopping – need to be sacrificed to make time for that work.

So what should you do? Make good friends and make them early – my closest friends are still people I met at secondary school – so that all your life you have a pool of support to draw on when you need it. Then reach out as much as you can. You love it when people call and ask you out. So call and ask them out – for walks, for films, for supper. Get to know your neighbours and talk to the people behind the counter in your local shop. Become part of your local community. Be married if you can find the right person to connect to.* To the best of your ability make yourself emotionally connected to other people. You'll feel a lot better as a result. People make people happy.

As an aside to this, a quick defence of the mobile phone which, while much maligned, is a gift to the modern woman. We are criticized endlessly for never being able to be alone for a minute without calling someone but what's wrong with that? These contacts make us happy. I call at least one of my sisters, my mother and my father most days. I talk to my grandmother several times a week and make a conscious effort to call a friend every few days. Talking to all these people makes me happy.

2 BUY EXPERIENCE NOT STUFF

Thanks to the process of hedonic adjustment discussed above, we know that the joy that comes from owning material goods diminishes over time, which makes buying them pointless in the pursuit of happiness. But that isn't the case with experiences, says behavioural finance expert James Montier. Instead 'experiences

---

*David Blanchflower and Andrew Oswald released a study in 2004 based on huge global surveys that told us that people in long-term faithful marriages are the happiest of all – they are more stable, have a greater sense of well-being, live longer and look younger.

seem to be open to positive review'. In a paper on the subject of happiness Montier refers to a diving trip he took to the Red Sea. The boat he was living on during his trip was 'an unmitigated disaster, from fires in the engine to diesel fumes being pumped into the cabin'. However, looking back, the things he remembered and now talks about most were not these downsides but 'a couple of stunning dives'. The result? In retrospect the experience actually seems better than it really was. 'We create our own revisionist histories with experience,' says Montier. 'This isn't available to a solid, hard, material possession.'

The other plus point of spending money on experience not stuff is that 'experiences are relatively unique'. Each dive you take is different. Each concert you attend is different. Each ride in a riding holiday different and so on. You have a different experience each time, something that stops hedonic adjustment from kicking in. Finally, says Montier, experiences have much greater 'social value' than things. You can't tell everyone about your new Ferrari for long without boring them all to tears but chatting about 'the highways of Pakistan' and so on is more interesting: 'people thrive on stories'.

3 LIVE ABSOLUTELY

One of the main things that makes us unhappy is that we don't judge our own possessions in absolute terms (I'm so lucky to be able to afford these lovely new shoes). We judge them in relative terms (I wish I could afford to buy as many new shoes as that woman next door). So the more other people have, the more we think we need in order to be happy too – we all have 'reference anxiety'.

This desperation to keep up with the Joneses means we are constantly caught up in a spiral of unsatisfactory consumption but are never quite able to come out on top: someone else always has more than us. If the people next door get richer we will be more dissatisfied than before regardless of the fact that our own condition has not changed at all, and if we get richer it will only make us happier than before, albeit temporarily, if no one else gets any richer at the same time. In his book *Luxury Fever*, Robert H. Frank suggests that this influence is so strong that most people would agree to make less money as long as they were absolutely guaranteed to make more than their neighbours: they would prefer to make £40,000 when everyone else is making £30,000 than £50,000 when everyone else is making £60,000.

"Some people think they are worth a lot of money just because they have it." Fannie Hurst

So what can you do to avoid reference anxiety? For starters you can stop watching television. Most of us watch it for about three hours a day, something that not only stops us increasing our happiness by taking away valuable socializing time, but which can also make us actively unhappy. Why? Because it doesn't show us ordinary lives. It shows us extreme lives. We see levels of violence that we end up thinking are normal, something that increases our day-to-day anxiety, but, worse, we see an endless parade of the rich and glamorous and their possessions and homes, which makes us dissatisfied with our own possessions and homes.

TV raises the standards of comparison: the Joneses are no longer living in a similar sort of house to ours next door but in a

$2 million house in Palm Beach; they don't drive a slightly better version of our car but choose each morning from a selection of Ferraris. And it isn't just the programmes about the very rich that throw us off kilter (although the celebrity homes programme *MTV Cribs* which has made half the world think that the other half has a double-size gold-plated Jacuzzi and a his'n'hers walk-in closet has a lot to answer for) but the more ordinary shows too: people on *Location, Location, Location,* on *Property Ladder* and on all the insane buying property overseas shows have more ready cash to hand than the man in the street used to dare to dream of. The upshot is that the more we watch TV the more we think we are poorer and have less stuff than other people (even when it isn't true) and the less happy we feel.

Television aside, all you can do is to try to live your life in absolute not relative terms. Every time you buy something ask if you really need it, and constantly try to remember how lucky you are to have what you have rather than how unlucky you are not to have what Paris Hilton has. And if you can't do that, pack your bags and move somewhere where everyone is poorer than you; conventional wisdom says one should always buy the worst house on the best street if you want to make money but the theory of happiness suggests we should instead buy the best house in the worst possible area (with no TV reception).

4 LAUGH

It seems the wrong way around, I know, but you can actually make yourself happy by laughing. Research shows that it can make you less stressed, reduce your blood pressure, boost your immunity and produce dopamine, one of our body's feel-good chemicals. There is even evidence that regular laughter reduces the chances of repeat heart attacks and best of all from our point of view increases your chances of a successful pregnancy via IVF. I am absolutely not suggesting that you indulge the therapy industry by attending laughter classes (yes, they are on offer) but it might be worth both being silly on a regular basis and making sure you often see people who make you laugh (in my case this is my family). Laughter is infectious so the more you do it the more everyone else will do it and the better you will feel.

5 GET RELIGION

One of the things that research constantly finds is that the religious are happier than the rest of us. Note, for example, that the Latin American countries that scored so highly on the life satisfaction index mentioned above all have a strong Catholic tradition as does Malta, officially the happiest place on earth. Scans of the brains of meditating Buddhists show they suffer less stress than the rest of us; the religious get divorced less often (and we know divorce is a great source of unhappiness); they are generally better educated; and they even earn more. According to Professor Leslie Francis of the University of Wales, doubling your church attendance lifts your income by 10%! All this sounds bizarre but it makes some sense. We have already noted that one of the main ingredients of happiness is a good social life and those who go to regular religious ceremonies get one of these automatically – simply by turning up they get access to a network of support that helps them to cope.

But there is more to religion than just making friends. Being religious also gives a sense of purpose. It's easier to stop being stressed about day-to-day life, to find an inner peace, if you think there's a different – and better – kind of life after death. Being part of an embracing system that tells you there is an eternal life suggests there's some kind of point to your current life. And as the Queen herself pointed out when she opened the Church of England's General Synod in 2005, with the modern world so much in flux 'there is a renewed hunger for that which endures and gives meaning'.

Those of us who just can't make ourselves believe are forced to look for our inner peace elsewhere. And look we do. We go to yoga classes, we detox constantly, we practise breathing exercises, we buy scented candles, special tension-releasing bracelets and whale music CDs and we indulge ourselves with endless therapy. Every time we feel bad we turn to one or other part of the self-help industry to sort ourselves out. Even sleeping has recently become a huge industry, with hundreds of millions of pounds spent every year around the world on various sleep therapies. Sleep therapists charge hundreds of pounds a day to help you to learn to sleep better, while gaining some kind of peace has even become the main selling point of business class on airlines.

But none of this lifestyle pseudo religion quite works. Why? Because it encourages us, like the diary writer above, to look in not out. To set off on a perpetual path of self-improvement that is designed to help no one but ourselves. The self-help industry is worth £2 billion a year in the UK alone but while millions of us have become slaves to it, I've never come across anyone who's actually found peace via a how-to-breathe-better book and a scented candle. Indeed I've often found that the more scented candles a woman owns the more miserable she is. The fact is that you can't fill the emotional voids in your life with spiritual products and you can't buy the kind of serenity that comes with a firm belief in eternal life.

That you can't pay for serenity doesn't bode particularly well for the nation's future: a survey done for National Kids' Day in 2005 asked children what they cared about most. The number 1 answer was being rich. Number 2 was being famous. Then came animals, nice food, computer games and, finally, at number 10, God.

But on the plus side, you can give yourself a sense of outward purpose without finding God. James Montier quotes a Dutch study that looked at the aspirations of business students and student teachers. The business students were looking for wealth and reputation in their careers. The teachers just wanted to contribute to the community. Over time the teachers, despite earning less, turned out to be happier. Again this makes sense. Even if you don't think your life will be eternal, knowing that when you go you will be leaving something worthwhile behind feels good too. This doesn't necessarily need to mean charity work although research shows that it does raise your well-being levels; it can be anything that, while not always actively enjoyable, brings help or enjoyment to others – think environmental work, community work, fostering children and so on. For ideas on how to offer your do-gooding services see **www.raleigh.org.uk**, **www.yearofthevolunteer.com**, **www.vso.org.uk**, **www.crisis.org.uk**.

6 BE CHALLENGED

We long for lives in which we could lounge around doing nothing all day, but if we had them we'd be bored to tears. A happy life is not one that is entirely free from stress of any kind. We need to have a challenge ahead of us and then to succeed in it: working towards a series of goals brings first hope and then great satisfaction. A team from Gothenburg University in Sweden completed a study in 2005 that concluded that the basic key to happiness is work. By this they didn't mean any old work but goal-orientated work. And just like one handbag, one goal isn't enough. Achieving brings joy for a while, says researcher Dr Bengt Bruelde, but then you hit the 'habituation effect' – you get used to the new situation and 'the joy is over'. So you need to find a new goal and start striving all over again.

It doesn't necessarily matter what you are striving to achieve, as long as it means something to you, challenges you and keeps challenging you. And it certainly doesn't have to be work-related (although it's nice if you can get happiness from your work): much joy has come out of decade-long searches for the perfect gluten-free chocolate cake recipe and hours spent drawing the perfect geranium. A good challenge might also give you 'flow' – that wonderful feeling of being so deeply involved in something that you lose yourself in it. You know when you get it and it is deeply, deeply satisfying. Sudden challenges also bring great satisfaction: activities that get our adrenaline going such as bungee jumping, parachuting, or even a round or two of karaoke have the double advantage of being both an experience (and so being better in retrospect) and stretching us out of our comfort zones.

Once you've moved into a lifestyle that constantly challenges you, you will, with a bit of luck, find yourself in a virtual circle of achievement and happiness: according to a survey of 275,000 people in the US, the 'chronically happy' consistently achieved much more than the miserable, thanks to the fact that by seeking out more in the way of challenge they ended up with more in the way of both career and relationship success. Happiness is created by good outcomes but it also goes on to create more of them.

7 TRY EVERYTHING

My mother always told me to accept every invitation I ever got, to go everywhere I could and take every possible opportunity for experience. As a teenager I thought she was nuts – every invitation accepted seemed to me just to open the door to the possibility of embarrassment or boredom. However, she was, of course, completely right. Studies show that people always think they will regret doing things that turn out to be foolish but in fact they don't. Instead they regret the things they did not do – opportunities they didn't grasp, jobs they didn't apply for, trips they didn't take, friends they didn't call and so on.

The reason for this, says Daniel Gilbert in his book *Stumbling on Happiness*, is that we have a 'more difficult time manufacturing positive and credible views of inactions than actions'. So if we marry an axe murderer we can still console ourselves by thinking of what we have learned from the experience. If we reject a proposal from someone who later becomes a movie star we can't console ourselves by thinking of what we learned from the experience 'because, well, there wasn't one'. This means, says Gilbert, that Ingrid Bergman would probably have felt just fine had she stayed with Bogart on the tarmac in *Casablanca* instead of listening to his claim that if she didn't leave with her husband Victor she'd regret it: 'Maybe not today. Maybe not tomorrow. But soon and for the rest of your life.' Instead she probably spent the rest of her life wondering 'what if?'.

8 COMMIT RANDOM ACTS OF KINDNESS

I read some years ago research from the University of California that suggested that the best way to be happy was to commit random acts of kindness at least five times a week – carrying old ladies' shopping, helping women with prams down steps, stopping to chat to lonely-looking people and so on. These acts, said the writer, will give you a little glow that will stay with you all day. So I tried it. And you know what? It works. Going out of your way to be kind really does give you a little buzz: there is a kind of gratification to be found in being selfless. Try it and see.

"One must be poor to know the luxury of giving".
George Eliot

It's also worth thinking about giving more of your surplus cash to charity to generate the same effect. I don't mean setting up a standing order to Oxfam but every few months sitting down with whatever you can afford and choosing a small and deserving charity to send it to. They'll be grateful and you'll feel good, particularly given that they get more than you send: charity giving is tax free so they can claim back the tax you paid on your contribution.

9 LOVE EVERY DAY

Like many of her generation my grandmother has had a lot of sad times in her life. She's lost a child, her husband, both her siblings and large numbers of her friends. Yet she's the happiest person I know. I asked her why. Simple, she said. 'The key to happiness is to banish sadness.' It is, she insists, that easy. Wake up every morning and remind yourself how lucky you are to have what you have, then determine to enjoy the day as it comes. Again this makes complete sense. In general people are happier if they choose the right attitude, says Richard Layard author of *Happiness: Lessons from a New Science*. If you are compassionate and thankful for what you have you will always have a base of happiness to work from.

So how can we be more like Granny? Simple. We can stop obsessing about all the terrible things that might or might not have happened to us in our childhoods or teen years, stop worrying about other people's failure to recognize our specialness and start loving simple pleasures: walking to the shop to get the paper, having bacon on toast for breakfast, the smell of our babies' hair, the first glass of wine on a Friday night and so on. Most of us, it seems, will eventually find our contentment in the mildly enjoyable and the seemingly mundane. Happiness makes happiness.

All in all, no one thing can make us happy so obsessing about any one on the list above is silly. We just need a sense of balance. A happy woman probably doesn't have her head in a self-help book and her diary full of yoga appointments. She isn't obsessed with her sense of self. She has her finances well under control so that money worries do not too often intrude on her peace of mind. She has a sense of purpose that she finds in her work, her community, her religion or all three but most of all she has close family and friends and she is determined to keep close to them.

Money is a key ingredient to our happiness in that it gives us a base of security to work from but money can't work alone. We can use it to buy ourselves time and flexibility but we then have to use that time to connect with the world around us properly. To turn the title of this book on its head: money is not enough, women need love too.

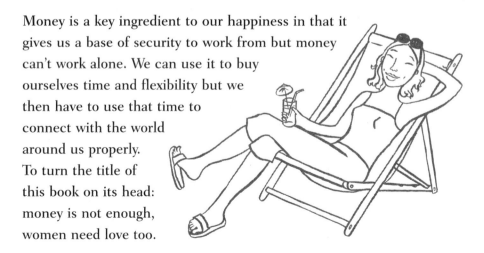

WHAT Do I Do Now?

✳ Ask if you are happy.

✳ If not, change: happiness is as much a state of mind as anything else.

✳ Never confuse pleasure (a fleeting feeling) with happiness (long-term contentment).

✳ Don't delay gratification too much. The future needs to be considered but so does the present.

✳ Commit random acts of kindness.

✳ Put real effort into making friendships and relationships work.

53 Money-Saving Tips

1 Drink less coffee out. One latte a day will add up to nearly £500 over a year.

2 Breastfeed your babies.

3 Never order cocktails. Stick to wine or beer in bars. Better still, never buy your own drinks.

4 Keep your weight constant: if you rarely change size you can buy quality pieces of clothing and wear them for years. Consider making that constant weight a lowish one too: thin people pay less for insurance.

5 Wash more, dry-clean less: whatever it says on the label woollens really don't need dry-cleaning. Even pashminas come out of the woollen cycle just fine as long as you iron them when a little damp. Wash cashmere on a gentle cycle and lay it flat between two towels to dry.

6 Packed lunches. We all know it's the right thing to do so why do so few of us do it? Spending £4 on lunch out every day adds up to £1,044 a year.

7 Ignore your hairdresser's insistence you get your hair cut every 6–8 weeks. Do it every 10 weeks instead.

8 Do your own nails: it really isn't complicated.

9 Buy sports equipment – skis, golf clubs and the like – on eBay. And if you have them and have never used them sell them on eBay and use the proceeds to pay down your credit card debt.

10 Stop going to the gym and walk home from work instead. If you aren't a professional body builder you don't need to go to a gym. Recent research also shows that doing light exercise for 5–6 minutes five times a day will do you just as much good as a big gym session.

11 Do your own cleaning (do it properly and you really, really don't need to go to a gym).

12 Never buy anything in a sale that you didn't long for before the sale.

13 Go public: if you live in a city you really don't need taxis. Make them a treat.

14 If you are flying on a budget airline book as far in advance as possible.

15 Cook from scratch. It's cheaper and nicer than having take-aways or ready meals and comes with an added bonus: once you aren't eating all those disgusting additives and sugars you'll lose weight too.

16 Cancel your subscriptions to women's magazines. They're pretty much the same every month so why not just read them in the hairdresser's and be done with it?

17 Never spend money on whale music CDs or aromatherapy scented candles. They won't make your life better.

18 Dump your home phone – aren't you always on your mobile anyway?

19 Check your bank statement every month. Banks make endless mistakes and odds are over the course of a year you'll catch a few that are working against you. Did all your deposits make it to your bank account? Are all your direct debits as they should be? Have you been charged fees you can challenge?

20 Get all your condoms for free from family planning clinics.

21 If you live in London sell your car and travel on a scooter – you won't have to pay the congestion charge and you'll look good too: men look silly on scooters, women look very glamorous.

22 If you must have designer clothes call the designer and ask for invitations to their sample sales. All designers have them and the discounts are huge.

23 If you can't go to sample sales shop in TK Maxx. Lots of designers. Low prices.

24 Stop drinking bottled water. Britons spend approximately £915 million a year on bottled water – around £25 each. Yet, according to Oxfam, it only costs an average of £15 to provide clean water

for life to one of the 1 billion people in the world who go without. That makes buying bottled water not just expensive but evil too.

25 If you won't drink tap water don't buy bottled water. Distil your own at home and take it to work. A 3 litre filter jug costs about £15 so given that a 1.5 litre bottle of water costs 80p you'll only have to use it 19 times to get value.

26 Never leave a hotel without a bar of soap.

27 Stop smoking: if you smoke 20 a day your habit is costing you around £1,700 a year – that's not far off 10% of the average person's income.

28 Overpay on your mortgage as much as possible – it could save you thousands in interest.

29 Watch out for Christmas: studies have shown that as many as half of all gifts given are never used – they go straight into the bin or off to the charity shop so make sure that you aren't throwing your money away as you buy: ask people what they want before you shop. Also make budgets and stick to them; you might think they will but your children will honestly not suffer long-term psychological damage if they don't get the exact trainers they want.

30 Buy next year's Christmas presents in the January sales.

31 Never do your grocery shopping when you are hungry. We throw away hundreds of pounds of food each every year. The less hungry you are when you shop the less you will buy and the less you will throw away.

32 Never buy a round but preserve your honour by not accepting other people's offers either. Buy your own drinks instead (and make them cheap ones).

33 Always buy own brands when you are supermarket shopping. They are very often made by the same manufacturers as the higher priced goods, they are just labelled differently.

34 Visit all the odd US moneysaving tip sites on the Internet: **miserlymoms.com**, **www.tightwad.com**, **www.cheapskatemonthly.com**. See also **www.flylady.com** and in the UK **www.moneysavingexpert.co.uk**.

35 Never buy anything that comes with a free gift in order to get the free gift. I'm talking about cosmetics. Beauty brands up the ante on free gifts every year. It used to be you got a nasty nylon make-up bag. Now it's specially designed make-up bags by the likes of Mulberry, properly nice handbags and beautifully designed umbrellas. But you don't need them and you very probably don't need the overpriced cosmetics you have to buy to get them either.

36 Switch to low-energy light bulbs. This will cut your electricity costs by £7 a year for each bulb that is on for more than three hours a day.

37 Buy your bike on **www.bumblebeeauctions.co.uk**. The site auctions property that the police have either seized from burglars and the like or had handed in and not been able to find owners for.

38 Turn your heating down by a few degrees. One degree down will save 10% off your heating bill, says the Energy Saving Trust.

39 Eat out less. People who live in Battersea spend on average 15% of their disposable income eating out, according to Barclays Business Banking. Silly people.

40 Buy your champagne in Netto and your clothes in Primark. It isn't embarrassing. It's clever.

41 Use **www.petrolprices.com** to find the cheapest petrol in your area. Enter your postcode and how far you are prepared to travel and it'll tell you where to go.

42 Don't buy detox products. Every January we are nagged by retailers to 'detox' our bodies with weird mixtures of seaweed, wheat grass and nettles. But according to the scientists there is no need. In fact the best way to sort yourself out after a period of indulgence is simply to have a good night's sleep and drink plenty of water (and tap water at that). Human bodies have their own mechanisms that allow them to break down and process most harmful chemicals, and fancy herbal teas and detox foot pads can't speed up the process, says Professor John Henry, a clinical toxicologist at St Mary's Hospital in London. Your liver can clear near lethal amounts of alcohol from your body in less than two days. No foot pad necessary. Never forget that the detox business is just that, a business. And one for which women's magazines and newspaper supplements work as promoters.

43 Don't buy diet books or go on celebrity diets. Just eat less (reduce portion sizes, never eat anything with refined sugar in it, give up snacking) and exercise

more. Giving up 500 calories a day will mean you lose around a pound a week. Not bad. If you are tempted by a diet book visit Amazon and find it there. Then look underneath at the 'customers who bought this also bought' section. You'll find that they bought other diet books. If any of them actually worked why would they have to do that? Same goes for fitness videos.

44 Declutter. Once you know what you have you won't find yourself buying it again. Keep your jewellery, shoes and the like on display so you use what you have.

45 Don't buy 'snack packs' of fruit or veg. An *Evening Standard* survey in 2006 showed that if you bought an 80g bag of carrot batons from Sainsbury's it would have cost you ten times the price of buying the carrots loose. Buying ready-to-eat pineapple from Waitrose would have cost you 750% more than buying a pineapple and cutting it up yourself.

46 Give up chocolate. I don't really advocate this one but it is worth noting that 4 bars a week at 50p a bar adds up to £104 a year.

47 Use coupons. You might think you will look silly and that you'll be embarrassed as you hold up the queue but you'll be saving money as you do it.

48 Don't have therapy unless you are seriously unwell – your doctor can tell you the difference.

49 Keep a budget book for a few weeks. It seems boring (and it is) but it will show you how your money disappears. Once you've written down how much you have spent on pointless muck you may stop doing it (this works

rather like food diaries for dieters – once you see how much you really eat written down you very often eat less).

50 Be very careful when renting cars. Most rental companies say they offer 'fully inclusive quotes' but in fact there is usually a large excess. If you so much as put a tiny dent in the car you will often find your entire excess seems to be needed to pay the bill. If you do damage the car ask to see the repair bill if you think you've been overcharged. That said, you don't necessarily want to buy extra insurance to cut the excess – it's usually much too expensive. Make sure you are there for the 'final inspection' too – it's amazing how much damage can be found when you aren't there. Always return your car full of fuel. It's so easy not to bother but you'll pay double the going rate for a tank of fuel so that bit of laziness will cost you a good £40. For more info on the dodgy ways car hire companies like to help themselves to your cash download the BVRLA Consumer Guide to Renting a Vehicle from their website.

51 Move the junk out of your garage and put the car in it. According to Saga Motor Insurance we miss out on £100 million worth of discounts a year by leaving our cars in more vulnerable positions on the road.

52 Skip the luxury face products and go old-fashioned: Pears' Soap, Vaseline, Nivea and so on. If you insist on having expensive products don't buy and then try. Go to the shop and get a free sample first. If you really love it then buy it (or ask for another sample).

53 If you are tempted to buy an expensive piece of designer gear remind yourself that no one will be able to tell the difference between your real one and a fake. A real Gucci bag will cost up to £1,000, a fake £10. And if no one can tell you have a real status symbol what's the point of having one at all?

The Final Checklist

Cut your spending

•

Pay off your debts

•

Start saving

•

Set up a SIPP

•

Talk about money with your husband

•

Teach your children about money

•

Commit random acts of kindness

Useful Websites

Bank charges
www.bankactiongroup.co.uk
www.bankchargeshell.co.uk
www.penaltycharges.co.uk

Benefits
www.direct.gov.uk/moneyandtaxbenefits
www.dwp.gov.uk

Car clubs
www.citycarclub.co.uk
www.mystreetcar.co.uk

Charity work
www.crisis.org.uk
www.raleigh.org.uk
www.vso.org.uk
www.yearofthevolunteer.com

Children
www.childcarelink.gov.uk
www.childtrustfund.gov.uk
www.sharingcare.co.uk

Clothes
www.bdbinvite.com
www.dwslondon,co.uk
www.londonfashionweekend.co.uk
www.outlet-firenze.com
www.tkmaxx.co.uk

Cohabitation
www.advicenow.org.gov/livingtogether

Credit agencies
www.callcredit.co.uk
www.equifax.co.uk
www.experian.co.uk

Debt
www.cccs.co.uk
www.citizensadvice.org.uk
www.creditaction.org.uk
www.nationaldebtline.co.uk

Divorce
www.collabfamilylaw.org.uk
www.divorce.co.uk

Education
www.education-fees.co.uk
www.isc.co.uk
www.slc.co.uk
www.studentswaps.com
www.ucas.com

Financial scams
www.419eater.com
www.homeworking.com

Furniture
www.homesandbargains.co.uk
www.showhomewarehouse.co.uk
www.trade-secret.co.uk

General finance
www.askdavidson.com

www.moneyexpert.com
www.moneyextra.com
www.moneyfacts.co.uk
www.moneysupermarket.com
www.moneyweek.com
www.onecompare.com
www.unbiased.com

Insurance
www.britishinsurance.com
www.confused.com
www.insureandgo.com
www.insuresupermarket.co.uk
www.paymentcare.co.uk

Investments
www.bloomberg.com
www.dmo.gov.uk
www.etfs.com
www.find.co.uk
www.fool.co.uk
www.funds-sp.com
www.idealing.com
www.iii.co.uk
www.ishares.com
www.morningstar.co.uk
www.snowdomes.com
www.trustnet.com
www.moneyweek.com

Money-saving tips
www.bumblebeeauctions.co.uk
www.cheapskatemonthly.com
www.flylady.com
www.miserlymoms.com
www.moneysavingexpert.co.uk
www.petrolprices.com
www.tightwad.com

Mortgages
www.fsa.gov.uk/register

Pensions
www.pensioncalculator.org
www.thepensionsregulator.gov.uk
www.worksmart.org.uk

Property
www.propertyfinder.com

Starting a business
www.businesslink.gov.uk
www.natwest.com/newbusiness
www.payontime.co.uk

Swapping and bartering
www.eswapit.co.uk
www.freecycle.co.uk
www.iswap.co.uk
www.mybookyourbook.com
www.ReadItSwapIt.co.uk
www.swapaskill.com
www.swopex.co.uk

Tax
www.hmrc.gov.uk
www.nannypayroll.co.uk
www.nannytax.co.uk

Utilities
www.energyhelpline.co.uk
www.simplyswitch.co.uk
www.uswitch.co.uk

Work
www.acas.org
www.eoc.org.uk
www.mumsandworking.co.uk
www.paywizard.co.uk
www.womenlikeus.org.uk
www.workingmums.co.uk

Index